KU-647-516

A Taste of History

10,000 Years of Food in Britain

Peter Brears, Maggie Black, Gill Corbishley
Jane Renfrew and Jennifer Stead

Introduction by Maggie Black

Illustrated by Peter Brears

English Heritage
IN ASSOCIATION WITH
BRITISH MUSEUM PRESS

Acknowledgements

Permission to reproduce extracts and recipes from published works has kindly been given by: BBC Enterprises (for 'Shellfish and Grapefruit Salad', 'Trout Marinated with Yoghurt and Spices' and 'Chablis Cup'); William Heinemann (for *The Soldier's Art*); Martin Books (for 'Redcurrant Flan' and 'Stir-Fried Ginger Beef'); Penguin Books (for 'Carrot Soup with Orange and Tarragon'); Reed International Books (for 'Bucks Fizz'); Delia Smith (for 'French Onion Soup'); Stones Restaurant, Avebury (for 'Imam Bayildi'. 'You too will faint ...' is a reference to the recipe name which translates as 'the Imam fainted' [with delight]). The authors and English Heritage have made every effort to find the owners of copyright of material and apologise to any we have not located.

Sources of illustrations: *Jost Amman* p. 164; *Breakfast table* p. 285; *Breaking eggs* p. 296; Roxburghe Collection, British Museum pp. 182, 184; *Dogspit* p. 243; *Fresh oysters* p. 220; *Pastry making* p. 302 all from Mary Evans Library. Botanical illustrations from *British Flora* by Fitch and Smith, L. Reeve & Co., London, 1916. Thanks to Norman Jacobs for the source of the illustration on p. 329.

© 1993 English Heritage

Published by British Museum Press
A division of British Museum Publications Ltd
46 Bloomsbury Street
London WC1B 3QQ

British Library Cataloguing-in-Publication Data
A catalogue record for this book is available
from the British Library

ISBN 0-7141-1732-3

Originally designed by Elizabeth Mander
This edition designed by Behram Kapadia

Printed and bound in Great Britain by The Bath Press

CONTENTS

INTRODUCTION

history of food spanning ten millennia may at first seem ambitiously broad. But if archaeological detective work is done, there is evidence to be found which makes it possible to recreate the daily fare of the inhabitants of the British Isles from earliest times. Discarded shells and animal bones, for example, have been dated as far back as 8,000 BC; cauldrons found in Iron Age burials suggest that appetising stews were enjoyed 4,000 years ago; and since the Middle Ages literate cooks have recorded recipes and methods which allow us to build a detailed history of meals and cooking equipment up to the present day.

This book is intended both as a history of food and as a guide to cooking authentic historic meals. In each chapter, the author has recreated dishes from archaeological evidence, or adapted recipes from early manuscripts, Georgian household cookery books, Victorian magazines or government pamphlets from the Second World War. Meats, wild herbs and seafoods recur as ingredients in good cooking over thousands of years. The reader can now trace the continuing affection for certain old dishes through the centuries. Familiar friends such as fried fish with parsley sauce, sweet cheese tarts and gingerbread are as popular now as they were five hundred years ago. And we must not forget the enduring attachment of the British to mushy peas! Recipes for this 'dish of necessity' occur in no less than four chapters of this book under various names.

More dramatically, conspicuous innovations in diet stand out among the recipes. The arrival of tea in the later seventeenth century was one. At first it was solely a recherché aristocratic drink served with elegant ceremony in delicate special cups. But in the late 1720s when the Vauxhall Pleasure Gardens were developed as a tea garden, both men and women of all classes except the very poor flocked there to drink tea and to listen to music. By the later eighteenth century, it had changed the English pattern of taking liquid refreshment radically and, it seems, permanently.

The British have always had a sweet tooth. The 'sugar paste' confections in Peter Brears' sixteenth century chapter show that English traders and pirates were then starting to deliver greater quantities of sugar than ever before. But the sweetmeats themselves were not novelties. Moulded sugar 'sculptures' for display along with rose and violet sugar for use as cough cures had been in use in the thirteenth century when Edward I was king of England, although only royalty and the immensely rich in church or state could afford them.

A luxury food gift, especially venison, was for centuries a potent symbol of love, or royal and political favour. Henry VIII courted Anne Boleyn in these words:

> Seeing my darling is absent, I can no less do than to send her some flesh, representing my name, which is hart flesh for Henry, prognosticating that hereafter, God willing, you must enjoy some of mine ... No more to you at this time, mine own darling, but that with a wish I would we were together an evening.
> With the hand of yours.
> H. R.

One of the best records of daily fare in the seventeenth century is the diary of Samuel Pepys. We can be grateful to him for his detailed records of the manners and meals of his time. Here is Pepys' description of his own table on 13 January 1663:

> My poor wife rose by 5 a-clock in the morning, before day, and went to market and bought fowle and many other things for dinner – with which I was highly pleased ... I had for them [his guests] after oysters – at first course, a hash of rabbits and lamb, and a rare chine of beef; next, a great dish of roasted fowl, cost me about 30s, and a tart; and then fruit and cheese. My dinner was noble and enough. I had my house mightly clean and neat, my room below with a good fire in it ... I find my new table very proper, and will hold nine or ten people well, but eight with great room ... At night to supper; had a good sack posset and cold meat and sent my guests away about 10 a-clock at night – both them and myself highly pleased with

our management of this day ... So weary to bed. I believe this day's feast will cost me near 5 pounds.

Almost 300 years earlier in 1355 the Calendar of Pleas and Memoranda Rolls of the City of London records the complaint of a less satisfied individual:

Henry de Walmesford, cook, was charged by Robert de Poke-brok, chaplain, with selling to him some veal for supper the preceding day which had been hashed up (recalfactas) and was stinking ... The veal was produced to the Court. It was declared by the Defendant to be sound. The meat was inspected by Thomas Maluele, John Wenge and Geoffrey Colman, Cooks of Bread Street, and John de Ware and John de Stoke, cooks of Ironmonger Lane, who said the meat was good. Judgement was given for the cook, who was acquitted.

This was hardly a satisfactory judgement, one would have thought, given the time that had passed since the incident, the unsavoury reputation of cooks for selling rotten meat or fish, and the number of cases in which they or their brethren the poulterers were found guilty of selling goods which were 'putrid, rotten, stinking and abominable to the human race, to the scandal, contempt and disgrace of the City'.

For the historian of food there is an ever-growing number of sources. Contemporary documentary records of kitchen accounts and bills of fare abound. A number of diarists have left commentaries on their meals and social life. Kitchen and still room equipment survives from pestle and mortar to the great iron ranges of the last century. These sources can now be supplemented by modern scientific research, including not only the results of investigative archaeology but also studies of nutrition and the relationship between diet and health. There are also the ingredients themselves, natural resources which have been reared or grown in Britain since prehistory. Salted whale is no longer commonly eaten, but fish, for example, was as central to the diet of medieval people as it is to the British in the twentieth century. In adapting established dishes for each new generation, we are able to share in the traditions of cooking and eating enjoyed by our ancestors.

MAGGIE BLACK

Tea time 1779, engraving by Taylor after Wale

Couch or Quitch

PREHISTORIC BRITAIN

Jane Renfrew

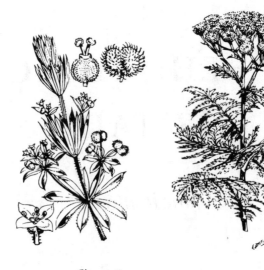

Cleavers, Goose-grass

Tansy

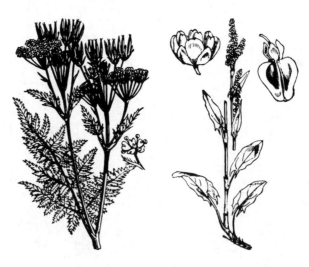

Sweet Cicely

Sorrel

12

M any people might imagine that the task of re-constructing the diet of our prehistoric ancestors would be completely impossible. In some ways they are right, but when archaeologists recover the remains of our distant forebears and their tools they also look for clues about their foods. The process is essentially one of detective work and the direct evidence may survive in a variety of different forms: as mounds of discarded sea shells, the bones of wild and domestic animals (sometimes showing butchery marks, traces of burning during cooking, or split to obtain the marrow). The remains of plants are also often preserved mainly as seeds or fruits, having been charred in the past or buried in other conditions which favour preservation, as in waterlogged soils, or else having been preserved as impressions in clay vessels or in daub. So whether it be the hunters of the palaeolithic or the first farmers of the neolithic or the celtic chieftains of the late iron age, we do have quite a number of clues to help us reconstruct their diet. But having discovered the ingredients which were available, our task is to work out what could have been made from them.

A further lead in this quest is given by studying the tools used for food preparation–for cutting, grinding, pounding and for cooking. Thus we can begin to understand the range of cooking techniques which were available at any given time in our prehistoric past, and to see how they developed through time.

Another aid in reconstructing the methods used by pre-historic cooks is to examine the different practices which have survived in the more remote parts of the British Isles, where the inhabitants had to make do with much the same ingredients as were available in later prehistory. The ingenuity of the islanders of Orkney and Shetland, for example, serves to remind us that when the ingredients were limited in range it was up to the cook to make them varied, interesting and palatable: in the recipes which follow I have drawn on their experience too.

The first men appear to have arrived in Britain sometime before 300,000 years ago. These men were hunters and lived in the Pleistocene during which Britain was subjected to the advances of the polar ice-cap which reached at its maximum extent as far south as London; when, however, it periodically retreated the interglacial periods were extremely warm. Naturally these huge changes in climate and vegetation led to a great variation in the sorts of animals and plants which formed the food supply of the hunters and gatherers. In the cold phases the exposed parts of southern Britain appear to have been roamed by mammoth, woolly rhinoceros, reindeer, bison, musk ox and arctic hare. In the warmer interglacials these species were replaced by the straight-tusked elephant, the Clacton fallow deer, bear, wild oxen, red deer, rhinoceros, hyena and even in some places hippopotamus. Their bones have been found in association with the characteristic flint handaxe tools of these early stone age hunters. From the camp sites so far excavated there has been little evidence for the plant food part of their diet, but on analogy with modern hunting communities up to 80 per cent of their diet may have consisted of vegetable foods. These hunters led a nomadic life following the herds of animals which they relied on for meat. This pattern of shifting hunters and gatherers continued to occupy Britain throughout the palaeolithic. Their tool kit gradually improved and, by the upper palaeolithic, projectile points helped to make their hunting weapons more effective and they began to make sharp flint knives from long blades struck from the cores. At the end of the palaeolithic many of the inhabitants of Britain were living in caves and were hunting horses, reindeer, giant Irish deer, elk, arctic fox, woolly rhino and mammoth.

With the retreat of the ice sheets the climate became progressively milder, and after about 10,000 BC the tundra vegetation gave way to a forested environment, first of birch, hazel and pine and then of oak and other deciduous trees such as elm, lime and alder. With the spread of forest conditions the large herds of wild animals were replaced by forest species: red and roe deer, elk and wild oxen and wild boar. Those hunters who lived close to the sea also began to exploit shellfish and sea fish, leaving huge mounds of shells and fishbones as evidence of their taste for marine foods. Thus from about 300,000 to about 3,500 BC the inhabitants of Britain lived exclusively by hunting and gathering.

About 3,500 BC the first farmers reached Britain from the Continent by sea (the land bridge which had joined us to the Continent during the palaeolithic had become submerged after the melting of the ice sheets before 6,000 BC). These early farmers brought with them bags of seed corn comprising two types of hulled wheat (Emmer and Einkorn), and the hulled and naked forms of six-row barley, and flax. They also brought young domestic cattle, sheep, goats and pigs. Their completely new life-style included living in more or less permanent settlements, using pottery containers, weaving cloth, making polished stone tools and constructing elaborate tombs and ritual monuments. Their arrival brought a truly fundamental change in the way of life of the inhabitants of these islands, and they laid the foundations of society as we know it today. These first farmers set the stage for various technological developments, the most important of which was the development of metallurgy – first with the making of copper, then bronze tools and later with iron working too. These had implications for cooking since it was now possible to have a wider range of tools, especially sharper knives, and later buckets and cauldrons, flesh-hooks, firedogs, spits and tripods, spoons and elegant drinking vessels.

The recipes which follow are supposed to reflect the development of the prehistoric economy in Britain, but several practical restraints have had to be introduced. First, it is rather difficult to give recipes which might relate to the palaeolithic since it is clearly difficult to obtain the ingredients – mammoth steaks or rhinoceros joints for example. So I have confined the recipes to the early post-glacial period and from then on to the end of the iron age immediately preceding the Roman invasion. I have also included only those wild foods which can be fairly easily recognized and are relatively abundant, so that anyone following the recipes will not subject themselves to the misfortune of consuming unpalatable or even poisonous plants by mistake, or to collecting plants which though once common are now rare and should be conserved.

The main difference between prehistoric food and that of today is that our distant ancestors cooked rather simply; they did not go in for elaborate sauces and having few ovens did not bake pies. Also there are a number of ingredients which we habitually use today which were not available to them, among the most important of which are the following: yeast (except the wild forms), baking powder, cream of tartar, spices, lemons, oranges, grapes, wine, vinegar, olive oil, onions, tomatoes, potatoes and cornflour. They did not have sugar, but used honey for sweetening.

They did, however, use much more of our wild vegetation than we do now and their edible plants probably reflected seasonal availability much more than do our modern-day vegetables. One reason for this is that deep freezing and freeze drying preserve our vegetables out of season; in the past vegetables and fruits could only be preserved by air drying, or by being made into preserves such as jam or jelly, or alcoholic beverages such as mead. As far as we know most vegetable foodstuffs were not preserved on a large scale outside their season of availability. The one exception to this is grain, which was stored in pits to provide a steady food supply through the winter and up to the next harvest.

The same problem of preservation was also important for animal products. Meat and fish could be air dried, sun dried, salted or smoked to preserve them through the scarce winter months, and this has been practised until recent times in the islands off our northern coasts.

Another feature that strikes one when looking at the uses of animals, birds and fish in these remote places is that nothing was wasted: udder, lights, tripe, brains, head, feet, tails, blood and even gristle were made into dishes which may not sound appetizing to our rather refined notions today, but which would be quite acceptable in the absence of any alternatives.

PREHISTORIC FOOD RESOURCES

T he sea and seashore were important sources of food for those who lived near. The occasional stranding of whales round our coasts must have provided a great bonus to those living in the vicinity, and it is not uncommon for up to four whales on average to be stranded on British shores each year. Olaus Magnus writing in 1555 described how a single whale might fill between 250 and 300 waggons and yield meat for salting, blubber for lighting and heating, small bones for fuel and large ones for housebuilding, and hide sufficient to clothe forty men, so one can understand what a windfall such a stranding might be. Perhaps the earliest example of man's exploitation of this resource is from Meiklewood near Stirling in Scotland where a mesolithic deer antler mattock was found propped against the skull of a Rorqual whale. Seals were also exploited off the Scottish coast and their bones occur in the mesolithic middens in Argyll and on Oronsay.

The mesolithic inhabitants of Oronsay already practised deep sea fishing from boats: they caught and ate conger eel, sea bream, saithe, wrasse, haddock, thornback ray, skate and shark. At Morton, Fife, on the east coast of Scotland, the mesolithic fishermen were also catching cod, salmon and sturgeon. In the Orkney Islands during the neolithic they were catching cod and coalfish; and finds of crushed fish bones in a mortar at Skara Brae may suggest that fishmeal was used as a famine food. Fish was probably best eaten fresh, being gutted and grilled over an open fire, or baked in hot embers. A large fish would be cut into steaks to facilitate quick and even cooking. Fish roes and livers also constituted rich foods much valued in the northern isles.

Crabs and lobsters were collected along the edge of the shoreline, or just beyond it, probably in weighted baskets– the forerunners of modern lobster pots. They were certainly appreciated by the mesolithic inhabitants of Oronsay and Oban and have probably been valued ever since.

Around the shores of Britain are a series of sites which consist of huge middens of shells, the discarded remains of many meals of shellfish which have been widely valued by the communities living by or visiting the seashore. This is not quite universally true, since in Orkney they have traditionally regarded 'ebb meat' as a last resource in times of hardship. Gathering shellfish may well be regarded as rather labour intensive. The most common species represented are oysters, limpets, mussels, and winkles. It has been argued that the limpets may have been used as fishing bait, but since they are found in such large numbers some at least may have been used for food, possibly as a tasty addition to a fish stew or soup. Sea urchins were also used for food on the late neolithic/early bronze age site at Northton, Harris. All these shellfish are best cooked by dropping them into boiling water and boiling them briskly for a short while before extracting them from their shells. They may also be roasted on hot stones. As soon as the shells open a piece of butter is put inside each, and the shellfish eaten immediately.

Sea birds also formed an important source of food on the coastal sites. Guillemots were present in the mesolithic site at Morton, Fife. They were also present at Skara Brae in Orkney, and on the Rousay sites. Here also were found gannets, eider ducks and their eggs, pink-footed geese, and swans. There is no doubt that these birds were valued for food as well as for their feathers. The inhabitants of St Kilda in the eighteenth century caught guillemots and gannets and either ate them fresh or salted them for use during the long winter months. They also ate large quantities of the birds' eggs boiled.

No finds of seaweed are known from early sites but it is likely that laver, *Porphyra umbilicalis*, which grows in the intertidal zone on the rocky coasts of western Britain, and also carragheen or Irish moss, *Chondrus crispus*, were probably both used, as they are up to this day. Both species are rich in iodine and vitamins. Seakale, *Crambe maritima*, a plant growing on the shingle beaches round our shores yields delicate tender shoots which can be cooked and eaten like asparagus, and marsh samphire, *Salicornia europaea*, which grows on the sandy mud of salt marshes, has succulent fleshy

Seakale   Marsh Samphire, Glasswort

stems of delicate flavour when boiled. Both these plants may have
been locally exploited but would leave no archaeological trace.

Inland, the hunters of the early post-glacial forests relied
heavily on game animals for their meat supply. The mesolithic
band which camped during the spring beside a lake at Star Carr,
Yorkshire, were hunting red and roe deer, elk, wild ox and wild pig
with the occasional wolf, pine marten, hedgehog and badger. The
presence of domestic dog at this site suggests that it was used by the
hunters in their food quest.

With the coming of agriculture, hunting still played a
significant role in the seasonal food supply. Elk disappeared by the
neolithic, and wild oxen by the end of that period. The neolithic
farmers hunted wild ox, especially in southern Britain where their
bones are often found associated with neolithic monuments. The
commonest animal hunted, however, was the red deer, found on
sites from the Orkneys to Dorset. Not only was it an important
source of food, but it also supplied the huge numbers of antlers
used as tools in the flint mines and in the construction of
earthworks. In general, the red deer appear to have been much
larger than contemporary Scottish deer. Of the other species of
deer, both roe and fallow deer have been found on neolithic sites in
the south and east of the country. Wild horse, wild boar, brown
bear and beaver have all been found on neolithic sites also.

At Glastonbury during the iron age the farmers hunted red and roe deer, wild boar, fox, wild cat, otter and beaver, also hedgehog, marten, weasel and polecat. It was probably in the iron age that hunting was first regarded as a sport, with the celtic warriors decorating their shields with wild boar emblems to show their prowess in the hunt.

The meat of these game animals would have to have been eaten at once, or else hung for a long while to tenderize in which case it would have been eaten 'high' as it still is today. We must imagine that all parts of game animals were eaten in some form or other. The gut may well have been used as a container for liver, lights and brains cut up and mixed with fat, and then either slowly roasted over the embers of a fire, or boiled; it is a type of dish which survives as the Scottish haggis.

It is possible that the early hunters ate the half-digested contents of the stomachs of their quarry. They certainly broke open the mandibles and long bones of the animals they hunted to extract the marrow.

Of the wild birds hunted in the late upper palaeolithic, the bones found at Kent's Cavern, Torquay, show that grouse, ptarmigan, grey-lag goose and whooper swan were being hunted for food. The first farmers also hunted goose, swans and ducks. It is possible that the art of falconry began to be practised during the bronze age as an aid in catching birds for food. There are a number of burials in Yorkshire where an archer is buried together with a hawk's head, for example in the beaker grave at Kelleythorpe.

The long list of birds, predominantly aquatic species, which were hunted by the iron age fowlers of the Somerset Lake Villages include: pelicans (and their young), cormorants, herons, bitterns, puffin, whooper swan, goose, wild duck, golden eye, teal, widgeon, pintail, shoveler, tufted duck, scaup, common pochard, red breasted merganser and common crane. At Meare the bones of black and red grouse and partridge were also found. One should not overlook the importance of birds' eggs in the diet too, in the long centuries before the introduction of the domestic fowl sometime in the later iron age.

The mesolithic fishermen on the inland waterways caught

freshwater fish such as pike by using fish spears or leisters armed with barbed antler points. Fish hooks were not introduced till much later. Fish traps and the use of fish nets must have a long prehistory here, as they do on the Continent. At Glastonbury, lead net sinkers were quite common and the villagers caught roach, perch, shad and trout. Pike and salmon were still caught using fish spears since they are much larger fish.

The first domestic animals arrived in Britain around 3,500 BC with the first farmers. They must have brought young animals in their skin boats across the Channel. Herds of sheep and goats, cattle and pigs were soon established. It seems possible that there may have been some subsequent crossing between the long-horned domestic cattle and the wild ox of the native forest before that species died out at the end of the neolithic. A small breed of goat was identified in the animal bones from Windmill Hill, and the sheep appear to have resembled the long-tailed Drenthe breed of Dutch heath sheep. The pig is also of a small form which persisted in Britain at least until the iron age. Both cattle and pigs would be happy browsing in the clearings in the forest, the sheep and goats would thrive better on the well-drained uplands. There is no evidence for the domestication of the horse before the bronze age. The neolithic dogs were of the large fox-terrier type.

Cattle appear to have been the most significant of the neolithic domestic animals. At many of the causewayed camps in southern Britain large numbers of young animals (under the age of one year) appear to have been poleaxed – we may imagine that quite a lot of veal was thus available for eating. Many of their bones show knife cuts at points suitable for the removal of sinew, flesh and skin. Many of the bones were split for the extraction of the marrow. The high proportion of young animals killed also implies that there must have been a good supply of milk available for human consumption, either fresh or in the form of butter and cheese. In the winter months the cattle were probably bled, the blood being mixed with flour and herbs to make black puddings.

Pigs may have been given less attention in neolithic times and allowed to forage at will through the forests until needed to supplement the food supply. Not only did they supply pork but

Lady's Bedstraw   *Butterwort*

also lard which was used in many dishes. Pigs may have sometimes been used, when confined in pens, to break up fallow land and manure it. If left long enough in a confined space they will even get rid of perennial weeds.

Sheep and goats were more important on higher ground, and they appear to have become more numerous during the later phases of British prehistory. Sheep were valued for mutton and for wool. Goats were probably kept for their milk as well as their meat.

Butter and cheese were milk products which could be kept for some time. Butter was probably made in much the same way as it was in the Orkneys until recent times. The milk was left to stand in the churn for two or three days until it thickened naturally. When the butter was slow in coming some red hot 'Kirnin' stones were thrown in to help the separation process. When the butter had gathered at the top it was lifted out into an earthenware dish and washed several times in cold water to remove any remaining milk, which would turn it sour quickly. It then had to be dehaired by passing a knife through it several times to remove any animal hairs on the knife edge. In many parts of Britain it was the custom to bury the butter in wooden vessels or baskets, or occasionally in cloth, bark or leather containers, in peat bogs. Many discoveries of this 'bog butter' have been made, ranging in quantity from a few pounds to as much as a hundredweight. The most rational explanation for this is that the surplus summer butter was stored in the cool bog for use in the winter. One Irish writer records that unsalted butter flavoured with wild garlic used to be put in a boghole and left to ripen.

Cheese is made by heating thick cream and adding rennet, which was obtained from the stomachs of calves. Occasionally plants were used as a substitute for rennet: the leaves of butterwort, *Pinguicula vulgaris,* lady's bedstraw, *Galium verum,* and nettle juice have all been used for this purpose, the last two being used in making Double Gloucester cheese. Simple cottage cheese is made by standing the milk till it separates into curds and whey, straining the curds through a muslin overnight, and then emptying them into a bowl and adding chopped herbs and salt to flavour it. My Cumbrian great-grandmother used to bury it in the garden for a week or so to improve the flavour. It should then be eaten fairly quickly as it does not keep well.

Together with their domestic animals, the neolithic farmers brought bags of seed corn and introduced a range of crop plants. They were the first people to cultivate the land and reap their harvests in autumn, storing it in pits to serve as the food supply through until the next harvest. Their chief crop was the hulled wheat called Emmer, but they also grew a little Einkorn wheat and brought two forms of the hulled six-row barley. Thus wheat and barley which had first been domesticated in the Near East some thousands of years earlier were introduced to the British Isles, and they still form our major cereals (though we now cultivate different species of wheat with better baking qualities). Oats and rye were not introduced, as far as we know, before the iron age, but spelt wheat may have been introduced before the end of the bronze age. The free-threshing forms of breadwheat were also known from this time onwards. The coarsely ground husked grains could have been baked into small unleavened loaves on the hearthstone beside the fire, or they could have been made into porridge or gruel, or added to stews or soups, cooked in pots which the first farmers also introduced.

The weeds that grew in the cornfields were probably harvested with the grain and had a food value often comparable to that of the cereals. Moreover, they were often incorporated into the cereal-based pottage and added flavour to it. A richer, more interesting soup resulted from the addition of fat or oil to the pot. Animal fat, or the oil-bearing seeds of flax would have been used. When the stomach contents of the iron age Tollund and Grauballe man were examined in Denmark, it was found that they had eaten a last meal which consisted of a cereal-based pottage mixed with linseed and a large number of weed seeds from a wide range of species. When the stomach contents of our newly discovered Wilmslow man are analysed we should have direct evidence of some part of the diet of iron age man in this country.

Barley was also used for making malt, and brewing beer. It appears that this process may well have been discovered by the end of the neolithic, and that the appearance of elegant beakers indicate the popularity of this beverage. The process of making malt is well described for the Orkney islands. Bere grain (hulled six-row barley) was set aside for malt. It was put in a large tub and covered with water. It was left to steep for forty-eight hours, then the water was drained off. The damp grain was then spread out on the barn floor for two to three days until germination took place. The grain was then collected in a heap, and two or three people began rubbing off the shoots with their feet by shuffling slowly

Iron age tankard of bronze and wood from Trawsfynydd, Merioneth

round the heap, twisting their toes and heels alternately, working to the centre of the heap. The malt was again heaped up and covered with straw and a mat to induce heat and further fermentation – the grain showed renewed signs of life and emitted a strong liquorous smell. It was rubbed down again before being dried in the kiln. All that remained was the grinding of the malt on a quern. This was done in small quantities for immediate use – a stone or half a stone was enough for brewing – the rest was stored away in a dry place until required. The ground malt was put in a barrel and scalded with boiling water. After infusing for two hours the liquid was drawn off. For special occasions the ale was made more intoxicating by adding an oat sheaf to the must (some people preferred to add heather for this purpose). The liquor (wort) was boiled for about half an hour then it was strained again, cooled and set aside for some days to ferment with added yeast. When fermentation ceased the ale was drawn off and stored in barrels or bottles in a cool place.

The pulse crops, peas and small broad beans, first appeared in Britain in the bronze age, and although they were useful as a different type of seed crop, which could be stored for use out of season and provide both starch and protein, they were never to become as popular crops as the cereals. They had two main uses as foodstuffs. When dried they could be ground up and added to cereal flour for breadmaking in time of dearth and, chiefly, they

Neolithic pottery and spoons. Left to right: pottery vessel from beside Sweet Track, Somerset, found with alder or hazel spurtle or porridge stirrer; pottery spoon, late neolithic grooved ware bowl and an early neolithic pot

could be used in soups or stews, for when simmered in broth they burst open to absorb the broth and fat and become a palatable purée. Young peas could also be eaten fresh, as they are very sweet.

The surviving evidence does not shed much light on the plant species which were collected and cooked as green vegetables. From finds of seeds we may however conclude that fat hen, *Chenopodium album*, was widely used as a green vegetable, probably cooked like spinach. Nettles, too, are well represented and may well have been gathered as young leaves and made into soups or eaten boiled. Other plants which have palatable leaves and may be cooked in these ways include common orache, *Atriplex patula*, easter ledge, *Polygonum bistorta*, white dead nettle, *Lamium album*, cleavers, *Galium aparine*, charlock, *Sinapis arvensis* and wild cabbage, *Brassica oleracea*.

Edible roots may also have played a part as a source of food since early post-glacial times. They were probably used in winter. The following species have been eaten in the more recent past: dandelion, wild parsnip, wild carrot, yellow goatsbeard, sow thistle and silverweed. A note of caution should be added – the roots are often rather small and those from old plants may be bitter or tough. The tuberous roots of the pignut, *Conopodium denudatum*, and the truffle, *Tuber aestivum*, have been regarded as delicacies. The roots of couch grass, *Agropyron repens*, were used as famine food.

In the early part of the year a number of young plants yield edible leaves suitable for use in salads. These include hairy bittercress, yellow rocket, ivy-leaved toadflax, lambs lettuce, sorrel, wood sorrel, dandelion, red clover, wild basil, sow thistle, salad burnet (beware of its strong flavour) and wild marjoram. Remember that there was no oil or vinegar for the salad dressing.

Many wild plants have been used as herbs to add flavour to various dishes. We have definite evidence that the seeds of mustard, coriander and poppies were used as flavourings in prehistoric Britain. It is very likely that some of the following wild plants were also used. Onion flavour may be obtained from the new leaves and shoots of jack by the hedge, *Alliera petiola*, and from the leaves and bulbs of wild garlic or ransoms, *Allium ursinum*. A

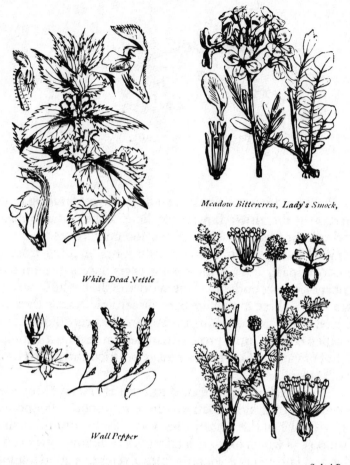

Meadow Bittercress, **Lady's Smock,**

White Dead Nettle

Wall Pepper

Salad Burnet

peppery flavour can be obtained from all parts of wall pepper, *Sedum acre,* and also from lady's smock, *Cardamine pratensis.* Sorrel leaves, *Rumex acetosa,* have a vinegary flavour. The leaves of salad burnet, *Poterium sanguisorba,* taste rather like cucumber, and those of sweet cecily, *Myrrhis oderata,* have an aniseed flavour. Corn mint, *Mentha arvensis,* tastes of mint, while water mint tastes of peppermint. The roots of herb bennet, *Geum urbanum,* have a strong clove flavour, and all parts of tansy, *Chrysanthemum vulgare,* have a strong flavour of ginger. Juniper berries form a good savoury spice.

Lime-tree

Pleasant drinks or tisanes can be made by pouring boiling water over the dried flowers of lime, elder, chamomile or woodruff, the fresh flowers of gorse, and mint leaves.

We have few remains of mushrooms or fungi from our prehistoric past, but an interesting exception is the find of a number of mature puffballs in the midden of the neolithic village of Skara Brae. These may have been discarded because they were overripe to use as food. Mushrooms are a useful source of food since they contain more protein than vegetables and a significant amount of vitamin D. They can easily be dried and stored for use out of season.

Before picking mushrooms to eat it is essential to become familiar with their identifications: there are about 3,000 species of fungi growing in the British Isles and only twenty of them are poisonous, of which four are fatally so. The following species are edible and fairly easy to identify (please refer to a good manual if you are not absolutely sure), they can be made into soups, added to stews or served in omelettes: morels, chanterelles, shaggy ink caps, saffron milk caps, shaggy parasols, ceps, blewits, field mushrooms, puffballs, beefsteak and oyster fungus.

All the fruits and nuts found on prehistoric sites in Britain belong to wild species. Many mesolithic camp sites have yielded large numbers of hazelnuts, suggesting that they were collected for winter use. The native woodland was rich in fruit- and nut-bearing trees whose produce was eaten fresh in due season: acorns, beechmast, hazelnuts, sloes, rosehips, haws, rowan berries, crab apples, wild pears, elderberries, strawberries, raspberries, blackberries and cranberries have all been found on prehistoric sites in Europe. In England, a beaker burial in the clay of the submerged coastline off Walton-on-the-Naze, Essex, was found to have about a pint of fruit seeds in the stomach region: these were chiefly the seeds of blackberries, mixed with rosehips and the seeds of *Atriplex*. We know from the impressions of apple pips in their pottery, that the first farmers ate crab apples. At Glastonbury the villagers had clearly been eating sloes – one mound produced nearly a barrow load of sloe stones. All these fruits can be used to make a storable jelly. In most cases it is necessary to add an equal amount of crab apple to the fruit in order to get enough pectin to make the jelly set. It is made by first bringing the fruit to the boil and simmering until mushy, it is then strained through muslin to separate the juice from the fibres and seeds. Measure the volume of liquid obtained and add to it an equal amount of honey. Bring to the boil, stirring well, and boil rapidly until the setting point is reached (220°F/104°C on a jam thermometer). Pour into sterilized jars and cover with waxed paper. When cool cover tightly with cellophane and store in a cool place.

Crab apples may have been made into verjuice and cider in prehistoric times. Verjuice would have formed a useful substitute for vinegar which was not known before the advent of the Romans. It is made by gathering the crab apples in a heap to sweat, discarding the stalks and any showing signs of decay. The apples are then mashed, using if possible a cider press to extract the juice. The liquid is then strained and stored for a month before it is ready for use. Crab apples were probably also halved and dried for use in the winter.

Crab Apple

Exotic early bronze age drinking cups.
Left, amber cup found at Hove;
right, the Rillaton gold cup

Honey was the only form of sweetening used in prehistoric Britain. We know from rock paintings that wild bees' nests were raided for honey in the late palaeolithic, and it seems likely that bees were actually being kept at least by the middle bronze age, for great quantities of wax were required for the casting of complex tools and weapons by the lost wax method. Wax would also be useful to seal up jars of jelly, verjuice, ale and mead for storage. Honey and salt were traditionally used together to season roast meat and fish in Ireland.

Mead was almost certainly produced in prehistoric times. Honey if left for a time will ferment of itself, and honey and water left together in a container would have produced an alcoholic drink, which could be flavoured with wild fruits and herbs. Traces of mead flavoured with cranberries and bog myrtle have been found in a birch bark container in a bronze age burial in Denmark. At Methilhill, near Kirkcaldy in Scotland, Mrs Camilla Dixon identified the pollen of small-leaved lime and meadowsweet inside a beaker in a grave. It appears that the beaker originally held mead made from lime honey and flavoured with meadowsweet flowers. Interestingly, the small-leaved lime does not grow nearer than the English Lake District, and so either honey or mead had been transported quite a distance.

Pots with perforated bases have been noted at several iron age sites and it has been suggested that they were honey strainers for separating the comb wax from the honey; examples come from Glastonbury and All Cannings Cross.

30

Cooking Techniques and Utensils

The use of preheated stones for cooking goes back at least to the mesolithic; Dr Paul Mellars has found deposits of fire-cracked pebbles in small pits in the mesolithic site in Oronsay. In the bronze age and later there is a whole category of sites known as 'mounds of burnt stones' which have been found from the New Forest to the Orkneys, in Wales and southern Ireland too. They appear to have been cooking places concerned with either (and more usually) boiling or roasting meat. Quite often they are found associated with a large watertight trough in which the meat was boiled. The technique of boiling/stewing in this way has been demonstrated by the late Professor O'Kelly in Ireland. A leg of mutton was wrapped in straw, tied securely with straw ropes, and lowered into boiling water in the trough. The water had been brought to the boil by successively dropping in red-hot stones which had been heated in a log fire beside the trough. The stones were transferred, with the ash, into the trough using a dampened wooden shovel, and in this way the water in the trough

Interior of neolithic house at Skara Brae.
A: hearth, B: bakestone, C: water-tight stone boxes,
D: saddle quern, E: stone dresser, F: knocking stone

was brought to the boil in about half an hour. Another stone was put in every few minutes to keep the temperature up. The 10 lb leg of mutton took 3 hours 40 minutes to cook in this way, and the trough which at first appeared enormous for its task was almost completely full of stones and ash. When the joint was removed it was found to be cooked through to the bone and was uncontaminated by the ash from the pot boilers.

As an addition to this experiment, Professor O'Kelly tried a different technique: that of roasting in a stone-lined pit. It was preheated by burning brushwood inside it, and then, after the ash was drawn out, another 10 lb leg of mutton was placed inside and surrounded by a rough dome of red-hot stones, preheated in a fire. Within twenty minutes the joint was sealed with a crisp brown crust which retained all the juices. The covering stones were changed seven times during the 3 hours 40 minutes cooking time, and at the end of the cooking time the meat was pronounced 'excellently cooked and most tasty'. The labour-intensive nature of the cooking must have given all concerned a good appetite.

The boiling of beef in a hide using pot boilers continued in some remote Scottish islands until the eighteenth century. Another method was outlined by Captain Edward Burt, who described how they put water into a block of wood which had been hollowed out with the help of a dirk and by burning. Then, using fairly large stones heated red-hot and successively quenched in the vessel, they kept the water boiling till the food was completely cooked.

In the prehistoric huts on Dartmoor each hut has a hearth sunk into the floor, and these are generally associated with heaps of

Late bronze age cauldron

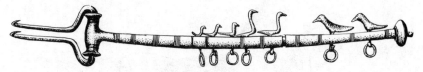

Late bronze age flesh-hook from Dunaverney, Co Antrim, probably used for removing food from cauldrons

fire-cracked pebbles, showing that pebbles heated in the hearth played an important part in cooking and in boiling water even round the domestic hearth. At Legis Tor a round-based pot was still in position in one of the stone-lined cooking holes, and had inside it a fire-cracked flint.

The most usual way of cooking meat was by grilling or roasting it over the red-hot embers of the fire, using some sort of spit. This need not have been more elaborate than a straight green pole or stick, barbecue fashion, resulting in the meat having an appetizing charcoal flavour when ready to eat. By the iron age, elegant firedogs had been developed which may have also supported spits.

The need for large containers for making stews was met in the late bronze age by the introduction of huge bronze cauldrons and their related hooks, chains and tripods for suspension over the fire. The meat was fished out from these vessels with elaborate, long-handled flesh-hooks.

One of the most extraordinary features of the prehistoric houses which have been explored is their lack of ovens. It is not that our prehistoric ancestors did not know about ovens, since we know of a number of examples from the neolithic in Orkney at the sites of Rinyo and the Links of Notland where there were small ovens beside the central hearth, but they were not found universally necessary. Even in the iron age villages of Glastonbury and Meare where every house was furnished with a central hearth, there are only two or three ovens in the whole village, and these were probably associated with some occupation other than cooking food. The exception is at Maiden Castle where three ovens were found in a single house. Thus, baking in ovens was not a commonly practised technique in prehistoric Britain.

*Saddle quern
for grinding grain*

Baking appears to have been done on a flat stone or bake-stone placed on or beside the central hearth. Sometimes bread may have been placed under an inverted pot which had hot embers piled over it. Emmer and Einkorn wheat do not make flour which stretches very much in the dough, and are thus better for making flat bread rather than leavened bread, though wild yeast may have been used to lighten the bread a little and add flavour to it.

The preparation of cereals for eating involved the use of pestles, mortars and querns. The houses at Skara Brae clearly show these two implements. The neolithic querns were of the saddle type with a bun-shaped upper stone which was rubbed backwards and forwards over a flat stone base. Rotary querns were introduced only in the iron age. They consisted of two circular stones: the lower with a convex upper surface and the upper with a concave lower surface, and a central hole through which the grain was fed. To prevent the upper stone slipping off the nether stone during grinding, a pin was fixed in the top of the nether stone and passed through a narrow bar of wood which crossed the feeding hole. At one side of the top stone a hole was drilled for the insertion of a wooden handle. The proximity of the two grindstones could be controlled by the insertion of leather washers under the wooden crossbar. In more recent times in Orkney the washer was inserted when oatmeal or malt was being ground, but not for the grinding of the finer barley meal.

Grain could have been prepared in three ways. It could have been prepared like graddan in the Hebrides up to the eighteenth century: a handful of ears of corn was held over the flames by the stalks, and the grains were beaten off at the moment when the husk was burnt but before the grain became charred. It was then winnowed and ground and baked within an hour of being harvested. Oats were 'burned in the sheaf' in a similar manner in Ireland in the past.

Another method was to make toasted grain, or 'burstin' as it is called in the Orkney islands. Barley grains were put in a pot beside the fire and the pot was tilted over on one side. To get the grains evenly dried and browned it was constantly stirred, and any which became burnt were discarded as they would give the burstin a dark colour and bitter taste. After being thoroughly toasted the grain was well sieved and then ground.

For making porridge or thickening soup the Orcadians used to use handfuls of threshed barley grains which were put in the 'knocking stane' or mortar with a little warm water, and were then lightly bruised with a mallet to break the husk. The husks were floated off by steeping in water and the grains were used just like pearl barley today. Last century boiled cabbage and 'knocked corn' formed a substantial part of the diet of these islanders.

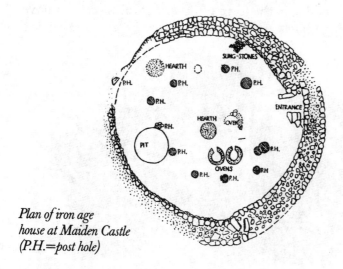

Plan of iron age
house at Maiden Castle
(P.H.=post hole)

Serving Prehistoric Food

Apart from flint-bladed knives there is little evidence of the eating equipment of our mesolithic ancestors, though they may well have had containers made from leather or wood from which they ate their meals. The first farmers introduced the use of pottery for storing, cooking and eating their food. The earliest pottery forms were round-based undecorated bowls – gradually through time impressed decoration began to appear round the necks and shoulders of the bowls. The round bases would have been more practical on an uneven floor, and in houses with no tables. By the late neolithic two types of flat-based pots, decorated with grooves or impressions over most of their surfaces, had become fashionable: the so-called Peterborough and grooved ware. The finds of pottery ladles from Sussex suggest that spoons may also have been made of wood, bone or horn, and a wooden spurtle was found in a bowl associated with the Sweet Track in the Somerset levels. A horn spoon was found in a beaker at Broomhead, Aberdeen.

The very finest prehistoric pottery made in Britain appeared in the late neolithic in the form of beakers, which seem to have been drinking vessels and are usually found in graves. They are

A beaker and two beaker mugs

*An early bronze age vessel
which may have been
used as a salt pot*

made from fine-grained clay and were decorated with horizontal
bands of impressions made with finely toothed combs. Some of
these beakers have handles and look as if they are copies in clay of
wooden tankards. We know that the beaker from Methilhill,
Scotland, had contained mead. It is possible that they may have
also been used for ale.

Drinking cups made from exotic materials are a feature of the
early bronze age in Britain: the Rillaton cup was made of gold, the
Hove cup was carved from a single piece of amber, and two cups
carved from shale were found near Amesbury, Wiltshire. One has
to ask whether these materials were used in order to reflect the
importance of the people using them, or of the liquid to be drunk
from them.

The pottery of the early bronze age falls into two groups: the
highly decorated flat-based, carinated bowls known as food
vessels, and the larger urns with decorated rims and collars usually
described as cinerary urns. Both are found associated with burials
and so we cannot be sure that they have anything to do with food.
Frequently associated with the large urns are small 'incense' or
pygmy vessels. They often have holes for suspension and are
decorated all over. Some are perforated, others have lids. I wonder
if they could have been used for salt, since we now have evidence
for the exploitation of salt in East Anglia at least as far back as the
early bronze age. It would have been extremely valuable as a
condiment to add piquancy to the bland food usually cooked.

The late bronze age saw the introduction of beaten metal
vessels – notably, from the culinary point of view, the cauldron and
the bucket. At this time also bronze knives were made, although
flint continued to be used to make cutting tools into the iron age.

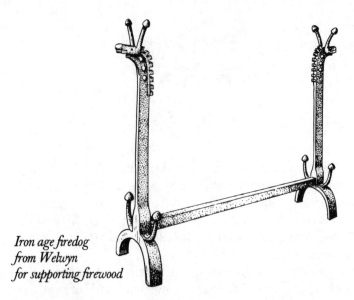

Iron age firedog
from Welwyn
for supporting firewood

Some of the early iron age pottery was decorated with a bright red haematite slip to make it resemble the burnished bronze vessels which were still luxury items. Some of the decorated pottery of the middle and late iron age is also rather attractive, especially that manufactured by the villagers of the Somerset levels, which is decorated with flowing lines and curvilinear patterns. The same style of decoration is also found on the wooden tub from Glastonbury. Here too were found both flint- and iron-bladed knives, and ladles and spoons made of wood. The curvilinear decoration is also to be found on the handles of bronze spoons which are characteristically found in pairs in Ireland and

Iron age bowl from
Glastonbury Lake
Village made
from bronze

northern England, and also on the handles of tankards, for example from Trawsfynydd, Merioneth. The cast-iron firedogs such as those from Capel Garmon, Denbigh, Welwyn, Hertfordshire, and Lord's Bridge, Cambridgeshire, were also works of art with their animal head terminals, and serve to underline the importance of the hearth to the iron age chieftains. Cauldrons, their hooks, chains and tripods, also feature at this time and are often found in graves.

In the first century BC the potter's wheel was introduced, and the pottery became much more stereotyped. Pedestalled bowls, platters, handled tankards and jars with countersunk handles became common pottery forms.

The rich burials of the Belgic chieftains show that already they had contact with the Roman world and were beginning to appreciate imported wine and olive oil. The grave goods found with the two burials uncovered at Welwyn at the beginning of this century include Mediterranean amphorae which must have contained wine, together with bronze and silver vessels for serving and drinking wine, firedogs, spits, and tripod cauldron hangers, pottery and wooden vessels – emphasizing the importance of feasting and drinking.

Future excavations, especially of waterlogged habitation sites, will no doubt shed new light on the foods, techniques of preparation, methods of cooking and serving of our prehistoric ancestors, but we have enough evidence to give us a glimpse into the way they utilized their available resources to provide an interesting and varied diet.

Wooden tub (left) and ladle from Glastonbury Lake Village together with a pottery bowl from Meare. Iron age

A pottery urn (centre) and two pottery food vessels from the early bronze age

RECIPES

The recipes which follow are based on recipes drawn from the following sources: pease pudding from Elizabeth Ayrton, *The Cookery of England*; roast goose, fried pike, grilled salmon, grilled ox tails, marrow bones, grilled breast of mutton from *Mrs Beeton's Cookery and Household Management;* leaven, Yorkshire riddle bread, flowerpot bread from Elizabeth David, *English Bread and Yeast Cookery*; roast venison from Jane Grigson, *English Food;* frumenty, nettle purée, tansy pudding from J. Hill, *The Wild Foods of Britain;* laverbread, carragheen sweet mousse, boiled samphire, easter ledge pudding from R. Phillips, *Wild Food*; slott, crab, blaanda bread from J. Simmons, *A Shetland Cook Book*; fish soup, hakka muggies, sowans, porridge, burstin and milk from M. B. Stout, *The Shetland Cookery Book.*

FISH SOUP

trimmings and head of a large fish
1 small haddock
salt
seasoning (optional)
flour
milk

Thoroughly clean the trimmings and put in a pan with the haddock. Cover with cold salted water. Bring slowly to the boil and skim. Add seasoning (if using), simmer for 40 minutes, strain and return to the pan. For every 2 pints (1.1 litres) stock, mix 2 tbls (30 ml) flour to a paste with some milk and add to the soup to thicken it. Bring to the boil, check seasoning and serve.

HAKKA MUGGIES

1 fish stomach (a ling muggie is best)
1 cod liver
seasoning
oatmeal

Wash the muggie carefully, and tie the small end tightly with string. Break up or slice the cod liver, season well, and fill the muggie with alternate layers of liver and oatmeal until two-thirds full. Close, leaving enough room for the oatmeal to swell, and tie tightly with string. Plunge into boiling salted water and boil gently for 25-30 minutes. Remove from the water, and serve hot with bread.

GRILLED HADDOCK

Have ready a clear red fire; allow one medium haddock per person. Gut the fish and then lay them on a grill across the hot embers. Allow to grill first on one side, then turn over and grill the other side. Rub with a pat of butter and serve immediately. The haddock may also be toasted in front of the fire, retaining all the juices and the flavour of the fish.

SLOTT

1 cod roe
flour
salt

Beat the roe until creamy, then add a little flour and salt and form into small dumplings. Drop them into boiling well-salted water, and cook for 20-25 minutes. When ready they will rise to the top. Eat hot, or when cold cut into slices and fry in butter.

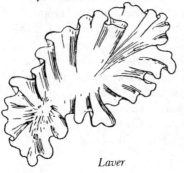

Laver

LAVERBREAD

Collect a good basketful of laver, avoiding any that are sandy. Break up the large pieces and wash thoroughly in cold water. Cook steadily for about 4 hours in a large pan of boiling water, checking every 30 minutes that it does not boil dry. It is cooked when the sheets of laver have broken up into tiny pieces, forming a smooth purée. Drain away excess liquid and store the puréed laverbread in the fridge until required. It will keep fresh for about a week. It is best served warm on fried bread garnished with bacon, since this helps complement the unusual texture and appearance of this excellent food.

SEA URCHINS

Sea urchins are usually eaten boiled like an egg. Boil briskly in salted water for 5 minutes. Drain, then open the urchins by cutting the concave side. Drain completely, discarding the excremental parts. To eat, dip buttered bread fingers into the yellow substance clinging to the inside of the shell. Sea urchins can also be eaten raw, as they are nowadays in the region around Marseilles.

CRAB

Choose a crab that is heavy in proportion to its size. Wash well and remove any adhering seaweed. Fill any holes in the shell with bread to prevent the meat becoming waterlogged in cooking. Drop into boiling salted water and cook for 15 minutes. When cold, break off the claws and take out the body – discard the green parts, gills and stomach. Chop the white and brown meats and arrange separately within the crab shell. Serve with warm bread rolls or bannocks.

BOILED SAMPHIRE

Samphire is a great delicacy. Pick marsh samphire during July or August at low tide. It should be carefully washed soon after collection and is best eaten very fresh. Tie the washed samphire, with the roots still intact, in bundles and boil in shallow unsalted water for 8-10 minutes. Cut the string and serve with melted butter. Eat the samphire by picking each stem up by the root and biting lightly, pulling the fleshy part away from the woody core.

CARRAGHEEN SWEET MOUSSE

¼ oz (7g) dried carragheen
1 pt (575 ml) milk
1 egg, separated
½ oz (15g) sugar or honey
fresh raspberries, to decorate (optional)

Soak the dried carragheen for 15 minutes in water, then pick out the dried ends and discard the water. Add the carragheen to the milk in a saucepan and slowly bring to the boil. Simmer for about 10 minutes, or until the mixture is quite thick. Beat the egg yolk with the honey or sugar. Strain the carragheen mixture and add the honey mixture to it. Beat the egg white until stiff, then fold into the mixture, stirring well, and pour into a bowl to set. The mousse takes 2-3 hours to set. It is nice to eat by itself, but is excellent with fresh or stewed fruit. If you omit the egg the mixture will set just as well and make a nourishing blancmange.

Carragheen (Irish Moss)

FRIED PIKE

1 pike, weighing 3-4 lb (1.4-1.8 kg)
salt
flour
1 egg, beaten
dry breadcrumbs for coating

Scale and clean the pike thoroughly, removing the head and tail. Cut the fish into slices and cover with very cold water. Remove when the fish feels firm. Dry well and rub lightly with salt and flour. Brush the slices of pike with the beaten egg, then coat in breadcrumbs. Fry in shallow fat for about 30 minutes until tender.

GRILLED SALMON

2-3 slices of middle cut salmon
2 tbls (30 ml) melted butter
salt
parsley butter, to garnish

Wipe the fish with a damp cloth, then brush with melted butter. Season with salt to taste. Place the fish slices on a well-greased grill rack, and grill for 6-8 minutes on each side according to thickness. Serve immediately, garnished with parsley butter.

ROAST VENISON

Venison is inclined to be hard and dry unless carefully cooked. Lard the joint and tie a jacket of fat pork round it to retain the moisture. It may be roasted on a spit, but it is probably more convenient to roast it in the oven at gas mark 4, 350°F (180°C), allowing 30 minutes per 1 lb (450g). Serve with wild mushrooms and rowan jelly.

MARROW BONES

8 oz (225 g) marrow bones per serving
flour
salt
dry toast, to serve

Scrape and wash the bones and saw in half across the shaft (the butcher will do this for you). Make a stiff paste of flour and water and roll it out. Cover the ends of the bones with the paste, to seal in the marrow, and tie the bones in a floured cloth. Stand upright in a pan of boiling salted water and simmer slowly for about 2 hours, refilling the pan with boiling water if necessary. Untie the cloth and remove the paste from each bone. Fasten a paper napkin round each one and serve with dry toast.

ROAST GOOSE

2 oz (50g) butter
salt
1 young goose (up to 4 months old)
watercress, to garnish

Mix the butter and salt together
and place inside the bird. Truss,
and cook in a moderate oven, gas
mark 4-5, 350-375°F (180-190°C)
for about 1 hour, basting if
necessary. Place the bird on a
serving dish and garnish with
watercress. Instead of roasting in
an oven the goose could be spit
roasted over an open fire.

GRILLED OX TAILS

2 ox tails
1½ pt (850 ml) well-flavoured stock
1 egg, beaten
dry breadcrumbs for coating
melted butter

Wash and dry the ox tails and
divide them into pieces at the
joints. Put into a saucepan with
the stock. Simmer gently for
2½ hours until tender. Drain well
and leave until cold. Dip the ox
tail pieces into the egg, then coat
with the beadcrumbs. Brush with
melted butter and grill until
browned.

GRILLED BREAST OF MUTTON

1 breast of mutton
salt

Divide the breast into serving
portions. Remove surplus fat and
skin and season the mutton with
salt. Grill quickly under a hot grill
or over hot embers to seal the
surface, then reduce the heat and
grill for a further 15-20 minutes,
turning the meat frequently.

CUTLETS OF WILD BOAR

Sauté the cutlets in oil or butter
until tender, and arrange them on
croutons of fried bread. Pour
over them the pan juices mixed
with a little thick cream and a few
crushed juniper berries (1-2 per
cutlet). Serve with unsweetened
apple sauce.

Juniper

PEASE PUDDING

Originally the peas were probably tied in a floured cloth and hung to cook in the cauldron in which a large piece of pork was being boiled.

8 oz (250 g) dried green peas, soaked overnight
a few sprigs of mint and thyme
1 oz (25 g) butter
salt

Boil the peas in water with the herbs until soft and the skins are well loosened. Drain thoroughly and put through a sieve or blender with the butter. Add salt to taste. Press into a well-greased pudding basin, cover tightly with foil and steam for 1 hour. Turn out carefully, and serve with meat.

NETTLE PURÉE

Put young nettle tops into boiling water and boil until tender. Drain well and chop finely. Reheat, adding butter and salt to taste. Sorrel, dandelion, spinach, sow thistle, watercress and lady's smock may all be mixed for this purée (if the more bitter herbs dandelion and sow thistle are used alone, change the water after 5 minutes boiling). Cooking in a liberal amount of fast-boiling water will conserve the vitamins better than slow, gentle cooking.

SOWANS OR VIRPA

1 lb (450 g) fine oatmeal
3 lb (1.4 kg) wheatmeal
16 pt (9 L) water

Put both meals in a stone crock. Stir in 14 pints (8 litres) lukewarm water and let it stand for 5-8 days until sour. Pour off the clear liquid and let this stand a few more days until rather sharp: this is the swats, which makes a refreshing drink. The remainder in the crock will resemble thick starch. Add about 2 pints (1 litre) water to give the consistency of cream. Strain through a cheesecloth over a colander. The liquid which is passed through will contain all the nutritious properties of oatmeal, with only the husk remaining. Gentle rubbing with a wooden spoon and a final squeezing of the cloth by hand will hasten the process. This dish is good for invalids.

FRUMENTY

Half fill a jar with wheat grains, wash them, then cover with milk or water and set in a warm oven for 12 hours. The grains will swell and burst, and in this state are known as creed wheat. Frumenty may be eaten with cream and honey.

EASTER LEDGE
PUDDING

1 lb (450 g) young bistort leaves and
  nettle tops (dandelion leaves and
  lady's mantle may also be used for
  added flavour)
4 oz (125 g) pot barley, washed
salt
1 egg
a large knob of butter

Chop the greens and sprinkle the
washed barley among them,
adding some salt. Boil in a muslin
bag for about 2 hours. Before
serving, beat the mixture in a
bowl with the egg, butter and salt
to taste. Form into cakes and fry
in shallow fat. Recommended as
a good spring tonic.

PORRIDGE

1 pt (575 ml) water
a pinch of salt
2 oz (50 g) oatmeal
milk and honey (optional), to serve

Bring the water to the boil and
add the salt. Sprinkle in the
oatmeal very gradually, stirring
well after each addition, then
bring to the boil. Boil gently for
20 minutes if using fine oatmeal
or 30 minutes for coarse. Serve
with cold milk, and honey if
desired.

BURSTIN
AND MILK

Burstin is made from hulled six-
row barley grains which are dried
in a pot by the fire until roasted
and then hand ground on a
quern, making a rich brown meal.
Put the burstin meal in a basin,
heat some milk and pour over.
Serve hot. This may also be made
with cold milk or with buttermilk.

TANSY PUDDING

½ pt (275 ml) milk
½ oz (15 g) butter
3 oz (75 g) fresh white breadcrumbs
1 oz (25 g) sugar or honey
2 tsps (10 ml) finely chopped tansy
  leaves
2 eggs, beaten
honey and cream, to serve

Boil the milk and butter together
and pour over the breadcrumbs.
Set aside for 30 minutes. Add the
sugar or honey and the tansy
leaves to the eggs, then mix with
the breadcrumbs and bake the
mixture in a moderate oven, gas
mark 4, 350°F (180°C), until set.
Eat cold with honey and cream.

BLAANDA BREAD

10 tbls (150 ml) barley meal
10 tbls (150 ml) oatmeal
a pinch of salt
2 oz (50 g) butter
milk, to mix

Mix the two meals and the salt in a bowl, then rub in the fat. Gradually add the milk to make a dough which is firm but not sticky. Shape into a round flat bannock and bake slowly on a griddle over the fire.

FLOWERPOT BREAD

1 lb 6 oz (600 g) wheatmeal flour
½ oz (15 g) leaven (see below)
½ oz (15 g) salt
about 12-15 fl oz (350-425 ml) milk
    and water, mixed

For these quantities use two terracotta flowerpots, about 5½ inches (14 cm) in diameter. Temper the pots by coating with oil and putting into a hot oven. Repeat this process three or four times. Once the pots are well sealed they will need very little greasing.
Mix the ingredients together to make a dough. Leave to rise for 2 hours, work the dough, then leave to rise again for a further 2 hours. Divide the risen dough between the pots and leave to prove for 45 minutes. Invert on a baking sheet and bake for 30 minutes at gas mark 7–8, 425–450°F (220–230°C). Remove the pots, reduce the heat to gas mark 2½–4, 320–350°F (160–180°C) and bake for 10–15 minutes more.

LEAVEN

Mix a small quantity of barley flour with warm water into a dough. Form into a round shape and make a dent in the centre to go about half-way through. Put the dough on a plate, cross it lightly with a knife twice, and fill the dent with warm water. Set it aside for a few days when the dough will have fermented and split like an overripe fruit. It is then ready to use as yeast to 'plum' the bread.

YORKSHIRE RIDDLE BREAD

Mix a quantity of pinhead oatmeal with water to make a thick porridge. Leave overnight in a warm room. Next day add salt to taste and place spoonfuls on to a hot bakestone or griddle. As the bread cooks it bubbles up, giving a characteristic appearance. Brown the cakes on one side only.

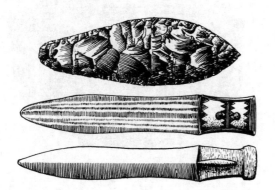

Flint knife and two bronze age knives

Roman Britain

Jane Renfrew

A Roman meal in an extremely affluent household. Few British families could have expected to eat in such luxury

hen the Roman legions invaded Britain in AD 43 they heralded many changes for these islands and, by bringing us into the Roman Empire, they gave us access to a new world of sophisticated tastes. These were apparent in many spheres but not least in agriculture, foods and cooking.

In reconstructing the diet of Roman Britain we have several sources of evidence to draw on. There is the physical evidence of the bones and seeds recovered during excavations, there is the literary evidence which comes in two forms: the letters preserved at Vindolanda, written by soldiers serving on Hadrian's Wall to their families, where they list their foods as in one case 'spice, goats' milk, salt, young pig, ham, corn, venison and flour'; in another letter, vintage wine, Celtic beer, ordinary wine, fish sauce and pork fat are mentioned. The other literary evidence is of a more general kind: the cookery book of Apicius, the agricultural treatises of Cato, Varro, Columella and Palladius, Pliny's great work on Natural History and the descriptions of notable feasts such as Trimalchio's feast as described by Petronius. Finally, there are illustrations of foods and dining scenes both in wall paintings and on mosaics, and hunting and vintage scenes are depicted on pottery.

The Romans were responsible for the import into Britain of a number of sources of food. The game introduced included pheasants, peacocks, guinea fowl and fallow deer. They introduced the following fruit and nut-bearing trees into cultivation here: vines, fig, walnut, medlar, mulberry, sweet chestnut. Among the great range of herbs and plants they used in cooking, especially in their sauces, were the following which have remained in cultivation more or less ever since: parsley, alexanders, borage, chervil, coriander, dill, fennel, mint, thyme, garlic, leek, onion, shallot, hyssop, rosemary, rue, sage, savory, sweet marjoram, radish. The vegetables brought into cultivation at this time include cabbage, lettuce, endive, turnip, mallow, orache, corn salad and fat hen – the last four have now gone out of cultivation but can still be found wild.

Besides introducing animals and crops for rearing and growing in this country, the Romans also imported a number of commodities which they valued in their diet. Among these were dates, almonds, olives, wine, olive oil, pine cones and kernels, fermented fish sauce, pepper, ginger and cinnamon.

Before we examine the Roman diet in closer detail it would probably be useful to sketch in outline the main events and developments in Britain under Roman rule. The Roman occupation of Britain was established after the Claudian invasion of AD 43 which was largely successful because of the prior trade established between the iron age chieftains and Roman merchants in the first century BC. The Roman troops (four legions) landed in Kent, at Richborough, Dover and Lympne, and gradually pushed northwards and westwards. Under Suetonius Paulinus and Petillus Cerialis, Wales was subdued by AD 78, and by AD 81 Agricola had established a northern frontier line between the Forth and the Clyde, and had penetrated further north into the Highlands establishing a forward position at Inchtuthil. Not that the conquest was by any means easy. The most dramatic reverse occurred in the winter of AD 60-61 when Boudicca, widow of King Pratsutagus of the Iceni, with the help of the neighbouring Trinovantes sacked and burnt the newly established provincial capital of Camolodunum (Colchester). The revolt then spread and Londinium (London) and Verulamium (St Albans) were also captured, before the rebellion was put down. Later, about AD 117, further trouble came in the north, probably in south-west Scotland, which involved heavy Roman casualties and resulted in the withdrawal of the Ninth Legion from York. Hadrian resolved to build an artificial line of defence between the Solway and the Tyne; work began in AD 122 and took about a decade to complete. Beyond the western end of the wall a system of towers and milecastles extended down the Cumberland coast to Maryport. By AD 140 when Antoninus Pius became emperor, a decision was taken to construct a new military frontier along the Forth–Clyde line, which became known as the Antonine Wall. Serious trouble in the northern province of Brigantia however, led to the immediate evacuation of the Antonine Wall in AD 154 and to the reinforcement of the three northern legions with additional troops from the Rhineland. Hadrian's Wall was restored for active service and many forts in its hinterland were rebuilt or strengthened. Again in AD 159 there was a concerted effort to re-establish the Scottish frontier line, and more forts were constructed along Dere Street to subdue the Selgovae and Novantae tribes but with little success.

Meanwhile in AD 192 the Emperor Commodus died and his succession was hotly contended by, amongst others, Clodius Albinus, Governor of Britain. He gathered together an army from the British garrisons, crossed the Channel and marched south-east across Gaul to Lyons where he met and was defeated by Septimus Severus. This left Britain open to attack and the native inhabitants of southern Scotland, northern England and Wales were not slow to seize the opportunity to wreck such empty forts as they could find – including possibly the legionary fortress at York. Many of the towns and villages of southern Britain were defended by strong fortifications and were not attacked.

On his succession Severus sent a series of governors to Britain to re-establish law and order especially in the north. Gradually they rebuilt the destroyed forts. In AD 208 Severus came himself, with two of his sons and considerable reinforcements of troops, but three years of military campaigns did not bring a decisive outcome. In AD 211 Severus died in York and was succeeded by his son Caracalla, who seems to have made a successful treaty with the enemy which lasted for many years and brought peace and prosperity to the northern province. The frontier was now firmly established on Hadrian's Wall.

An external threat from across the North Sea led to the establishment, early in the third century, of new forts to guard the entrance to the Thames (at Reculver) and the Wash (at Brancaster). These were to be the forerunners of a much more extensive coastal defence system known as the Saxon Shore, established by the end of the third century.

Once the military conquest had brought peace and good communications, civilian settlements began to be established, and Britain saw the founding of its first urban settlements. The abandoned legionary fortress at Colchester was used to form the nucleus of the first town to be established, by the soldiers who had been discharged from the army's XX Legion. In the years which followed Agricola's campaigns, further discharges from the army were made and towns were established at Lincoln and Gloucester. Once again legionary forts were reused.

Native urbanization started slowly and received important help from Roman military architects and surveyors. The first of these towns appear to have been established at Verulamium (St Albans) and Canterbury. Meanwhile civil settlements developed round many of the forts. They and their garrisons represented a continuous demand and a stable market for the sale of surplus agricultural produce, and a stimulus to produce more. It has been estimated that at the time of the establishment of the Antonine Wall 6,000 tons of wheat per annum was needed to feed the garrison north of Hadrian's Wall.

Once the military operations moved to the north, the lowlands of southern England had to be governed by a civilian system of local government based on the iron age tribal structure, with *civitas* capitals in each region serving as administrative centres. By the end of the first century Cirencester, Silchester, Winchester, Exeter and Verulamium had become established, and the next half century saw the founding of Leicester, Wroxeter and Caistor-by-Norwich. These new towns acted primarily as market and servicing centres for the surrounding catchment areas of rural population. Such towns were equipped with a forum, basilica, a *mansio* or inn, public baths and often a theatre or amphitheatre, shops, arcaded streets, a good water supply (sometimes brought in by aquaduct), drainage system, good-quality private housing and well-surfaced streets.

Some towns were associated with particular industries: Charterhouse-in-Mendip with lead mining, Kenchester and Weston-under-Penyard with iron-ore mining in the Forest of Dean, Manchester near Nuneaton with extensive potteries on Watling Street, Wilderspool, Cheshire, with pottery, glass and metal-working industries.

The rural populations were basically administered through a system of villas intimately connected to the towns and villages. They were the centres of agricultural estates, and the main dwelling house was flanked by a series of barns and ranges of other farm buildings. The villas in Britain fall into two main types: the corridor type, in which several rooms open off a single corridor and are often flanked by short wings on either side (an example can be seen at Newport), or the extensive courtyard type, in which blocks of rooms forming separate wings are ranged around one or more courtyards (as at Chedworth and North Leigh). Even the smallest villa was equipped with a hypocaust central-heating system, mosaic floors and painted wall plaster, and most also had their own bath house. However, a large part of the countryside remained uninfluenced by Roman civilization and the people continued to live in their traditional native settlements. They used Roman pottery and coins when they came their way, and sometimes reused Roman tiles and other building materials in their traditional settlements.

In the immediate vicinity of the large garrison on Hadrian's Wall a large number of native farmstead settlements must reflect a policy of encouraging the local farmers to intensify their activities to feed the troops. Elsewhere in Britain, especially in the south, large quantities of wheat were being grown to meet the *annona* or corn tax, and much of the surplus thus raised was exported to feed the troops on the Rhine.

The Roman occupation of Britain lasted until AD 410. The withdrawal of Roman influence was a gradual affair which began about the middle of the fourth century. The troublesome tribes of southern Scotland began to attack the forts north of Hadrian's Wall, and the Scots in Ireland also began to get restless. In AD 367 Britain was overwhelmed by a great barbarian conspiracy of concerted attacks from the Picts, Scots and Saxons. Hadrian's Wall was over-run and Nectardius, the Count of the Saxon Shore, was killed. Theodosius came to Britain in AD 369 to review the situation and repair the defences. He constructed a system of signal stations along the Yorkshire coast, and strengthened defences on Hadrian's Wall. He seems to have been effective in these measures, for the towns and villages appear to have continued to prosper until the end of the fourth century. The military situation was not so secure because in AD 383 the Dux Britanniarum (commander of land forces in Britain), Magnus Maximus, revolted, removed troops from Wales and northern England and crossed to the Continent with them. The Irish immediately began to attack Wales, and the Picts, Scots and Saxons increased the frequency of their raids. By AD 401 more Roman troops were withdrawn from Britain to defend Italy and in 407 Constantine

III removed the last of the garrison from Britain to the Continent. The Emporor Honorius had no option but to tell the British cities which had sent a plea for help in AD 410 that they would have to defend themselves. Thus after nearly four centuries the Roman rule in Britain came to an end.

The Romans had a profound influence on the development of civilization, and although not all the new ways were adopted by the indigenous population a great many of their sophisticated systems of doing things continued to be copied for centuries. In the case of cooking and cuisine we shall see that they introduced many items into the diet which are still common today, together with methods of cooking with which we are very familiar. If one asks what are the main differences between Roman cooking and that of today the answer must be that they had an extraordinary fondness for using a sauce made from the fermented entrails of fish, which was used equally often in sweet as in savoury dishes, often combined with liberal amounts of pepper. They also used large amounts of honey in their cooking, and were fond of using a wide range of herbs to flavour their dishes. In their more elaborate feasts great store was set by making dishes look as if they were made from other ingredients–playing a sort of identification game with the guests.

Food animals depicted on Romano-British objects. Top left, bull's head bucket-handle mount, Felmersham on Ouse, Bedfordshire; top right, bronze figure of a boar, Hounslow; centre, hare brooch, Lincoln; bottom left, cockerel brooch, Brough Castle, Cumbria; bottom right, bronze figure of a roped stag, Milber Down Fort, Devon

ROMAN BANQUETS

Perhaps the best introduction to Roman cooking is to look at the descriptions of some of the most elaborate banquets recorded – bearing in mind that they are exceptions rather than the rule, they give one a vivid insight into the extravagant aspirations and achievements of the Roman cooks. The Romans often sacrificed their culinary skills to the presentation, ostentation and setting of their banquets. At one meal Heliogabalus served his guests with 600 ostrich brains, peas mixed with grains of gold, lentils with precious stones, and other dishes mixed with pearls and amber – which may have satisfied the guests in some senses, but hardly gastronomically.

The dining room in which the Romans took their meals was known as the *triclinium,* so called because it was usual to arrange three couches around a central dining table, leaving the fourth side open for the serving slaves. Usually three people reclined on each couch to take their meal, with their left arm supported on a cushion. The guests brought their own napkins. Slaves removed the guests' shoes and replaced them with sandals. They performed their ablutions after each course. When eating they wore a fine white napkin around their necks and had another beside them to wipe their fingers.

After invoking Penates, Lares and Jupiter, the feast began. It was usually in three parts. The first course was an hors-d'oeuvre. The second was the *coena* or meal proper, after which sacrifices were made to the Lares in great solemnity – the pieces reserved for this were taken to the fire, as was the ancient custom, and a slave offered an oblation to propitious gods from a special goblet. The third course was a dessert which usually consisted of fresh or dried fruit, or fruit in pastries, or honey cakes. Sometimes guests would pick off rose petals and drop them into the wine. Musicians, dancers, acrobats and clowns and even gladiators might appear at important feasts to entertain the guests between courses. The combination of rich surroundings, sumptuous and inventive cooking and dazzling entertainment gave the Roman banquets a magnificence seldom achieved since.

Undoubtedly Trimalchio's feast, described by Petronius, was quite exceptional even among the great banquets of imperial Rome, but it is worth recalling in outline here for the atmosphere it conveys. The first course was as usual an hors-d'oeuvre. A Corinthian bronze statuette of a horse carrying twin baskets, one filled with black olives, the other with green, was brought in on a tray of relishes. On the back of the animal were two silver dishes with Trimalchio's name engraved on the rim, together with the weight of the metal. Salvers moulded like bridges contained dormice seasoned with poppy seeds and honey. There were also sizzling sausages placed on a silver gridiron with Syrian plums and pomegranate seeds placed beneath it. A tray was placed on the table containing a basket in which sat a carved wooden hen, as if sitting on a nest. Two slaves then revealed that the nest was filled with pea-fowl eggs, and distributed them to the guests. On breaking them they were found to be made of light pastry. Inside were deliciously spiced garden warblers hidden within the yolks.

Crystal flagons, still sealed and bearing labels inscribed 'Falernian Opimian Wine 100 years old' were then brought in, opened and their contents served to the guests. Whilst they were drinking, a slave put a perfectly made silver model of a skeleton on the table, and demonstrated how the joints and backbone could be articulated in all directions by working a series of springs.

The guests were not quite sure what to make of the second course when it first arrived. It was served on a globe-shaped tray with twelve signs of the Zodiac reproduced on its rim in a circle. Above each sign the chef had placed dishes which in their shape or nature had some analogy with the particular constellation: over Aries the Ram there were chickpeas, over Taurus the Bull a piece of beef, over Gemini the Twins kidneys and testicles, over Cancer the Crab a simple crown, over Leo the Lion African figs, over Virgo the Virgin the uterus of a sow, over Libra the Scales a pair of scales with a pie on one side and a cake on the other, over Scorpio the Scorpion a small sea fish, over Sagittarius the Archer a hare, over Capricorn the Goat a lobster, over Aquarius the Water-bearer a goose and over Pisces the Fish two mullets. In the middle of this contraption was a honeycomb sitting on an artistically-cut piece of turf. An Egyptian slave served hot bread to everyone from a silver dish. As the guests were enthusiastically preparing to taste this fare Trimalchio said, 'Let us eat, believe me you have the most succulent of meals before you.'

As he spoke four slaves removed the top of the globe-shaped table to reveal plump chickens, sows' udders, a hare with wings fastened to its back symbolizing Pegasus. At the corners of the tray were four figures of Marsyas with highly seasoned fish sauce dripping from their bellies over the fish, which were floating about as if they were in a regular canal. The slaves spread over the couches covers embroidered with hunting scenes. Suddenly there was a loud roar and Laconian hounds burst into the room and began to run round the table followed by an enormous platter on which lay a wild boar, two baskets lined with palm-leaves hanging from its tusks – one filled with Syrian dates and the other with Theban dates. Little sucking pigs made out of pastry were offered to the guests who were allowed to take them away. Drawing his hunting knife a slave gave the wild boar a great stab in the belly and suddenly from out of the opening flew a number of thrushes. They tried in vain to fly out of the room but were caught in nets and offered to the guests.

When the table had been cleared three pigs, muzzled and hung with small bells were driven in, and the host asked the guests which they would like to eat. He then ordered the oldest to be slaughtered. Then the guests were offered more wine grown in his own vineyard.

An enormous pig was served up which covered most of the table and the guests were amazed at the speed of the cook. Trimalchio examining it, summoned the cook and declared that it had not been gutted before cooking and made as if to have him beaten. Then he asked the cook to gut it there on the spot. When the stomach of the pig was slashed open, out poured black puddings and sausages with which it had been stuffed. The cook was given the privilege of drinking with them and received a silver crown. It certainly seems that to enjoy a Roman feast one had to have a sound constitution.

THE EVIDENCE FOR THE FOODS EATEN IN ROMAN BRITAIN

There can be no doubt that shellfish were highly prized as food in Roman Britain. Oysters were especially important and may well have been transported live in tanks to inland sites. Oysters from the coast near Colchester and near Richborough were famous, and even valued in Rome. The consumption of oysters was so great that the proximity of Roman sites is almost always shown by the presence of large quantities of oyster shells. In one deposit in Silchester more than a million oyster shells were recovered. Other shellfish were also valued for food: periwinkles, mussels, whelks, cockles and scallops have also been found on Roman sites. It appears that both at Caerwent and Silchester shellfish shops may have been situated in the east wing of the forum.

Sea fish were also popular: cod, ling, haddock, grey mullet, herring and sea bream were caught, probably with a line and barbed bronze hooks which have also been found. Crabs and lobsters were taken inshore. Whale bones found at Caerwent may indicate that the occasional stranded whale was also fully utilized for its food potential.

Romano-British earthenware cooking pots

The most characteristic of all ingredients used in Roman cooking was *liquamen* or *garum*. It was made in many different parts of the Empire: several towns were specially renowned for their liquamen factories, especially Pompeii and Leptis Magna. The best account of it is given in *Geoponica* XX, chapter 46,1-6.

> This so-called liquamen is made as follows: the entrails of fish are thrown into a vessel and salted. Take small fish either atherinae or red mullet or sprats or anchovy and salt all together, and leave out in the sun, shaking it frequently. When it has become dry from heat extract the garum from it as follows: take a fine-meshed basket and place it in the middle of the vessel with the above mentioned fish, and in this way the so-called liquamen put through the basket can be taken up. If you wish to use the garum at once i.e. not expose it to the sun but boil it – make it in the following manner. Take brine and test its strength by throwing an egg into it to try if it floats: if it sinks the brine does not contain enough salt. Put the fish into the brine in a new earthenware pot, add origan, put it on a good fire till it boils... let it cool and strain it over two or three times until clear, seal and store away. The best garum is made by taking the entrails of tunny fish and its gills, juice and blood, and add sufficient salt. Leave it in a vessel for two months at most, then pierce the side of the vessel and the garum, called Haimation, will flow out.

The general effect of these mixtures is something resembling anchovy essence. The recipes will give some indications of the ways in which it was used.

The Romans were probably the first people to have the idea of enclosing vast tracts of land as game parks. In these they kept and hunted red, roe and fallow deer, wild boar and the bears that lived in the remoter parts of Wales and Scotland. Martial (vii, 3) describes how some British bears were taken to Rome to take part in wild beast shows. Hunting scenes are depicted on Castor ware pottery made in the Nene Valley which show running figures of dogs, hares and deer in low relief. Game was eaten either roasted or boiled and served with highly flavoured sauces. Venison sauces sometimes include dates in Apicius's recipes.

Not only were large game kept in parks, small game such as hares were kept in *leporia* or hare gardens attached to the villas of the more well-to-do Romans so that they would be quickly available when needed for the table.

Even smaller animals were kept in confined spaces. Dormice were kept in close captivity enclosed in pottery vessels and fed upon acorns and chestnuts. They were eaten at banquets after having been stuffed with minced pork and dormice meat, and baked in the oven. So far we have little direct evidence for this practice in Britain, though it was very common in other parts of the Empire.

Snails were another delicacy which was treated with care. The snails had to be kept on land entirely surrounded by water to prevent their escape. They were deliberately fed on milk, wine must and spelt wheat. For their final fattening they were kept in jars with air holes. When they became so fat that they could not get back into their shells they were fried in oil and served with liquamen mixed with wine. Shells of Roman snails have been found on many Romano-British villa sites, indicating that this was a popular form of food.

Wild fowl were also an important source of food; at Silchester swan, goose, wild duck, teal, widgeon, woodcock, plover, crane and stork appear to have been eaten as food. The larger wild fowl were hung for some days to tenderize them. There was a special sauce for those that were 'high' which was strongly flavoured with pepper, lovage, thyme, dried mint, filbert nut, Jericho date, honey vinegar, wine, liquamen, oil, wine must and mustard. The problem of removing the sinews from cranes was tackled by cooking them with their heads outside the water. When cooked, the birds were wrapped in a warm cloth and held tightly whilst the head was pulled off with all the sinews attached so that only the meat and bone remained. Roast barnacle goose, *cherneros,* was decribed by Pliny as the 'most sumptuous dish known to the Britons'.

The Romans practised intensive rearing of delicate birds in special enclosures. They introduced pheasants, peacocks and guinea fowl into Britain, and they may also have kept partridges in captivity as they did in Italy. Peacock meat was so tough that it could only be made palatable if it was killed at least a week in advance, and then was converted into rissoles. They were stewed in broth to which a little honey and pepper was added after cooking.

Wood pigeons were encouraged to roost in man-made pigeon houses or *columbaria* built in the form of high towers with niches inside, where the birds could nest and breed. People living in towns may have had earthenware dovecots built on the roof tiles of their houses as in the Mediterranean area today. Pigeons can play an important part in supplying meat, and are especially handy if they live in pigeon houses close by.

We have little evidence for the kinds of freshwater fish which were caught, but at Silchester eel, dace, perch, pike and carp are reported, together with bronze fish hooks and remains of frogs which may also have been eaten.

Salt was obtained from brine by boiling it in an evaporating furnace. Remains of this activity have been identified at Goldhanger and Cooling, Kent; Canewdon, Essex; Dymchurch, Sussex; and in the Fens and on the Lincolnshire coast. Salt springs were probably also used at Droitwich and Middlewich in Cheshire.

The arrival of the Romans brought new farming practices to this country. In southern England villas of the Italian type were built and new domestic animals were introduced. The treatises of successful landowners on the Continent were read and noted and the management of livestock became much more scientific. The main object was to secure a better supply of meat, though milk, dairy products, hides and wool were also important. The new farming methods included the improved feeding of livestock, and turnips made a significant contribution to the winter fodder.

British cattle were exported to the Continent even before the Romans arrived. Beef appears to have been the preferred meat of Roman Britain, and was supplied as the meat ration of the Roman garrison. There appear to have been several breeds of cattle represented in bones collected from Roman sites; there was the shorthorn, *Bos longifrons,* the larger *Bos taurus,* and an even larger form closely similar in size to the wild white Chillingham cattle. Oxen were also present and were the principal beast of burden. They provided milk, butter and cheese for the diet, also meat and leather, bone and horn and glue. Most of the cattle on the military sites in the north of England were of the shorthorn type. The animals represented are usually mature (though some young cattle were present at Newstead), and often their bones had been split for the extraction of the marrow. In one place at Silchester (Insula VI) a deposit of 2,500 lower jaws of cattle were discovered, and at another place on the same site were found 60 cattle horn cores – both deposits may be the refuse from some industrial activities but they do show that cattle were available in quite large numbers. At Cirencester the find below a shop floor of pits filled with cut and sawn bones has suggested that it was in fact a butcher's shop. At the Roman villa at Bignor, Sussex, there were stalls for 55 head of cattle, and a byre for 12 yoke of oxen.

When beef or veal was cooked it was often sliced and then served up in an elaborate sauce. Fried veal was given a sweet and sour sauce composed of raisins, honey, vinegar, pepper, dried onions and herbs.

Pigs were also plentiful, especially in the south and east of the country. Pork was prized by the Roman soldiers and lard was part of their daily rations. The farmers introduced the practice of keeping pigs in sties to fatten them up. Pig sties have been found on two villa sites, at Pitney, Somerset, and Woolaston Pill in Gloucestershire.

Sucking pig was roasted in the oven and then served with a thickened sauce flavoured with pepper, lovage, caraway, celery seed, asafoetida root, rue, liquamen, wine must and olive oil. Sow's udder was put in a mixed *patina* with fish, chicken meat and small birds.

Hams and bacon were either dry salted or pickled in their own brine. Ham and shoulder bacon were recognized as two different meats. According to Apicius they were both first boiled with dried figs; then the ham was baked in a flour and oil paste, while the bacon was ready to be served with a wine and pepper sauce. An early Roman grave at Grange Road, Winchester, contained a shale tray with a meal set out on it. There were two joints of pork, a Samian ware cup and platter, two knives and a spoon.

The soldiers on Hadrian's Wall and on the Antonine Wall also consumed a fair amount of mutton – large quantities of sheep bones were found at Corbridge and at Barr Hill. The Romano-British sheep seem to have been of light build, somewhat resembling the Soay sheep of St Kilda today. Sheep pens for 197 sheep have been found at Bignor Roman villa together with what appears to have been a lambing enclosure.

Two varieties of goats were also kept, probably as much for their milk as their meat. It may have been the practice to kill and salt the meat of unfit animals for human food, as it has been up till recent times.

There is some evidence that horse meat was eaten, possibly in the form of sausages; in Insula II at Verulamium there is a deposit of aged horse bones which have been dismembered and stripped of their flesh.

Among the remains of birds, those of domestic fowl predominate. There were apparently two varieties: one with small leg bones displaying the well-developed spur of the game cock resembled the modern bantam, the other was the ordinary domestic hen. They are found throughout Roman Britain. The other domestic bird was the goose, probably a variety of the grey lag goose. Boiled or roasted they were served with thick sauces, and they were often given elaborately spiced stuffings. Both birds produced a steady supply of eggs which were also used in cooking.

It seems likely that butter was used in cooking, but there is no evidence for it. The Romans were more accustomed to cooking with olive oil, or with lard.

The chief milk product we know to have been used was cheese. Pottery cheese strainers have been found on many Romano-British sites, for example the strainer found at Boxstead Farm, Lower Halstow, Kent. Cream cheeses may have been made in the shallow bowls known as *mortaria* (see below). Milk could be left in such bowls to curdle, the whey then being poured off through a spout on the rim. The grits on the inner surface of the bowl would retain the curd-forming bacteria from one cheese-making day to the next, thus obviating the need to use rennet, herbs or old whey to set the milk working. Curd cheeses were flavoured with herbs.

Mortarium *or grinding bowl showing coarse grit fired into the inside surface to make it rough*

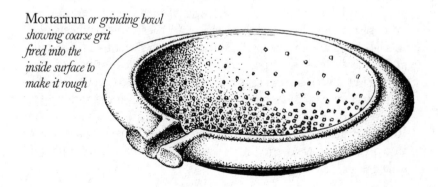

An earthenware cheese mould from Boxtead Farm, Lower Halstead, Kent

Cheese may have been eaten by itself with bread, but it could also be incorporated in other dishes. Hard cheeses were sometimes sliced into salads. Softer curd cheeses were used in *patina* dishes mixed with other meat or fish ingredients, hard-boiled eggs, nuts and seasonings.

Honey was a popular flavouring. Columella and Palladius describe how wild swarms of bees are to be trapped in empty hives or pots placed near the observed watering places of bees. The colonies are then installed in hives on the farm. Pottery hives – the worst sort on account of the great extremes of temperature to which the bees are subjected – have been found at Casterley Camp, Wiltshire, and at Rockbourne villa, Hampshire. Both take the form of an ordinary large jar suitably pierced with holes. Hives of wood or straw may have been used but have not survived. Two-handled jars from Silchester and Colchester may have been used as honey pots.

Various forms of wheat were cultivated in Roman Britain. The old hulled varieties of emmer and einkorn wheat continued to be grown, and to these increasing amounts of spelt wheat were added – probably to meet the corn tax or *annona*. All these hulled wheats need special drying treatment to release their grains efficiently in threshing, and it may be for this purpose that the considerable numbers of corn-drying kilns were erected especially on villa sites, so that the spikelets of hulled wheat could be parched before threshing and grinding. The naked forms of wheat, bread and club wheat, are also known from Roman Britain but in much smaller quantities. They are much easier to process and gave rise to the varieties of wheat which are cultivated today.

Both the naked and hulled varieties of six-row barley were grown too, but to a smaller extent and it seems that they used barley as punishment rations for soldiers on Hadrian's Wall and for fodder for the horses. Barley may also have been used for brewing although we do not have direct evidence for this.

Sprouted grains of rye were noted by Helbaek in the grain stored in a granary in Verulamium, but this is probably due to dampness: the hulled wheat stored in the same building had probably been parched, but in any case showed no signs of sprouting. Sprouted grains of wheat and rye were found together at Carleon in a situation which strongly suggests that they were deliberately sprouted to make malt. The manufacture of beer consists of two processes: malting and fermentation. In the first the starch contained in the grain is converted to sugar by the release of the enzyme diastase during the natural germination process. This is encouraged by spreading the grain thinly over a warm floor and giving it a circulation of air and moisture. When the sprouts reach the length of the grain (after a few days) the germination is stopped by giving the malt a mild roasting. The next stage is to steep the malt in water, then to boil it with herbs to give flavour. The fermentation takes place when yeast is added to the wort. The liquid is then drawn off and stored in tightly sealed bottles or barrels.

Plain Samian ware bowls

Possible bases of brewing vats have been found at Silchester where they have been described as 'round furnaces', often associated with long hearths. In a barn at the Wilcote villa, Oxfordshire, there was a similar round furnace with a flue, in which remains of a brewing vat were found. It was situated beside, but at a safe distance from, a granary.

Cereal grains were used for baking and for making porridge and gruel. Flour was normally ground at home on rotary hand querns, but there were also some commercial bakers who appear to have used larger hour-glass shaped querns which were driven by donkeys. On Hadrian's Wall water-driven mills have also been found.

There appears to have been a baker's shop in Canterbury, and at Verulamium an iron slice for removing loaves from the oven probably belonged to another bakery. An elaborate bread mould depicting a religious scene was found at Silchester. The Romans made a number of different kinds of bread: *autopyron* was a coarse, dark mixture of bran with a little flour made for the consumption of slaves and dogs; *athletae* was bread mixed with soft curd cheese, but otherwise unleavened; *buccellatum* was a biscuit or dried bread given to the troops; and *artophites* was a light leavened bread made from the best wheaten flour, and baked in a mould. It was loaves of this sort of bread which were found carbonized in Modestus's ovens at Pompeii.

For a long time the chief Roman food was a kind of gruel made from cereals, called *puls* or *pulmentus*, which was prepared from barley or spelt wheat which was roasted, pounded and cooked with water in a cauldron to make a porridge similar to the modern Italian *polenta*.

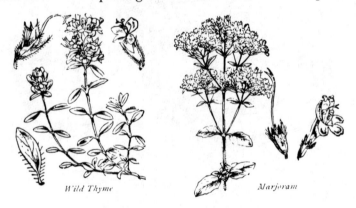

Wild Thyme   *Marjoram*

They also made a wheat starch product called *amulum,* which was used by the Roman cooks in the same way as we use cornflour today for thickening sauces. It was prepared by soaking wheat grains in fresh water in wooden tubs, and then straining the liquid through linen or wicker baskets before the grain turned sour. The liquid was poured on to a tiled floor spread with leaven, and left so as to thicken in the sun.

The Romans were enthusiastic about vegetables. They grew peas and beans and imported lentils into Britain. They introduced a number of vegetable crops such as cabbage, onion, leek, shallots, carrots, endive, globe artichokes, cucumber, marrow, asparagus, parsnip, turnip, radish and celery. They also ate a number of wild vegetable plants: at Silchester we know that they used Good King Henry, corn salad, nettles and pennycress.

Herbs were also extensively used in the Roman cuisine and many new ones were introduced to Britain at this time to supplement the poppy seeds, mustard and coriander already known in prehistoric times. The new herbs include alexanders, aniseed, borage, chervil, dill, fennel, garlic, hyssop, lovage, mint, parsley, rosemary, rue, sage, savory, sweet marjoram and thyme. The Romans much preferred to have their meat flavoured with herbs, either in stuffings or in sauces. One cook on the cook market in Plautus's *Pseudolus* (1, 810) said:

> 'I don't season a dinner the way other cooks do, who serve you up whole pickled meadows in their *patina*–men who make cows their mess mates, who thrust herbs at you then proceed to season those herbs with other herbs. They put in coriander, fennel, garlic and horse parsley, they serve up sorrel, cabbage, beet and spinach, pouring into this a pound of asafoetida and pounding up wicked mustard which makes the pounders' eyes water before they've finished. When they season their dinners they don't use condiments but screech owls, which eat out the intestines of the guests alive. That is why life is so short for men in this world, since they stuff their bellies with such like herbs, fearful to speak of, not just to eat. Men will eat herbs which the cows leave alone.'

A shop selling herb seeds at Colchester was burned down during Boudicca's rebellion, and the burnt seeds which survived include dill, coriander, aniseed, celery seed and poppy seed.

71

Salads, cooked vegetables, fungi and some light egg or fish dish supplied the hors-d'oeuvre of a Roman meal. Salads were served with a dressing of liquamen or *oenogarum* (liquamen mixed with wine).

Probably the most important fruit which the Romans introduced into Britain was the grape. Britain lies at the northernmost limit for the ripening of grapes in Europe, and their cultivation was restricted to the southern part of England. Direct evidence for the cultivation of vines comes from the finds of Sir John Evans in 1851 at Boxmoor villa in Hertfordshire. Here he reportedly found part of a vineyard with the vinestocks in position. Grape pips have been found widely on Roman sites and at Gloucester they were found together with grape skins and are thought to represent the debris from winemaking. A most interesting scene of a vine harvest is depicted on a barbotine pot from Colchester.

The local wine was, however, supplemented by imports of considerable quantities of wine-filled amphorae first from Spain and then from south-west France. Wine appears to have been imported in wooden barrels from this area to Silchester, where those that survive appear to have been made of silver fir, native to the Pyrenees. Wine was also imported from the Moselle region. The usual drink of the soldiers on the Wall was sour or ordinary wine though the letters from Vindolanda also list vintage wine.

Grapes may also have been imported in the form of raisins, sultanas or currants, sun-dried in the Mediterranean region.

A selection of storage jars. Standing up to about a metre high these were supported in frames or propped up in holes in the ground or simply stood against a wall. They were sealed with a stone and wax or a lump of clay

Vinegar was a very important product. It was manufactured from wine which had gone flat, or had been attacked by the vinegar bacteria during fermentation with additional yeast, salt and honey. Vinegar sharpened sauces and dressings, and was much used in the preservation of fruits, vegetables and even fish. Raw oysters were said to keep well if washed in it, as were pieces of fried fish if plunged into vinegar immediately after cooking. Diluted with several times its volume of water, vinegar made a refreshing drink, and was included in the rations for soldiers on the march. It is possible that the beer-based alegar was also coming into use in Roman times.

Wine intended for use in cooking was reduced by boiling before it was stored. This concentrated its sugars and made it keep better. The boiled-down must or defructum was also added to sharp new wines to help them keep.

Wine merchants' shops have been identified at Verulamium, York and Lincoln, usually by the presence of a large number of broken amphorae.

The fig is another Roman introduction and may well have been grown in southern England but, because the fruits which ripen here are parthenocarpic and bear their fruit without pollination, they do not develop hard seeds. This means that figs identified by the presence of their seeds alone must come from fruits which have been fertilized through the action of the blastophaga wasp, and have been imported to this country from warmer climates.

Among the other orchard crops introduced at this time are the medlar, the mulberry, damsons, plums and cultivated cherries. Apples and pears were also being grown in orchards. The dates found at Colchester and the olives from London must have been imported.

Various nut-bearing trees were introduced from Europe at this time including the walnut, the sweet chestnut, the almond and the stone pine whose cones and kernels seem to have had a ritual as well as culinary significance.

There is ample evidence that the local wild fruits were used in season. Seeds of blackberry, raspberry, strawberry, crab apple, bullace and elder were found at Silchester, for example, and the Bearsden Fort in Scotland also had seeds of raspberry, wild strawberry and hazelnuts.

Techniques for Food Preparation

A s mentioned above, corn-drying kilns were mainly found in association with villas. At Hambledon, Buckinghamshire, there was a huge capacity for drying corn (there were at least eight corn-drying kilns in the farmyard but curiously no granaries for storing it). These kilns are thought to have been used for drying and parching the hulled wheats to facilitate the threshing of the grain from the spikelets. They could also have served as suitable places to sprout grain to make malt for brewing. During the third and fourth centuries they occur in increasing numbers, sometimes inserted into the main house, as at Brading on the Isle of Wight.

The standard plans of Roman forts include two *horrea* or granaries. These are always buttressed and have raised floors to keep their contents dry. They often have a loading platform at one end. South Shields, which served as the supply base for Severus's campaigns in Scotland, contains no less than twenty-two granaries. The best preserved examples are at Corbridge, which show ventilation slits between the buttresses. The most likely internal arrangement was a central aisle lined with rows of bins.

Grain storage is always a tricky business and it appears that the granaries at York were subject to infestations of grain weevils, the contents having to be burnt to eradicate this menace.

One unusual find at Carvoran on Hadrian's Wall is of a *modius* or dry measure for grain. It is now in the Clayton Museum at Chester. It is made of bronze in the shape of a truncated cone about 8 inches (20cm) high.

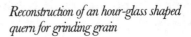

Reconstruction of an hour-glass shaped quern for grinding grain

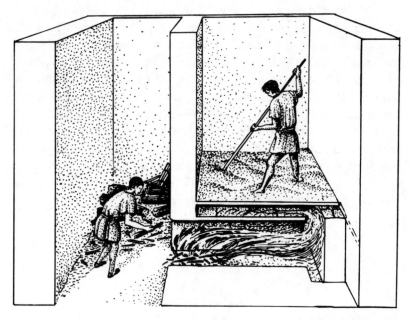

Romano-British corn-drier

Its capacity of 2.494 gallons (11.337 litres) is unexpected since it exceeds the standard measure of a modius by about 10 per cent. It has been suggested that this was a device to defraud provincials who were obliged to deliver a certain amount of wheat, but Roman certified measures are usually quite accurate and it is possible that the gauge, set lower than the rim, is missing.

The querns of Roman Britain were all rotary. The army imported a large number of them from the Rhineland made of Andernach lava. The normal method of grinding corn was by means of rotary hand querns made from millstone grit or imported Andernach lava. The lower stone was fixed in position and its slightly convex upper surface fitted snugly into the inversely coned lower surface of the upper stone. The upper stone revolved round its axis by means of a wooden or metal handle. Some of these querns are thought to have been ossilatory, the movement of the upper stone being only a quarter turn rather than the normal full rotation.

A larger type of mill, rarely found in Britain but common at Pompeii has a bi-conical or hour-glass shaped upper stone which revolves round a steeply conical lower stone by means of a heavy wooden lever to which a donkey or mule was sometimes attached. One example of such a mill, made of Andernach lava, was found at Princes Street, London; another is known from Canterbury. At Silchester flour appears to have been mainly ground at home, but one establishment seems to have been devoted to grinding flour on a commercial scale. A large hall (XVIII A 3) contained a series of masonry platforms running parallel to the long walls and about 5 feet (1.5m) away from the nearest one. These seem likely to have been bases for large querns of the hour-glass type.

Reconstruction of a Roman kitchen as displayed at the Museum of London

Cooking Equipment

The complex Roman recipes required more careful cooking than the simpler stews, roasts and pottages of the preceding prehistoric cooking tradition, and so it is not surprising to find that the Romans used more sophisticated cooking equipment. Much of the Roman cooking was done on a raised brick hearth, on top of which was a charcoal fire above which cooking vessels stood on tripods or gridirons. Meat and fish could be directly grilled over burning charcoal on the gridiron. It is possible that wood was burnt on the raised hearths too, especially in the case of dishes which Apicius describes as being smoked. Some very ornamental water heaters were discovered at Pompeii which may have been used for keeping food warm, or possibly for cooking by the bain-marie method. For boiling sucking pig in a cauldron it was likely, at any rate in country kitchens, that it was suspended by chains from the rafters over a more conventional open fire. Wild boar and other large animals were also roasted on spits over wood fires. Ovens were used for baking and roasting. They were constructed of rubble and tiles, shaped like low beehives, and provided with a flue to give a draught. Wood or charcoal fires were then lit inside them, the ashes were raked out as soon as the required temperature was reached, the food was put in and the opening of the oven was covered to retain the heat. There were also a range of portable ovens *(clibanus)* made of earthenware or iron. They were used for baking bread, or keeping dishes warm. Literary sources indicate that they had a rounded vault, wider at the base than at the top, with double walls. A charcoal fire must have been made under the inner floor, the heat percolating between the walls and the fumes escaping through small holes in the outer wall.

Built ovens have been recorded from a number of different sites: at Cirencester a row of fourth-century shops (insula V) were all equipped with ovens and may have been bakeries. They are a feature on many villa sites (good examples of kitchens with ovens occur at Great Witcombe and Chedworth), and they have been found on military sites, sometimes backing on to the ramparts as at Carleon.

Meat was cooked by roasting over a low fire, either on a gridiron or in a portable oven. The latter was suitable for roast neck of mutton, sucking kid or lamb, kidneys and stuffed dormice. Larger joints were either cooked in a baker's oven or grilled on spits over an open fire.

Meat was also stewed in an iron cauldron suspended over an open hearth. Sometimes animals such as stuffed sucking pig were suspended in a basket within the cauldron while cooking. Metal vessels became much more widespread and small cauldrons were mass-produced and thus became cheaply available.

A hoard of bronze cooking vessels together with a gridiron were found at the legionary fortress at Newstead. All the pans show signs of hard wear and some are even repaired with bronze patches soldered

Romano-British kitchen equipment.
Left to right: iron frying pan with folding handle, bronze pot,
iron gridiron with bronze cooking pot, bronze saucepan or paterae

into place. More frequently cooking pots were used and because they were cheap and widely available they could be thrown away when they became foul and unfit for service. Porous clay vessels are almost impossible to clean effectively.

A number of specialized cooking pans have been found. The frying pan (*fretale* or *sartago*) was sometimes equipped with a folding handle so that it could be put inside the portable oven as well as used for cooking over the gridiron. The *patella* was a round shallow pan with a handle, a little deeper than the frying pan, which was used on the table as well as in the kitchen. The *patina* appears to have been a deeper vessel still and was used for making complex dishes with many ingredients; it was somewhat like a casserole without a lid.

There were two other vessels which featured in the kitchen: mortaria and amphorae. *Mortaria* were special pottery bowls with roughened inner surfaces and a spout on the rim. They were general-purpose mixing bowls with heavy rims for lifting, and were first introduced by the Roman army. Gradually local potteries began to make them. There are also a number of huge mortaria, perhaps for use in bakeries, which were made in the second century by Verecundus of Soller, Kreis Durren, Germany, and imported into Britain.

Amphorae, or two-handled jars, were used in large quantities by the Romans for transporting and storing wine and oil, and remains of many hundreds of them have been found in Britain. After serving their primary purpose they were often adapted for other uses – they may be set into floors to store water, and they were even used as coffins. They varied in shape from the early carrot-shaped type with small handles to amphorae with long necks and elongated handles, still keeping their pointed bases, and globular forms with short necks and smaller handles. In general it seems that the tall amphorae came from France and contained wine whereas the globular amphorae came from Spain full of precious olive oil. It should be remembered that wine was also imported in wooden barrels, as is indicated by the Silchester finds.

SERVING THE FOOD

The Romans ate a good deal of their food with their fingers, hence their use of napkins, but they did have cutlery in the form of knives and spoons, but no forks. Knives were made in all sizes and are frequently found, usually with iron or bronze blades and bronze, wood or bone handles. Spoons were used for eating soft foods and sauces. They are also found quite frequently and are made from silver, bronze or bone and have either round or oval bowls. A small spoon known as a *cocleare* was used at the bowl end for eating eggs and the pointed handle end for picking shellfish out of their shells. The round-bowled spoons are earlier, whereas the oval, lyre-shaped bowl forms predominated in the third and fourth centuries. Larger spoons and ladles of bronze or iron may have been used for serving up food.

Equipment for serving wine was often very elaborate. It was sometimes imported, and often made from silver. It includes elaborate strainers with the perforations arranged in patterns, silver jugs, dishes, cups and goblets, enamelled wine ladles, cups and jars and finger bowls.

Dining tables were sometimes equipped with elaborate lamps, candelabra and sets of heated dishes. There can be little doubt that the

Knives and spoons. From the top anti-clockwise, iron knife with bone handle, iron knife from London, silver spoon from Dorchester, bronze spoon, London, and bone spatula from Dowkerbottom Cave, Yorkshire

furnishing of the table together with the interior decor of the dining room were the signs by which the Romans judged social standing.

The table was also furnished with plates, made either of pewter (examples are known from fourth-century London and Appleshaw, Hampshire), silver (the most exotic known in this country are from the magnificent Mildenhall Treasure and were probably not intended for use, but rather for show), or from the cheerful, bright red Samian ware. This was imported from France and comes in two forms: large bowls with decoration in relief and a range of smaller bowls and platters which are undecorated.

Glass was much less common than pottery but included bowls, beakers, bottles and jugs usually of a pale greenish colour (but examples of white, amber, dark blue and yellowish green glass are known and there are a few examples with the late polychrome glass from Roman London).

Two forms of metal jugs are also known to have been made in either pewter or bronze. There is a rather bulky wide-mouthed jug with a broad neck which merges without division into the body; and a relatively narrow-necked form which is much more graceful and has its neck clearly separated from the bulbous body by a line of decoration.

There can be little doubt that the Romans gave a great deal of thought and went to some trouble in order to serve their food as elegantly and imaginatively as possible.

Some rare examples of fine Roman glassware

RECIPES

All these recipes are based on those of Apicius, whose cookery book is the only one to have come down to us from Roman times. M. Gaius Apicius lived at the time of Tiberius, in the first century, and apparently wrote two books on cooking: a recipe book and a book on sauces. It appears that the manuscripts which have survived are those of a late fourth-century or early fifth-century edition which also includes extracts from a Greek cookery book of the Imperial period. The best edition to consult is *The Roman Cookery Book, a critical translation of The Art of Cooking by Apicius* by Barbara Flower and Elizabeth Rosenbaum. Readers are referred to this book if they want to experiment further; the recipes given below were selected to give a range of dishes which it is more or less practical to try out today and which give an idea of the tastes of the Romans and of their culinary skills. Apicius is rather cavalier with his cooking instructions and so I have given much fuller details of quantities, cooking times, and procedures based on contemporary practice, but each cook must feel free to vary the quantities especially of herbs, spices and flavourings according to their own personal preferences and experience.

A number of standard ingredients may need explanation. *Liquamen* has already been discussed, and anchovy essence in diluted form, or soy sauce, may be used as substitutes. *Defrutum* is a cooking wine which has been reduced to at least half its volume by boiling down before use, to give it a thick consistency. *Caroenum* is a very sweet wine, similarly reduced to a third of its volume and mixed with honey. *Passum* is another, sweeter cooking wine for which a sweet Spanish wine can be substituted successfully. *Mulsum* is a mixture of honey and wine which was used as a drink to accompany the first course of a meal. Most of the sauces were thickened with *amulum*, a type of wheat starch, for which cornflour is an excellent substitute. *Asafoetida* extract may be obtained from the chemist, but use it very sparingly as it is extremely strong and only the tiniest drop is needed to give flavour.

BOILED MUSSELS

1-1½ pt (0.5-0.8L) mussels per person
a pinch of each of the following: celery
*   seeds, rue, peppercorns*
1 tbls (15ml) honey
1 tbls (15ml) passum
1 tbls (15ml) olive oil
1 tsp (5ml) anchovy essence
1 tbls (15ml) cornflour

Prepare and cook the mussels as in the preceding recipe. Remove from their shells, and keep warm. Pound the celery seed, rue, pepper and honey together in a mortar. Add *passum*, olive oil and anchovy essence, and put in a pan. Blend in the cornflour and bring to the boil stirring all the time, until the sauce thickens. Pour over the mussels, sprinkle with pepper and/serve.

PRAWN RISSOLES

24 cooked shelled prawns
a pinch of pepper
1 tsp (5ml) anchovy essence
1 egg, beaten
flour

Pound the prawns in a mortar with the pepper and anchovy essence. Mix in the beaten egg to bind and form into rissoles. Roll in flour and fry gently in oil until lightly browned on both sides.

MUSSELS WITH LENTILS

1-1½ pt (0.5-0.8L) mussels per person
12 oz (350g) lentils
1 onion, chopped
a pinch of each of the following:
*   peppercorns, cumin seeds, coriander*
*   seeds, dried mint, rue, pennyroyal*
1 tbls (15ml) vinegar
1 tbls (15ml) honey
1 tbls (15ml) defructum
1 tsp (5ml) anchovy essence
olive oil, to serve

Clean the mussels thoroughly, discarding any that are open, place in a rinsed wide pan and cover closely with a folded damp tea-towel. Heat quickly, shaking the pan at intervals, for about 5-7 minutes until the shells open. Take the mussels from their shells, removing the beards. Pound in a mortar. Put the lentils in a pan of cold water with the onion and bring to the boil. Cook until the lentils are soft. Pound the pepper, cumin, coriander, mint, rue and pennyroyal in a mortar, then mix in the vinegar, honey, *defructum* and anchovy essence, and pour into the pan with the lentils. Add the mussels to the lentils, and bring them to the boil, stirring. Serve hot, sprinkled with a few drops of best olive oil.

MILK-FED SNAILS

6 edible snails per person
2 pt (1.1L) milk
salt
1 tsp (5ml) anchovy essence
1 tbls (15ml) wine

Clean the snails with a sponge and remove the membranes so that they can come out of their shells. Put in a vessel with half the milk and salt for 1 day, then in a fresh vessel with the remaining milk for 1 more day, cleaning away the excrement every hour. When the snails are fattened to the point that they cannot return to their shells, fry them in oil. Serve with a dressing of anchovy essence and wine.

SAUCE FOR YOUNG TUNNY FISH

a pinch of each of the following: pepper, lovage, origano, fresh coriander
1 onion, thinly sliced
2 oz (50g) stoned raisins
1 tbls (15ml) passum
1 tbls (15ml) vinegar
1 tbls (15ml) defructum
1 tbls (15ml) olive oil
1 tsp (5ml) anchovy essence
honey (optional)

Pound the pepper, herbs, onion and raisins in a mortar. Put in a saucepan with the liquid ingredients, and bring to the boil. Add honey to taste if liked. Serve with grilled or boiled tunny fish.

PATINA OF FILLETS OF HAKE

4 oz (100g) shelled pine kernels
1 hake fillet per person
2 leeks, chopped
2 sticks celery, chopped
1lb (450g) spinach, cooked to a purée
8 oz (225g) cooked chicken breast, sliced
4 oz (100g) salami, sliced
4 eggs, hard-boiled and halved
8 oz (225g) pork sausages, cooked and chopped
3 oysters per person, shelled (or 1 can smoked oysters in oil)
2 oz (50g) cheese, grated
1 oz (25g) peppercorns
½ pt (275ml) milk
a pinch of each of the following: pepper, lovage, celery seeds
1 drop asafoetida essence
2 eggs, beaten
sea urchins, to garnish (optional)

Soak the pine kernels, and let them dry. Fry the hake fillets. Take a shallow ovenproof dish and layer in it the leeks, celery, spinach purée, chicken, salami, hard-boiled eggs, sausages, oysters and cheese. Sprinkle the pine kernels and peppercorns over the top. Put the milk in a saucepan, add the pepper, lovage and celery seed, and bring to the boil. Add the asafoetida essence and remove from the heat. Mix in the beaten eggs, then pour the sauce over the patina and cook in a moderate oven, gas mark 4, 350°F (180°C), until set. Garnish if wished with sea urchins.

SAUCE FOR SEA BREAM

a pinch of each of the following:
    peppercorns, lovage, caraway seeds,
    celery seeds, dried onion
1 drop asafoetida essence
1 tbls (15ml) wine
1 tbls (15ml) passum
1 tbls (15ml) vinegar
1 tbls (15ml) olive oil
1 tsp (5ml) anchovy essence
1 tbls (15ml) cornflour

Grind together the pepper, lovage, caraway, celery seed and dried onion in a mortar. Moisten with a drop of asafoetida essence and add the wine, *passum*, vinegar, olive oil and anchovy essence. Put the mixture in a saucepan, blend in the cornflour and heat until boiling, stirring all the time. Remove from heat when the sauce has thickened, and serve with sea bream.

OYSTERS

3-4 oysters per person
a pinch of pepper
a pinch of ground lovage
2 egg yolks
1 tbls (15ml) vinegar
1 tbls (15ml) olive oil
1 tbls (15ml) wine
1 tsp (5ml) anchovy essence
1 tbls (15ml) honey (optional)

Ask your fishmonger to open the oyster shells for you, as near as possible to the time of eating. They can be served raw or stewed or baked, then covered with the following sauce to serve. Mix the pepper and lovage with the egg yolks, then add the vinegar, a drop at a time, to make a smooth mixture. Stir in the olive oil, wine and anchovy essence. Honey may be added if liked. Mix all thoroughly together, pour over the oysters and serve.

FISH COOKED IN ITS OWN JUICE

1 salmon, salmon trout or ordinary trout
1 tbls (15ml) salt
1 tbls (15ml) coriander seeds
1 tbls (15ml) vinegar

Clean, wash and dry the fish. Pound the salt and the coriander seed in a mortar. Roll the fish in this mixture. Place the fish in an ovenproof frying pan, seal by frying quickly on both sides, then cover with a lid. Put the pan in the oven and bake at gas mark 4, 350°F (180°C) until the fish is cooked through. When it is cooked, remove from the oven, sprinkle with strong vinegar and serve.

SUCKING PIG À LA FLACCUS

1 sucking pig
salt
a pinch of each of the following: pepper,
*   lovage, caraway seeds, celery seeds, rue*
1 drop asafoetida essence
1 tsp (5ml) anchovy essence
3 tbls (45ml) wine
1 tbls (15ml) passum
2 tsps (10ml) olive oil
1 tbls (15ml) cornflour
ground celery seed, to serve

Clean the pig. Sprinkle with salt
and roast at gas mark 4, 350°F
(180°C), allowing 25 minutes per lb
(450g) plus 25 minutes. While it is
cooking pound the pepper, lovage,
caraway, celery seed and rue in a
mortar. Moisten with asafoetida
essence and anchovy essence, then
blend in the wine and *passum*. Put
in a saucepan with the olive oil and
bring to the boil. Thicken with
cornflour mixed with water. Add
the juices from the roast sucking
pig, bring to the boil and simmer
gently until thickened. Pour over
the pig, and sprinkle with ground
celery seed. Serve hot.

HOT BOILED GOOSE WITH COLD SAUCE

a pinch of each of the following: pepper,
*   lovage, coriander seeds, mint, rue*
1 tsp (5ml) anchovy essence
1 tbls (15ml) olive oil

Place the goose in a large saucepan.
Barely cover with cold water and
simmer the bird for approximately
2½ hours until tender. Dry with a
clean cloth and keep warm. Pound
the pepper, lovage, coriander seed,
mint and rue in a mortar. Add the
anchovy essence and olive oil,
together with the juices from the
pan. Pour over the bird and serve.

BOILED PARTRIDGE

1 partridge
a pinch of each of the following: pepper,
*   lovage, celery seeds, mint, myrtle*
*   berries or raisins*
1 tbls (15ml) wine
1 tbls (15ml) vinegar
1 tbls (15ml) olive oil
1 tsp (5ml) anchovy essence
1 tbls (15ml) honey

Place the partridge with its feathers
on in a large saucepan. Cover with
cold water and simmer gently for
about 45 minutes over a low heat.
Pluck the bird when cooled but still
wet. A freshly killed partridge may
be plucked first and then braised in
the sauce so that it does not get
tough. To make the sauce, pound
together the pepper, lovage, celery
seed, mint, myrtle berries or raisins
in a mortar, and then mix them
with the wine, vinegar, olive oil,
anchovy essence and honey. This
makes a pleasant cold dressing to
serve with the cooled partridge.

HOT SAUCE
FOR ROAST VENISON

a pinch of each of the following: pepper,
*   lovage, parsley*
8 oz (225g) dried damsons, soaked
*   overnight*
1 tbls (15ml) honey
1 tbls (15ml) wine
1 tbls (15ml) vinegar
1 tsp (5ml) anchovy essence
olive oil
1 leek, chopped
1 savory plant

Put the pepper, lovage, parsley, the drained damsons, honey, wine, vinegar, anchovy essence and a drop of olive oil in a pan and stir them together with the leek and savory plant. Cook slowly over a low heat for about 1 hour. Serve with roast venison.

STUFFED HARE

8 oz (225g) whole pine kernels
4 oz (100g) shelled almonds
4 oz (100g) chopped mixed nuts
1 oz (25g) peppercorns
1 hare
2 eggs, beaten
a pinch of each of the following: rue,
*   pepper, savory*
1 small onion, chopped
4 oz (100g) stoned dates
1 tsp (5ml) anchovy essence
2 tbls (30ml) spiced wine

Mix together the pine kernels, almonds, chopped mixed nuts, peppercorns and the chopped giblets of the hare. Bind with the eggs and use the mixture to stuff the hare. Wrap the hare in baking foil and roast in the oven at gas mark 5, 375°F (190°C) for 1-1½ hours until tender. To make the sauce, put the rue, pepper, savory, chopped onion, dates, anchovy essence, spiced wine and the juices from the roast hare in a saucepan. Let this boil gently until thickened, then pour over the hare.

SAUCE FOR
ROAST WOOD PIGEONS

a pinch of each of the following: pepper,
*   lovage, fresh coriander, mint, dried*
*   onion*
4 oz (100g) stoned dates
1 egg yolk
1 tbls (15ml) wine
1 tbls (15ml) vinegar
1 tbls (15ml) olive oil
1 tbls (15ml) honey
1 tsp (5ml) anchovy essence

Pound the pepper, herbs and onion together in a mortar. Add the dates and egg yolk and pound until smooth. Mix the remaining ingredients in a pan, add the mixture from the mortar, and heat gently until the sauce thickens, stirring all the time. Pour over roast pigeons and serve.

BOILED CHICKEN

1 boiling chicken
a pinch of each of the following: pepper,
    cumin, thyme, fennel seeds, mint, rue
1 drop asafoetida essence
2 tbls (30ml) vinegar
4 oz (100g) stoned dates
1 tbls (15ml) honey
1 tbls (15ml) olive oil
1 tsp (5ml) anchovy essence

Put the chicken in a saucepan.
Cover with water and simmer
gently for 2½-3 hours until
thoroughly cooked. Dry well.
Pound the pepper, cumin, thyme,
fennel seed, mint and rue in a
mortar and moisten with a drop of
asafoetida essence. Add the vinegar
and dates and pound until well
blended. Stir in the honey, oil and
anchovy essence. Pour over the
chicken and serve either hot or
cold.

HOT LAMB STEW

1½-2 lb (700-900g) lean loin, neck or
    breast of lamb, cubed
1 small onion, finely chopped
1 tsp (5ml) coriander seeds
a pinch of each of the following: pepper,
    lovage, cumin
1 tsp (5ml) anchovy essence
1 tbls (15ml) olive oil
1 tbls (15ml) wine
1 tbls (15ml) cornflour

Put the pieces of meat into a
saucepan and toss in hot oil to seal.
Pound the onion, coriander seed,
pepper, lovage and cumin in a
mortar. Mix with the anchovy
essence, olive oil and wine. Pour
this mixture over the meat in the
pan and simmer gently for about 2
hours, until tender. Mix the
cornflour with a little water and
add to the stew to thicken the
sauce. Stir until boiling. Serve hot.

SAUCE FOR MEAT SLICES

a pinch of each of the following: pepper,
    lovage, caraway seeds, dried mint,
    spikenard
1 egg yolk
1 tbls (15ml) honey
1 tbls (15ml) vinegar
1 tbls (15ml) olive oil
1 tsp (5ml) anchovy essence
1 bay leaf
1 tbls (15ml) cornflour

Pound the pepper, lovage,
caraway, mint and spikenard in a
mortar, then mix together with the
egg yolk, honey, vinegar, olive oil
and anchovy essence. Place in a
pan over a low heat, and add the
bay leaf. A leek may also be added
for extra flavour if desired. Blend
in the cornflour and stir until
thickened. Remove leek and bay
leaf and pour immediately over
meat slices.

SAUCE FOR SOFT-BOILED EGGS

4 oz (100g) shelled pine kernels
a pinch of pepper
a pinch of lovage
1 tbls (15ml) honey
1 tbls (15ml) vinegar

Soak the pine kernels and let them dry. Pound the pepper, lovage and pine kernels in a mortar until smooth. Mix with honey and vinegar, and pour this sauce over freshly boiled eggs which have been removed from their shells.

TRUFFLES

12 large truffles
salt
1 tbls (15ml) olive oil
1 tsp (5ml) anchovy essence
1 tbls (15ml) wine
1 tbls (15ml) caroenum
1 tbls (15ml) honey
a pinch of pepper
2 tsps (10ml) cornflour

Scrape the truffles and put in a saucepan with some water. Boil until just tender, sprinkle with salt and thread on to skewers. Grill lightly. Put the oil, anchovy essence, wine, *caroenum,* honey and pepper in a saucepan and bring to the boil. Add the cornflour mixed with a little water and stir until thickened. Remove/truffles from skewers and serve with the sauce.

MEAT PIECES À LA APICIUS

T-bone beef steaks, or pork chops, or leg
steaks of pork or mutton
a pinch of each of the following: pepper,
lovage, cyperus, cumin
1 tsp (5ml) anchovy essence
2 tbls (30ml) passum

Bone the meat, roll up the pieces, tie together with string and put in the oven to seal at gas mark 7, 425°F (220°C) for about 10 minutes. Remove from oven and put under a low grill, taking care not to burn them. Pound the pepper, lovage, cyperus and cumin in a mortar and blend with the anchovy essence and *passum.* Put the meat in a pan with this sauce and simmer gently until completely cooked. Remove the meat from the pan with a slotted spoon and serve without the sauce, sprinkled with pepper.

PEAS À LA VITELLIUS

1½ lb (700g) dried peas, soaked
    overnight
a pinch of each of the following: pepper,
    lovage, ginger
yolks of 2 hard-boiled eggs
3 tbls (45ml) honey
1 tsp (5ml) anchovy essence
1 tbls (15ml) wine
1 tbls (15ml) vinegar
1 tbls (15ml) olive oil

Boil the peas gently for about 1½
hours until very soft. Stir to make a
smooth mixture. Pound the
pepper, lovage and ginger in a
mortar and mix with the hard-
boiled egg yolks, honey, anchovy
essence, wine and vinegar. Put the
pounded mixture in a saucepan,
add the olive oil and bring to the
boil. Add to the peas, stirring until
smooth and heated through, then
serve.

LENTILS WITH CHESTNUTS

4 oz (100g) lentils
4 oz (100g) shelled chestnuts
½ tsp (2.5ml) bicarbonate of soda
a pinch of each of the following: pepper,
    cumin, coriander seeds, mint, rue,
    pennyroyal
1 drop asafoetida essence
1 tsp (5ml) anchovy essence
1 tbls (15ml) vinegar
1 tbls (15ml) honey
1 tbls (15ml) olive oil

Cover the lentils with water and
simmer gently for 30 minutes. Put
the chestnuts in another pan, cover
with water, add bicarbonate of
soda and bring to the boil. Cook
until tender. Pound the pepper,
cumin, coriander, mint, rue and
pennyroyal in a mortar. Moisten
with asafoetida essence, anchovy
essence, vinegar and honey, and
pour over the cooked chestnuts.
Add olive oil and bring to the boil,
stirring all the time. Mix with the
lentils. Taste and adjust flavouring
if necessary, serve hot.

PURÉE OF LETTUCE LEAVES
WITH ONIONS

6 small lettuces
½ tsp (2.5ml) bicarbonate of soda
a pinch of each of the following: pepper,
    lovage, celery seeds, dried mint,
    origano
1 onion, finely chopped
1 tbls (15ml) wine
1 tbls (15ml) olive oil
1 tsp (5ml) anchovy essence

Plunge the lettuces into a pan of
boiling water with the bicarbonate
of soda, and simmer for 2 minutes,
drain, then chop finely. Pound the
pepper, lovage, celery seed, mint,
origano and onion in a mortar.
Add the wine, oil and anchovy
essence. Cook gently in a saucepan
for 30 minutes, pour over the
lettuce, and serve.

JULIAN POTTAGE

8 oz (225g) whole wheat grains, soaked overnight
1 tbls (15ml) olive oil
2 cooked brains
8 oz (225g) minced meat
a pinch of each of the following: pepper, lovage, fennel seeds,
1 tsp (5ml) anchovy essence
1 tbls (15ml) wine
2 pt (1.1L) stock

Drain the wheat grains and bring them to the boil in a pan of water. Simmer until soft, add the olive oil and continue to cook until thickened to a creamy consistency. Pound the brains and minced meat in a mortar, then put in a saucepan. Pound the pepper, lovage and fennel seed, and moisten with anchovy essence and wine. Add this to the meat in the pan. Bring gently to the boil and add the stock. Add this mixture gradually to the wheat, mixing it in by the ladleful, and stir until smooth, to the consistency of thick soup.

PATINA OF ELDERBERRIES

6 bunches of elderberries
½ tsp (2.5ml) pepper
1 tsp (5ml) anchovy essence
4 floz (125ml) wine
4 floz (125 ml) passum
4 floz (125ml) olive oil
6 eggs

Remove the fruits from the stems of the elderberry bunches with a fork. Wash them, place in a saucepan with a little water, and simmer gently until just softened. Drain and arrange in a greased shallow pan. Add the pepper, moisten with anchovy essence, then add the wine and *passum* and mix well. Finally, add the olive oil and bring to the boil. When the mixture is boiling, break the eggs into it and stir well to bind it together. When set, sprinkle pepper over it and serve hot or cold.

A pewter jug from Moorgate

STUFFED DATES

6 dates per person
shelled almonds, hazelnuts or pine kernels
  (1 per date)
pepper
salt
3 tbls (45ml) honey

Stone the dates and stuff with the nuts and a little pepper. Roll the dates in salt, then heat the honey in a frying pan, fry the dates briskly, and serve.

HONEY OMELETTE

4 eggs
½ pt (275ml) milk
1 tbls (15ml) olive oil
3 tbls (45ml) honey
pepper

Mix together the eggs, milk and oil. Pour a little oil into a frying pan and heat. When it is sizzling add the prepared mixture. When thoroughly cooked on one side turn out on to a round dish, warm the honey and pour it over the omelette. Sprinkle with pepper and serve.

A silver cup
from
Water Newton

SWEET WINE CAKES

1 lb (450g) self-raising flour
1 tbls (15ml) sweet white wine
a pinch of aniseed
a pinch of cumin
2 oz (50g) lard
1 oz (25g) cheese, grated
1 egg, beaten
12 bay leaves

Moisten the flour with the wine and add the aniseed and cumin. Rub in the lard and grated cheese and bind the mixture with egg. Shape into 12 small cakes and place each one on a bay leaf. Bake in the oven at gas mark 6, 400°F (200°C) for about 25-30 minutes.

HONEY CAKES

12 stale sweet wine cakes (see above)
2 pt (1.1L) milk
3 tbls (45ml) honey
pepper

Remove the crusts from the cakes and steep them in milk. When they are saturated put them in the oven at gas mark 4, 350°F (180°C) for about 20 minutes, Warm the honey and pour it over the hot cakes, pricking them to absorb more honey. Sprinkle with pepper and serve.

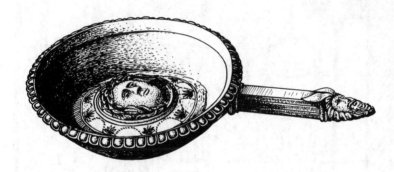

A bronze skillet from Faversham

MEDIEVAL BRITAIN

Maggie Black

Fourteenth-century cooking and serving, from the Luttrell psalter

The earliest surviving English recipe books date from about 1390 when *The Forme of Cury* was written by order of King Richard II. Our knowledge of English medieval cooking in general comes mostly from indirect sources, such as government and church regulations, account and rent books, and a few books about table manners and diet. Pictures and poems such as Chaucer's *Canterbury Tales* fill further social detail.

To give a coherent picture, the notes which follow describe, by and large, how people ate in the late fourteenth and early fifteenth centuries, and the recipes come from books of the same period.

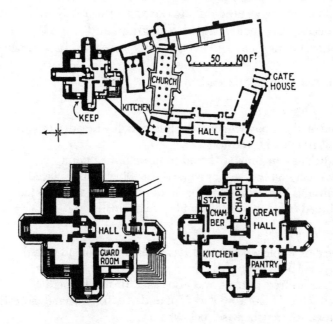

Warkworth Castle. The main kitchen was outside the keep. Steps led up into the keep which was on two floors. There was a small kitchen on the upper floor off the great hall, presumably for reheating food

FOOD CHOICE

Bread was everyone's staple food but the grain it was made from varied from place to place, and with one's income. Wheat made the finest, whitest bread but only grew on good soil; and only the lord of the manor, that is the feudal holder of a large estate, could afford to have land dug over and manured for it. The commonest bread, called maslin, was made from wheat and rye flour mixed; darker loaves were made from rye flour alone. Barley and other oats were the breadcorns of the north and west where the climate was wet and cold. Nearly always, weed seeds were included with any grain, and when the harvest was poor, beans, peas and even acorns were used in the cheapest bread.

The main types of bread were:

White Breads

Pandemain or paynemaine, the finest quality bread, from flour sifted two or three times.

Wastel, also first-quality bread from well-sifted flour.

Cocket, a slightly cheaper white bread which was replaced around 1500 with small loaves or rolls of top-quality white bread called manchets (hand-sized breads).

Other Breads

Cheat or whole wheat bread was whole wheat bread with the coarse bran removed.

Tourte (or trete or treet) was also called Brown Bread. It contained husk as well as flour and may have been the bread used for trenchers (see below).

Maslin, mesclin or miscellin was mixed wheat and rye bread.

Horse bread included peas, beans, and any other grain to hand.

There were also the cheap breads 'of all grains', bran bread (made mostly with bran) and in the north and west especially, various kinds of barley bread and oatcakes which are still called havercakes or clapbread.

The most important use of brown bread for the wealthy was as trenchers (plates). The trenchers were made by cutting large loaves, preferably four days old, into thick slices with a slight hollow in the centre. An ordinary person would have only one or two plate trenchers for a whole meal, but a great personage would have several stacked up for him. These trenchers were gathered up in a basket and given to the poor after dinner.

Plain or toasted bread was used a great deal in cooked dishes. Breadcrumbs were a standard way of thickening sauces and of stiffening custards so that they could be sliced. Gingerbread was just a heavily spiced breadcrumb and honey mixture, heavily decorated with box leaves stuck on with whole cloves. Other cakes and buns were really just sweetened, spiced pieces of bread dough.

Most country people baked their own bread, but in the towns, professional bakers operated, and were notorious as crafty swindlers. In 1267, therefore, by royal order, a set of regulations for assessing bread prices was laid down, called the Assize of Bread, to try to make sure that everyone paid a fair price for a loaf and no more. It was difficult to enforce, especially in small rural markets, but bakers who were caught flouting it were punished severely, and it was at least a responsible attempt to see that ordinary people could afford a very basic product.

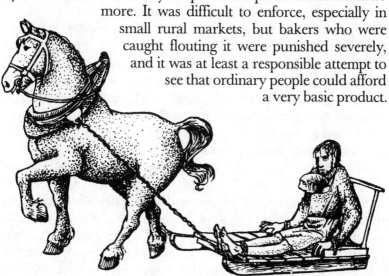

A baker of short-weight loaves being punished by being dragged through the streets on a sledge

Poorer people had another grievance besides bread prices; by about 1350, servants and serfs were complaining that they were only issued with coarse maslin or brown bread, and free labourers also resented not getting wheaten bread. Their masters justified it by saying that branny brown bread sustained those who did heavy manual work for long hours, but that it caused wind in people who lived sedentary lives; in fact, they really reserved it because it was a status symbol.

Fish was almost as vital as bread to medieval people. The Roman Catholic Church to which everyone belonged laid down that on Fridays (and until late in the period, Saturdays and Wednesdays) no one might eat meat; and throughout Lent, eggs and other dairy foods were forbidden too. This meant that for about half the days in the year everyone had to eat fish.

Churchmen had even more restricted meals. Officially the Rule of St Benedict forbade 'the meat of quadrupeds' to monks except for the sick, but from the thirteenth century the dietary strictures were respected less and less and by the fifteenth century were usually honoured only at formal banquets.

For ordinary people, fish meant salted or pickled herrings. England's herring fleets caught thousands of fish throughout the summer, and there was a big salting and pickling industry to process them; it was the only way to preserve them for travel inland. Apart from dried cod, called stockfish, which was as hard as board, poor people inland got no other sea fish. Londoners and people living near the east coast were luckier because they could get oysters and whelks quite cheaply.

In summer, when Lent was past, ordinary people inland could also sometimes widen their choice by catching river fish and collecting eels. The wealthy had a wide choice of sea fish, including those we know now, such as plaice, haddock and mackerel, and more exotic ones. Seals were eaten, and so were the 'royal' fish, whale, sturgeon and porpoise, which belonged to the king but which he often gave away. Shellfish such as crab and lobster were common and popular too.

Besides these, landowners had plentiful river fish such as salmon, trout, grayling, bream and tench. Most estates of any size

A twelfth-century fish-day meal. The man in the centre holds a knife and trencher. The page holds a beaker which will be shared by the guests

also had their own fishponds, called stews, in which they bred carp (a luxury) and pike (fairly common). Pickled salmon was a luxury imported from Scotland and Ireland when out of season at home.

One would think that this gave enough choice, even for the large number of 'fish days' in the year; but there were some curious animals classified as 'fish'. For instance, barnacle geese and puffins were alleged to be 'fish' because they were said to be created at sea, while beavers, which still existed in Britain, were said to have fishes' tails.

Since so much salt fish had to be eaten, many spice and herb sauces were developed specially to serve with them. Fried parsley was already a favourite garnish for fish.

Throughout medieval times more sheep were kept in eastern England than cattle. Goats were also kept for milk and meat. The Normans gave sheep-meat the name we know it by now – mutton. It was second favourite to beef, but both these red meats were preferred to the white meats, veal and kid; they made more solid, satisfying roasts.

A pig was a poor man's standby, because the pig could forage for himself year-round in the woods, and fight off most foes. It looked and behaved like a wild pig, but when slaughtered the flesh made good pickling pork or bacon, the poor man's only winter meat. The 'innards' made blood puddings and other sausages, and the fat could be eaten on bread or used for cooking.

Unlike swine, cattle, sheep and goats could not feed themselves throughout the winter, so fodder was a constant problem. As a result, all beasts except breeding stock and milk animals were slaughtered at intervals throughout the winter, to provide fresh offal and salted joints. Beef sides, or goat and mutton hams, were salted and smoked like pork.

Fresh mutton could be roasted if young, but was better boiled if elderly. It was about the same size as our well-aged lamb. All domesticated animals were small, scrubby creatures, very different and much less meaty than our specially-bred modern animals.

Game animals were designated personal property by the first Norman kings and nobles, and poachers were mutilated or executed if caught. But although hunting the wild bull, boar and deer remained an aristocratic privilege, hares and adult rabbits, which were called coneys, were made poor men's prey and free meat at the beginning of the thirteenth century. Wild cattle were getting rare, but boars were common almost until Tudor times and provided traditional Christmas brawn for all large feudal households. Roasting cuts of venison and pasties were 'top table' fare, but 'umbles' (liver and lights) made pies for the huntsmen and the lower tables at a household feast.

Poultry, game birds, small birds and waterfowl were enjoyed by everyone, especially the clergy, who were officially allowed to eat 'two-legged' but not 'four-legged' meat.

Apart from hunting wildfowl with falcons, a noble household would employ its own bird-catcher or bargain with a local poulterer for supplies, and would have its own dovecot and domestic poultry yard (for pheasants and partridges as well as hens, ducks and geese). Some of this backyard stock might be cooped and fattened; battery rearing and force-feeding were common. Even the poor kept hens, but eggs were precious, and so they would catch a wild bird or two for choice.

The birds which were eaten were much more varied than we eat today. Swan or peacock were served at a banquet or celebration, dressed up as a processional centrepiece for the top table. The bustard was another 'great fowle' for parties. They could weigh up to twenty-five pounds and could hardly fly. Other unusual meal choices were: crane, heron (especially the young ones called heronshewes), gull, curlew, egret, quail, plover, snipe, blackbird (the most expensive of the 'smale byrdes'), lapwing, thrush, bittern and greenfinch. Dishes of birds like these were served at almost all well-to-do meals, lay or clerical. At a feast, there might be as many as twenty dishes.

The milk of cows, sheep and goats alike was used throughout medieval times, although cow's milk came to be used most towards 1500 because it was less work to milk one cow than ten sheep. The milk, and the cream, butter and cheese made from it, together with eggs, were called 'white meats'.

Killing, butchering and salting a pig for winter

On large feudal estates, the milk was turned into cream, curds, soft cheese and butter for the lord's kitchen, and the residual whey and buttermilk made hard, skim-milk cheese for the servants and workers. This skim-milk cheese was sometimes so hard that it had to be soaked and beaten with a hammer before it could be eaten.

Well-to-do adults thought fresh milk was a drink only fit for children, the old and invalids, although they enjoyed thick rich cream and curded cream – alone or with strawberries (against their doctors' advice!). They thought butter too was unwholesome for grown men from midday onward, although children got bread and butter for breakfast *and* supper.

The kitchen of the medieval abbey at Foutevraud.
It is a separate building outside the hall.
Each of the small towers houses an oven

Cooked dairy foods, however, were another matter. Milk made hot beverages called possets or caudles, cream soups and delicious custards. Cream made even richer ones. Soft rich cream cheese called ruayn or rewain cheese made cheesecakes much like ours, to supplement the rich man's meat dishes.

Even a medieval peasant kept a cow if he could, and unlike his lord he relied on it for food. Curds and whey, buttermilk, heavily salted butter and cheese were his staples. In summer he made soft cheese called spermyse or 'green' cheese. Bread and hard skim-milk cheese (which kept all winter) were his daily diet in the fields, as he ploughed, sowed and harvested the vital breadcorn.

In medieval times, everyone, high or low, ate pottage daily.

This was broth or stock in which meat and/or vegetables had been boiled, with chopped meat, herbs, and very often cereals or pulses added. The result was a soup-stew rather like Scotch broth.

The pottage might be thick (running) or almost thick enough to slice (stondyng). One well-known thick cereal pottage was frumenty. Other thick, more luxurious pottages were called mortrews. A peasant made do with pease pottage, rather like runny pease pudding.

The commonest pottages, however, were vegetable ones, made with red or green cabbage, lettuces, leeks, onions and garlic, as in the recipe for lange wortys de chare (p.32). Leek pottage, or white porray as it was called, was especially popular, and was thickened with ground almonds for the rich in Lent. Green porray, made with green vegetables and flavoured with parsley and other herbs was also eaten a great deal. A green herb pottage simmering over the fire must have smelt delicious. Sadly, it was probably over-boiled and not very nourishing.

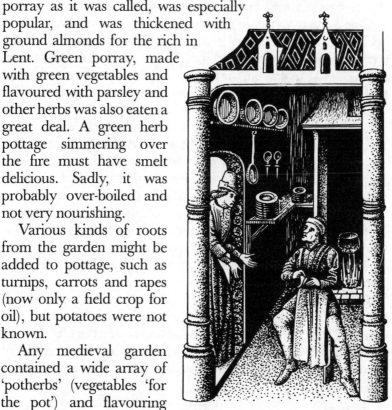

Various kinds of roots from the garden might be added to pottage, such as turnips, carrots and rapes (now only a field crop for oil), but potatoes were not known.

Any medieval garden contained a wide array of 'potherbs' (vegetables 'for the pot') and flavouring herbs because they were used so much for medicine

A fourteenth-century cook in his kitchen. Piles of pewter plates stand on the shelves

Sweet Violet   *Primrose*

as well as cooking. Salad vegetables had their place there too. The salad recipe on page 35 uses only a few of the ones generally grown.

One attractive idea which seems worth reviving was that of adding flowers to salads. Primroses, violets and borage flowers were among them. Fruits and roots were often pickled and added to salads too. Apart from the pickle juice, most salads were dressed with oil and vinegar as they are now.

Medieval people were somewhat suspicious of raw fruit because they thought it created fevers and diarrhoea, but wild fruits such as cherries were in fact eaten fairly freely. Grapes were grown for the table, and plums and damsons were eaten raw too. Apples and pears, including the large hard pears called wardens, were usually cooked. 'Roasted' (baked) apples were popular.

Citrus fruits began to be imported around 1290, and soon lemons were used both fresh and pickled, as well as Seville oranges. Both were very expensive. However, sweet lemon preserves were bought from importers, and, later, English housewives learnt to make their own.

Other imports, reserved at first almost entirely for the rich because of their price, were currants and raisins, figs, dates and prunes. Dried fruits together with spices created the character of typical medieval feast food. Dishes for the wealthy were full of them, and poorer people generally got some at Christmas and for feast-days.

The biggest luxury import was almonds. On fast-days, ground almonds could be substituted for pounded chicken as a thickening, or diluted to make a substitute for cow's milk. Almond milk features in dozens of recipes. The poor had to make do with oatmeal, but in season, they could gather and use or store wild hazelnuts and cobs as a useful addition to their diet.

We owe cane sugar to the Crusaders who tasted it in the East just before 1100. It was imported ready processed in the form of cones called loaves, white if refined and fairly pure, or dirty brown. It was however so rare and expensive even at the end of the medieval period that it was treated as a spice and kept under lock and key if possible.

Salt had been mined in England since early times, and was also made from evaporated sea water. Apart from the tons used for preserving, it was also a valued cooking spice. Mustard, like saffron, was also home-produced. Pepper was the only spice imported in large quantities. Everyone, high and low, used a great deal of it.

However, medieval people wanted more than just salt, pepper and mustard as condiments. Wealthy European cookery was aromatic and pungent with ginger and cinnamon, nutmeg, mace, cardomoms and cloves, and other spices we no longer use such as galingale, grains of paradise and cubebs. They were popular because they masked and improved the taste, not so much of tainted food (though they helped that too) but of the seemingly unending salted and dried winter foods.

These were more expensive for the British than anyone else because they were not imported in direct shipments but had to be bought at markets on the continent of Europe. The merchants who did this obviously charged for it.

Borage

Grocers also made up and sold to medieval housewives convenient ready-ground mixed spices. The most usual mixtures were called powdor fort and powdor douce. Recipes varied, but powdor fort, which was 'hot', generally included ginger, pepper and mace, and sometimes dried chives. Powdor douce contained ginger or cinnamon, nutmeg, sometimes cloves, a little black pepper and sugar.

We are often told that medieval cookery was thoroughly overspiced. Certainly some of it was for our tastes. But the number of spices used in a dish does not tell us how much of each was used, or their strength. Spices had been brought long distances, by sea or overland in all weather and must often have lost their original intensity of flavour by the time they arrived. Moreover, since they were so costly, they were hardly likely to be used overgenerously. Spicing may well have been no stronger than in the recipes below.

One other interesting aspect of medieval food might surprise us now. Not only was it spiced, it was highly scented and coloured as well. Jellies were set in different coloured layers for a striped effect, rice pudding was bi-coloured, custards were reddened and meatballs gilded. Saffron provided yellow, sandalwood red, parsley juice green, and turnsole purple. For a particularly ostentatious gift food was gilded with thin sheets of gold leaf.

There were times of desperate famine in the Middle Ages. The Black Death left villages depopulated, with few to till the soil or sow next year's grain. Local battles during the Wars of the Roses left the fields trampled flat, the livestock slaughtered or driven off, and the field workers gone. The few people left grubbed roots from the ground, ate marsh plants and trapped small wild creatures to survive.

Yet, in the years between, the land was kindly and there was still a wealth of natural food plants and creatures. Medieval people's food resources were restricted, and some which could have helped them greatly (such as fresh fruits and vegetables) were largely ignored or maltreated. But even a peasant had certain customary rights to land, grazing and food which a wise lord respected, and certain things of his own, such as his cow and strip of land in the communal field.

COOKING METHODS AND TOOLS

C ooking methods depend on cooking facilities. A rural cottager, whether free, tenant or serf, had only a one-room home with a fire built on a large flat stone in the centre, or against a wall if his hut had stone walls; the embers would keep the 'down-hearth' stone fairly hot. If a beam stretched across the hut, the housewife might have a cast-iron cauldron hanging from it; but she was more likely to use earthenware pots standing in the hot ashes beside the fire, or balanced on a tall stone among the embers.

She could seethe (boil) her pottage in this way, stirring it with a ladle or spurtle (wooden stick). But if she wanted to bake, she needed more equipment. Although the manorial lord demanded that his peasants should get their corn ground by his licensed miller for a fee, it was hard to enforce, and many people ground their small quantity of grain in a hardwood mortar, stone trough or in a hand-quern; they mixed it with water and baked their unleavened bread or oatcakes on the down-hearth under an upturned pot.

Instead of roasting, small birds, hedgehogs or a poached squirrel might be wrapped in clay and baked in the hottest ashes, as might fresh fish, but salt herring was best boiled.

A village tradesman or artisan lived almost as simply; but his home would probably have two rooms or at least partitions, with the fire in the living area. On each side of the down-hearth, there might be iron firedogs with hooked tops to support an iron rod from which a cauldron could be hung. Whereas the

Cauldrons were sometimes hung over the fire on a swinging chimney crane. The pot hook used here could be used to adjust the height of the cauldron

poor housewife would be lucky to have two or three pottery or wooden bowls to set her milk in for cream or cheese, and probably churned her butter by hand, her grander neighbour who kept a cow might well have a new-style plunger churn which worked like a pestle in a mortar with a lid.

The kitchen of a castle, manor house or monastery was generally stone-floored and walled, with great wide fireplaces where most of the cooking was done. Roasting, all done on spits, might take place here, or in a separate building because of the size of the fire needed to roast all the meat required, and the risk of conflagration. The king's new separate kitchens at Clarendon in 1206 each had fires which would roast two or three whole oxen.

Roasting spits were still simple, propped on firedogs and turned by apprentice cooks or kitchen-boys. There were no women cooks or kitchen maids yet. Boy scullions cleaned the spits, basting ladles, and the brushes and bowls used for applying egg-wash to gild the near-roasted joints. They lived in the kitchen and even slept on its floor. Scullions did not penetrate the other rooms in the kitchen complex. There were larders, storerooms and cellars, and between the kitchen and dining hall as a rule, a buttery where drink was stored and a pantry, from where bread, trenchers and salt were served.

The bakehouse was usually a separate building, with ovens' built out from the walls. Wood, peat or furze was lit in the oven and left to burn until the interior was hot enough. The spent fuel was then quickly drawn out, the floor of the oven was cleaned, and the bread was put in to bake, along with pies, tarts and enriched breads like pastries. Long-handled rakes were used to deal with fuel and ash, while flat hardwood peels were used to lift the loaves in and out of the ovens.

The dairy was another separate structure. Here, wide shallow panshons stood to hold the milk; ladles, skimmers, jugs and brushes hung on the walls, and a heavy cheese-press stood in a corner, with a tall churn beside it, and perhaps the dairymaid's pails and yoke.

Back in the main kitchen, the only large pieces of furniture were the heavy table used as a work-surface, where pottage vegetables

A baker, using a peel or long shovel, loads bread in a hot oven

were cut up, and the chopping block for meat joints. Boiling was done in cauldrons hooked on to pot-hangers over the fire. Other pots and pans, usually of heavy metal with long handles, could be held over the fire for making sauces or boiling eggs. There were also flatter, long-handled pans like our frying pans, and used for the same purposes.

The professional medieval cook had two other cooking appliances. One was a grid of metal bars on a long handle, on which food could be broiled over the fire (instead of under it as under a modern grill). The other resembled a two-sided waffle-iron, and was used to make crisp batter wafers.

He had, of course, other kitchen tools: cleavers, knives and mallets, tongs for cutting sugar, bunches of twigs for whisking and scouring, pestles and mortars of all sizes and weights, to name just a few. Plus cloths, scouring sand and tubs for washing up!

TABLE SERVICE AND ETIQUETTE

The way the usual two-course dinner was conducted in a fourteenth -or early fifteenth-century manorial household was important to everyone who took part. Whether he was serving or sat in the lowest seat, it showed that he had a rightful, allotted place in this intricate social and work hierarchy, with both duties and customary rights.

Every day, when at home, the lord of the manor dined with his household in his Great Hall. It was always a formal meal to some degree, to show his own status, but he would generally hear requests and complaints before or afterwards as well as hand out the odd favour or rebuke. It helped everyone to know more or less where he stood.

How well this worked depended on the lord's status. The king or an archbishop dined in state every day, and only great nobles or prelates could get near them; but a good lesser lord was usually approachable, except at a feast, which was mainly an occasion for display and entertainment.

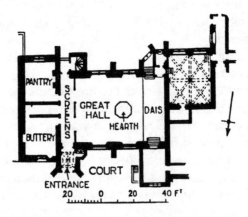

Penshurst Place in Kent still has the site of the early medieval fire in the centre of the Great Hall. The ground plan of the hall also shows the dais where the lord sat and buttery and pantry leading off the hall

Dinner in the fifteenth century. The cup-bearer approaches the lady of the house and, under the balcony, the steward stands watching the household servants

We know much more about medieval feasts, especially grand ones, than about ordinary dinners, because the method of serving, the seating arrangements and the menus of some of them were recorded in detail at the time, but the general plan of ordinary meals was the same, although the procedures were simplified.

At one end of the long hall was a raised platform or dais, on which the lord, his family and his frequent visitors were seated. They were placed along one long side of the table, facing the room and the musicians' gallery at its other end. The lord sat in the centre (under a canopy at a feast). In the body of the hall, tables were set along its length on both sides, to seat the household and lesser guests in order of rank. The table nearest the dais, on the lord's

Serving royalty in the fifteenth century. Elaborately piled dishes are carried by serving men with napkins draped over their shoulders

right, was the most senior, and was called the 'Rewarde' because it was served with the dishes from the lord's own table. The table opposite it was called the 'Second Messe', and the rest were graded similarly. (At a big feast, the lesser guests might spill over into several rooms, and even the gallery.)

Under the gallery, behind screens, there were doors leading to the kitchen, buttery, cellar and pantry and near them were serving tables called cubberdes (cup boards). At one side or in an adjoining room there was the ewery with basins for hand-washing before the meal.

There were a few regular items on the menu which everyone used, such as trencher bread, but apart from those, there had to be different dishes for each table in the hall, and more for the top tables than others. Then, at least once a week, most of the dishes had to be chosen to exclude meat (including meat-thickened sauces); and since both raw and cooked meat might 'go off' between Thursday and Sunday, butchering had to be carefully planned to leave as few leftovers as possible on Thursday night.

There were special groups of people to be fed too. Medical teaching of the time stated that young children should have a quite different diet from adults (excluding red meat and fruit, but including milk). Their nurse, who ate with them, ranked above most female servants. There were also the lord's almoner, secretary and accountant, who were all clerics. Then, even in a modest manor, there were several other groups to cater for.

In a great household, such as the king's or in a large monastery, planning a feast with guests of many different grades and their servants was an intricate affair. Besides the partly or wholly different menus for all the various secular groups, there had to be a wholly separate one for the clergy.

Any menu was served in two main courses, with a dessert course afterwards for special guests at a feast. Each course consisted of a number of poultry and meat (or fish) dishes and two or three sweet ones. They were handed round to those at the high table but were put on the other tables for people to help themselves. Each dish was portioned beforehand and two or four people shared a portion or 'messe', either eating it from the shared platter or transferring bits to their trenchers. Sometimes cups were shared too.

A feast might have three courses and had special treats included because at the end of each course, a 'sotelte' – a carved hard-sugar sculpture relevant to the occasion – was presented to the high table; everyone had a good look at it and if it were edible might get a taste. Then, when the table had been relaid for the second course, there might be a procession to bring in a decorated peacock or swan; and later the host would give presents to his main guests, there would be drinks, and diversions – a jester and mummers.

The highest-ranking nobles had a steward, who ran the household. Under him the chief official at dinner was the marshal, next in rank, in charge of different aspects of the meal, were the sewer (head waiter and taster), the pantler or panter (head of the pantry), the butler (in charge of drinks), the ewerer (in charge of hand-washing and linen), the chief cook, the carver and the lord's cup-bearer. All these except the last two had several grooms (trained staff) and underlings to help them: there were waiters, and assistant waiters who brought the food only as far as the hall; assistant cooks, their scullions and spit-boys; pot-boys and bottle-washers.

At a great English state feast, the duties of the major household officials were carried out by noblemen who would be rewarded with generous gifts; for instance the king's cup-bearer and taster might be given the solid gold cup he tasted from.

The everyday household officials always laid the tables. First, the senior ewerer laid two or three cloths on the high table and all the other tables, and set out a cloth at the ewery, a special basin for the lord and a cup from which to taste the water in it. Next, the pantler brought the lord's bread rolls wrapped in a napkin, his trenchers and the large ceremonial covered salt-cellar, together with special knives for cutting the bread, and a spoon. He laid each in a special spot in front of his master's place. This done, he saw that the other tables were provided with bread, trenchers, knives, spoons, and with small trenchers for salt.

When the cooks were ready, the company assembled, but only the lord sat down as yet. Everyone else went off to wash, the sewer, carver and cup-bearer going first. These three were then equipped with towels and napkins, elaborately draped over one shoulder, and then the assay or tasting ritual took place.

Advancing towards his master with three bows, the carver went down on his knees, uncovered and moved the salt, unwrapped the lord's bread, and cut a small cornet (cone) of both white and trencher bread for the pantler to taste. At the same time, the marshal and cup-bearer advanced with the lord's hand-washing basin, tasted the water and kissed the towel he should use. The first course of dishes were by this time on the serving tables, and the sewer attacked them, giving the chief cook and the lord's chief steward a taste of them all. Every dish was marginally mutilated for fear of poison.

The carver at work on a nobleman's dinner in 1415.
From the Book of Hours *of the Duke of Berry*

Once these tastings were done, lesser guests sat down and the carver came to the fore. There were elaborate medieval instructions for dressing and carving the various meats and birds, and each creature was handled differently, a skilled carver priding himself on the speed and dexterity of his performance. Once he had completed his task, the first course could at last be served.

Only one thing remained to be tasted, and that was the drink. This was the job of the marshal, butler and cup-bearer and was performed with the same flourishes as the food tastings. The tasting and serving of the ale (and wine for senior ranks) was timed to coincide with the service of the first roast.

*The Royal Gold Cup was made in
France in the fourteenth century but
later was brought to England
and from the reign of Henry VI
to James I it was part of the
English royal treasure*

It was perhaps as well that the senior officials had tasted so many dishes, because they now had to remain on their feet throughout the meal, making sure that each dish was served with the right sauce, that everyone was served properly and that no important guest was left with an empty cup or a soiled trencher.

Then, when the meal was ended, the tables were cleared, and if the lord had guests, sweet wine was served, with perhaps wafers and whole spices as dessert. Finally grace was said, and the lord got on his feet to drink a toast as a signal that dinner was over, after which everyone went off, back to work.

Medieval table manners were carefully described in etiquette books for young people. Most of the precepts concerned personal cleanliness and how to share one's 'messe' courteously with one's neighbour. The student is told to have clean nails, and not to leave fingermarks on the table. He must not drink from a shared cup with his mouth full lest he soil it, nor drink his soup noisily. Neither must he pick his teeth with his knife, blow on his food to cool it, or wipe his mouth on the tablecloth. For his neighbour's sake, he should clean his spoon properly, not leave it in the dish (there were no forks in those days). He should not dip his fingers too deep in the shared dish, nor crumble bread into it in case his hands were sweaty. He should definitely not gnaw bones, nor tear meat to bits with his teeth or fingers. Scratching his head at table was unacceptable, and there were other specific instructions about spitting and belching.

These basic directions seem a curious contrast to the fanciful etiquette of preparing the table, tasting and serving. But even a manorial household or similar group still consisted largely of people with a peasant and farming background; even lordlings had been brought up in close contact with peasant life and ways, in which there were no facilities for courteous living.

In teaching them manners, it is significant that cleanliness and courtesy were considered priorities for both the enjoyment of food and for communal living generally. So much so that the instructions were laboriously written down by hand for generations of lords and ladies in the making to learn.

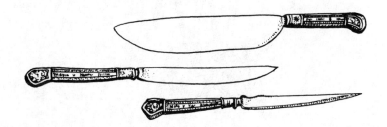

A fifteenth-century carving knife and two table knives. The pointed blades were used to lift food to the mouth before forks became fashionable

Chief cooks were high-ranking household officials in England and France in the fourteenth century. This is the effigy on the tomb of a great medieval chef called Taillevent. His coat of arms shows three cooking pots

RECIPES
Flesh-day dishes

BEEF OR MUTTON OLIVES

Alows de beef or de motoun: 'Take fayre Bef of the quyschons, and motoun of the bottes, and kytte in the maner of Stekys; then take raw Percely, and Oynonys smal y-scredde, and yolkys of Eyroun sothe hard, and Marow or swette, and hew alle thes to-geder smal; than caste ther-on poudere of Gyngere and Saffroun, and tolle hem to-gederys with thin hond, and lay hem on the Stekys al a-brode, and caste Salt ther-to; then rolle to-gederys, and putte hem roste hem til they ben y-now; than lay hem in a dyssche, and pore ther-on Vynegre and a lityl verious, and pouder Pepir ther-on y-now, and Gyngere, and Canelle, and a fewe yolkys of hard Eyroun y-kremyd ther-on; and serue forth.'

Today, use lamb instead of mutton, and a little extra cider vinegar instead of verjuice (sour grape or apple juice). If you wish, brush the olives with beaten egg shortly before the end of the cooking time. This was called endoring, and was often done to give spit-roasted meats a golden colour.

4 thin slices of beef topside or lamb rump
1 large onion
6 hard-boiled egg yolks
1 tbls (15 ml) shredded suet
2 tsps (10 ml) finely chopped parsley
a pinch of ground ginger
a pinch of powdered saffron
salt
a little butter
cider vinegar for sprinkling
a little ground ginger, cinnamon and
*   black pepper, mixed, for sprinkling*

Beat the meat thin and flat with a cutlet bat. Chop the onion finely with 4 egg yolks. Add the suet, parsley, ginger, saffron and salt to taste. Knead and squeeze until pasty, using the onion liquid to bind. (If necessary, add a few drops of water or a little extra parsley.)
Spread the stuffing on the meat slices and roll them up like small Swiss rolls. Secure with wooden toothpicks. Lay side by side in a greased baking tin, with the cut edges underneath. Dot with butter. Bake, turning once, at gas mark 4, 350°F (180°C) for 35-40 minutes. Baste once or twice while baking.
Lay the olives on a warmed serving dish. Just before serving, sprinkle with vinegar and spices, and garnish with the remaining egg yolks, crumbled.

Harleian MS 279

BROILED VENISON OR
BEEF STEAKS

*Stekys of venson or bef: 'Take Venyson
or Bef, & leche & gredyl it up broun;
then take Vynegre & a litel verious, & a
lytil Wyne, & putte pouder perpir ther-
on y-now, and pouder Gyngere; & atte
the dressoure straw on pouder Canelle
y-now, that the stekys be al y-helid ther-
wyth, & but a little Sawce; & than
serue it forth.'*

*4 venison or beef steaks, each weighing
    6 oz (175 g), about ¾ - 1 in
    (2-2.5 cm) thick*
cooking fat (optional)
½ pt (275 ml) red wine (not too dry)
2 fl oz (50 ml) water
1 tsp (5 ml) brown sugar or to taste
1 tsp (5 ml) red wine vinegar
1 tsp (5 ml) lemon juice
a grinding of black pepper
a pinch of ginger
a sprinkling of cinnamon

Trim the steaks, and beat out
slightly. Brush lightly with
cooking fat if you wish. Heat a
thick-based frying pan or griddle,
and sear the steaks on both sides,
then reduce the heat and cook
slowly until done as you prefer,
turning as required. While
cooking, put all the remaining
ingredients except the cinnamon
in a small saucepan, and bring to
the boil. Leave off the heat to
infuse for 5 minutes. Taste and
add a little more water or sugar if
you wish. Take steaks to table
when ready, sprinkle lightly with
cinnamon and pour a little sauce
over each.

Harleian MS 279

● Southern French and
Mediterranean wines were
popular when this recipe was
used, especially the sweeter ones.
They were often thin and raw-
tasting, and might be drunk
watered. In this recipe, some
water and sugar have been
added. Lemon juice has been
substituted for verjuice.

GRAPE-STUFFED BOILED
CHICKEN

*Chykens in hocchee: 'Take chykens and
scald them, take parsel and sawge,
without any other erbes, take garlec and
grapes, and stoppe the chikens ful, and
seeth them in good broth, so that they
may esely be boyled thereinne. Messe
them and cast thereto powdor-douce.'*

*2 chickens, each weighing 2½ lb
    (1.1 kg)*
8 oz (225 g) green grapes
*minced parsley and fresh sage leaves,
    mixed, to coat grapes*
4 garlic cloves or to taste
salt
ground black pepper
at least 1½ pt (850 ml) chicken stock
powder-douce for sprinkling (see note)

Prepare the birds for boiling. Halve and seed the grapes, and coat them thickly with the minced herbs. Chop the garlic finely or crush it, and mix with the grapes. Season the mixture to taste, then stuff the birds with it. Truss the birds, enclosing the stuffing securely.

Place the birds on a thick cloth in a stewpan. Add enough stock to come three-quarters of the way up their sides. Bring slowly to the boil, lower the heat and simmer for about 45-60 minutes until tender. Place on a warmed serving dish and sprinkle with the powder-douce.

Mrs Groundes-Peace's Old Cookery Notebook

● For the powder-douce in this case, mix ½ tsp (2.5 ml) each of ground cinnamon, grated nutmeg and ground black pepper, and 1 tsp (5 ml) white sugar. Recipes varied, but always included either cinnamon or ginger.

STUFFED CHICKEN

Grapes, when in season, were suggested as an alternative to onions for the stuffing and sheep's fat as an alternative to lard. The bird was roasted on a simple, hand-turned spit over a wood fire.

3½ lb (1.6 kg) chicken
4 hard-boiled eggs
2 medium onions
½ pt (275 ml) chicken stock
1 small bunch parsley
2-3 tbls (30-45 ml) lard
salt
pepper
¼ tsp (1.5 ml) ground ginger
¼ tsp (1.5 ml) cinnamon

Prepare the chicken for stuffing and for spit or oven roasting. Separate the egg whites and yolks. Slice the onions thinly. Bring the stock to the boil, and blanch the onions and parsley for 2-3 minutes. Remove the parsley, and cook the onions until soft. Drain, reserving the remaining stock. Cool.

Cut off the parsley stalks and chop the leaves with the egg yolks, lard, seasoning and spices. Add the onion. Stuff the chicken with the mixture, then truss it. Roast the chicken in the usual way, with the reserved stock in the drip-tray or roasting tin. Use it to baste the chicken and to make a thin or slightly thickened gravy with the pan juices and some extra stock. If wished, garnish the chicken with the egg whites, chopped, and a little extra parsley.

Harleian MS 4016

BEEF AND VEGETABLE POTTAGE

Pottage was everyone's fare, at feasts and everyday meals alike. More often than not, the broth was just made with vegetables, but it was based on bone stock and had meat added when the Church and one's pocket allowed. This particular pottage was called 'lange wortys de chare'.

2 lb (900 g) shin of beef
4-6 short pieces of marrow bone
4 pt (2.3 L) water
2 leeks
2 sticks celery
2 onions
¼ firm white cabbage without outside leaves
4 oz (100 g) 'white' breadcrumbs (see note)
a few saffron strands
2 tsps (10 ml) salt
ground black pepper

Cut the meat into 2 inch (5 cm) cubes. Put in a stewpan with the bones and water. Bring to the boil, and skim well. Reduce the heat, and simmer, uncovered, for about 2-2½ hours. Meanwhile, prepare the vegetables and boil in a separate pan, whole or in large pieces, for 10 minutes. Drain and cut into thick slices. When the beef is just about ready, remove the marrow bones and add the vegetables. Continue simmering until the vegetables are soft. Stir in the breadcrumbs, saffron and plenty of seasoning. Bring back to the boil, and cook for 2-3 minutes. Skim off any excess fat before serving.

Harleian MS 279

● The old recipe specifies a loaf of white bread which would have been a small, bun-like loaf made with unbleached soft wheat and raised with ale yeast. A large scone round made with unbleached or low-extraction flour (or a mixture of white and wholemeal flour) would be something like it.

DRESSED SWAN OR PEACOCK

The flesh of both birds was thought tough and indigestible from early times. However, one or the other was served in full plumage at most great banquets because it was so handsome. Probably, as today, a cured skin with feathers, feathered head with beak and a bunch of tail feathers were kept for dressing a bird each time it was needed. The bird was presented as if sitting upright on its nest, the head being held erect by a rod or skewer thrust through the mouth, down the throat into the breast.
The swan was the more expensive (it cost 3s 4d in 1380). It was presented garlanded and crowned, on a silver or gold stand, with its wings erect, neck

arched backwards, head erect, at least at royal banquets. It was much more commonly served than peacock, and is occasionally still served today. Both the Vintners' Company and the Dyers' Company hold swan-upping dinners.

Swan dight: 'Kutte a Swan in the rove of the mouthe toward the brayne enlonge, and lete him blede, and kepe the blode for chawdewyn; or elles knytte a knot on his nek, And so late his nekke breke; then skald him. Drawe him and rost him even as thou doest goce in all pyntes, and serue him forth with chawd-wyne.'

● Chaudron (chawdron) was a special sauce for swans. It was made of the bird's own guts, cut small and boiled in broth with its blood and vinegar and strong spices. It looked blackish, and was served hot. (Swan was quite often served as an ordinary dish, without the head.)

Pecok dight: 'Take a Pecok, breke his necke, and kutte his throte, And fle him, the skyn and the ffethurs togidre, and the hede still to the skyn of the nekke, And kepe the skyn and the ffethurs hole togiders; draw him as an hen, and kepe the bone to the necke hole, and roste him, And set the bone of the necke aboue the broche, as he was wonte to sitte a lyve, And abowe the legges to the body, as he was wonte to sitte a-lyve; And whan he is rosted ynowe, take him of, And lete him kele; And then wynde the skyn with the fethurs and the taile abought the body, And serue him forthe as he were a-live; or elles pull him dry, And roste him, and serue him as thou doest a henne.'

In other words, truss in erect position after flaying; roast, cool, then cover with skin and feathers like a jacket. Present like a swan, but with gilded comb instead of a crown, and a gold chain instead of a garland.

Harleian MS 4016

A peacock, its tail displayed, served by a lady of high rank

Late medieval earthenware jug

STEWED MUTTON

'*Take faire Mutton that hath ben roste,
or elles Capons, or suche other flessh,
and mynce it faire; put hit into a
possenet, or elles bitwen ij siluer disshes;
caste thereto faire parcely, And oynons
small mynced; then caste there-to wyn,
and a litel vynegre or vergeous, pouder
of peper, Canel, salt and saffron, and
lete it stue on the faire coles, And then
serue hit forthe; if he have no wyne ne
vynegre, take Ale, Mustard, and A
quantite of vergeous, and do this in the
stede of vyne or vinegre.*'

about 1 lb (450 g) cold roast lamb
2 tsps (10 ml) chopped parsley
1 medium onion, finely chopped
2 in (5 cm) piece cinnamon stick
salt
pepper
a pinch of saffron strands
2 tsps (10 ml) red wine vinegar
7 fl oz (200 ml) red wine

Dice or chop the meat into small
pieces, and put in a flameproof
pot or a saucepan. Add the
parsley, onion and cinnamon
stick. Season well. Sprinkle the
saffron strands over the meat,
then pour over it the vinegar and
wine. Bring to the boil, and cook
until the onion is soft and the
meat well heated through. Add a
little extra wine if the 'stew' looks
like drying out, but do not make
it sloppy. When served, the liquid
should be almost reduced to a
syrup or glaze.

Harleian MS 4016

● Add a little brown sugar or
honey to the stew if you wish.
● In most recipes, it has been
assumed that a kitchen-boy had
ground the spices, if not to the
fineness we are used to. In this
recipe, a piece of cinnamon stick
would certainly have been used,
so it has been kept.

SALAD

*Salat: 'Take parsel, sawge, garlec,
chibollas, oynons, leek, borage, myntes,
porrectes, fenel, and ton tressis, rew,
rosemarye, purslayne, lave, and
waisshe hem clene. Pike hem, pluk hem
small with thyn hond and myng hem
wel with rawe oile. Lay on vynegar and
salt and serve it forth.'*

Use some or all of the following
fresh vegetables and herbs:

spring onions	*parsley*
leeks	*sage*
baby onions	*borage*
large onions	*mint*
fennel	*watercress*
garlic	*rue*
purslane	*rosemary*

For the dressing:
olive or walnut oil
white wine vinegar
salt

Wash and clean the vegetables
and herbs. Pick over, prepare and
slice the vegetables thinly, and
grate the garlic. Shred the herbs
by hand. Mix with enough oil to
moisten. Sprinkle with vinegar
and salt, and serve at once.

John Russell's Boke of Nurture

RASTONS

*These were small round loaves or large
rolls, made of sweetened bread dough
enriched with eggs, like a brioche paste.
After baking, the tops were cut off 'in
the maner of a crown', and the crumb
was removed, leaving hollow shells.
The crumb was finely chopped with a
knife and mixed with clarified butter. It
was then replaced in the hollowed bread
crusts. The tops were replaced and the
loaves or rolls were returned to the oven
for a few moments to heat through.*

Small rolls are more practical for
modern meals. Make a brioche
paste, and bake it in deep bun
tins. When baked, cut off the
tops, remove the crumb with a
spoon, crumble, and mix with
just enough clarified butter to
moisten. Replace the tops and
return to the oven for 5-7
minutes. Serve hot.

Harleian MS 279

Parsley

127

Lenten and fish-day dishes

HOT WINE BEVERAGE

A caudle was a hot wine drink thickened with eggs, which was drunk at breakfast or bedtime. This was a version for Lent or Fridays when, strictly, eggs were not allowed.

½ pt (275 ml) water
1½ pt (850 ml) white wine
8 oz (225 g) ground almonds
½ tsp (2.5 ml) ground ginger
1 tsp (5 ml) clear honey or white sugar
a good pinch of salt
a good pinch of powdered saffron or a
few drops of yellow food colouring

Bring the water and wine to the boil in a saucepan. Tip in the almonds, and add the ginger, honey or sugar and salt. Stir in the saffron or food colouring, and leave off the heat to steep for 15-30 minutes. Bring back to the boil, and serve very hot, in small heatproof bowls.

The Forme of Cury

ALMOND MILK

'Cold milk of almondes' was a basic ingredient used as a fast-day substitute for other thickened liquids in many medieval dishes. Only one recipe is known, dated about 1467; it is quoted by Lorna Sass in her book To the King's Taste *and is for thick almond milk served cold. Modern ground almonds make a slightly gritty liquid; grinding in a blender before use helps, but do not let them 'oil'. Use the following proportions:*

2 oz (50 g) almonds, blanched, skinned
and ground
For thin milk:
½ tsp (2.5 ml) honey or white sugar
a good pinch of salt
7 fl oz (200 ml) boiling water
2 tbls (30 ml) white wine
For thick milk (like coating white sauce):
¼ tsp (1.5 ml) honey or white sugar
a good pinch of salt
2½ fl oz (65 ml) boiling water
1 tbls (15 ml) white wine

Put the almonds in a bowl. Add the honey or sugar and salt to the water, and pour over the almonds. Leave to stand for 15-30 minutes, stirring occasionally. Mix in the wine. Strain thin milk if a particular recipe requires it. Refrigerate in a covered container for up to 48 hours.

● The original recipe suggests boiling the water with the sweetening and salt, one suspects to a syrup – indicating that the medieval palate liked its sauces sweetened much more heavily than above. Add extra honey or sugar to dessert dishes.

LENTEN STEW

'Soupes dorroy' was listed as a pottage (soup-stew), so the original recipe can be interpreted as either a soup or a semi-solid main dish for my lord's Lenten dinner, depending on how much liquid is used. From the way it is written this version of the recipe (there are several) seems to be a main dish.

8 large onions
4 fl oz (125 ml) sunflower oil for frying
4 oz (100 g) ground almonds
½ tsp (2.5 ml) honey
a pinch of salt
¼ pt (150 ml) boiling water
¼ pt (150 ml) white wine
*8 rounds of 'white' bread or brioche,
   crusts removed, about 1¼ in (3 cm)
   thick*

Slice the onions into rings, and simmer them in the oil, turning often, until soft and golden. Leave aside in the pan. Put the almonds in a small saucepan. Mix the honey and salt into the water, and pour it over the almonds with half the wine. Leave to soak for 10 minutes, stirring occasionally. Meanwhile toast the bread lightly on both sides. Lay the slices side by side in a shallow dish. Add the remaining wine to the onions, and simmer until they are reheated through. Heat the almond milk until steaming and pour it over the toast slices. Pile onions on top.

Harleian MS 279

COOKING SUNDRY FISH

Floundres boiled: 'Take floundres and drawe hem in the side by the hede [gut through a slit below the head] . . . and make sauce of water and salt and a good quantite of ale; and whan hit biginneth to boile, skeme it, and caste hem there-to; And late hem sethe [boil]; and serue hem forth hote; and no sauce but salt, or as a man luste.'

Shrympes: 'Take shrympes, and seth hem in water and a litull salt, and lete hem boile ones or a litull more. And serue hem forthe colde; And no maner sauce but vinegre.'

Sole, boiled . . . or fryed: 'Take a sole and do away the hede, and drawe him as a plais [plaice – or flounder, see above] and fle [skin] him; And make sauce of water, parcelly and salt; And whan hit bygynneth to boile, skeme it clene, and lete boyle ynogh. And if thoy wilt haue him in sauce, take him whan he is y-sodde [add it after boiling] . . . Or elles take a sole, and do away the hede; draw him, and scalde him, and pryk him with a knyfe in diuerse [various] place for brekyng of the skin [to prevent curling]; And fry it in oyle, or elles in pured [clarified] buttur.'

Follow modern cooking methods, i.e. simmer or poach the fish, rather than boiling furiously. There is no need to skim impurities off modern salt, tap-water and beer.

Harleian MS 4016

PIKE WITH GALENTYNE SAUCE

You can boil the pike (in ale and water) as in the old recipe if you wish, but sousing it helps to dissolve the little hair bones which are such a trial to eat. The method was well known at this period. Galentyne sauce was strongly flavoured and more like a condiment. There were several versions of it; the one here is the version in the original recipe for pike except that sandalwood (which is almost unobtainable) has been omitted.
This recipe is for cold fish with hot sauce. Another version, which follows it closely, is for hot fish smothered in (stronger-flavoured) cold sauce. Lampreys were also served with sauce galentyne as dressing, and fillets of roast pork were served in a thickened spiced red wine sauce also called galentyne.

3 lb (1.4 kg) middle-cut pike, cleaned
1¼ pt (700 ml) malt vinegar
½ small carton pickling spice
4 bay leaves
For the sauce:
3 oz (75 g) dark rye breadcrumbs
4 tbls (60 ml) white wine
3-4 tbls (45-60 ml) water
2 tbls (30 ml) white wine vinegar
¼ tsp (1.5 ml) cinnamon
salt
ground black pepper
2 tbls (30 ml) grated onion
2 tsps (10 ml) sunflower oil

Put the fish in a non-metallic ovenproof dish and pour the malt vinegar over it. Add enough water to three-quarters cover the fish, and include the spice and bay leaves. Cover, and soak for 24-48 hours in a cool place. Then put in the oven at gas mark 2, 300°F (150°C) and cook for 2-2½ hours. Cool in the liquid, then drain and skin.
To make the sauce, put the breadcrumbs in a bowl. Add the wine, water and vinegar, and sprinkle with the spice and seasonings. Leave for 1-2 hours to soften. Meanwhile, simmer the onion in the oil until soft. Mash the bread sauce until pasty, adding a little extra water if over-strong or too solid. Stir in the fried onion. Put in a small saucepan, and bring to the boil. Pour over the cold fish just before serving.

Harleian MS 4016

● Substitute middle-cut cod for the pike, if you prefer.
● Medieval wines were often sweetened – if the completed sauce is too sharp, add a little sugar.

SAUCE VERT

'Take percely, myntes, diteyne, peletre, a foil or ij of cost marye, a cloue of garleke. And take faire brede, and stepe it with vynegre and piper, and salt; and grynde al this to-gedre, and tempre it up with wynegre, or with eisel, and serue it forthe.'

This was a very popular type of sauce in medieval times because it masked the taste of fish which was slightly 'off', over-salt or just muddy. Mint sauce is almost the only modern survivor. Dittany, pellitory, and costmary had almost 'gone out' by the end of Tudor times, when more pleasing herbs had come into use. Use any fresh herbs you can get, the more the better.

Suggested proportions:
leaves of 10-12 sprigs parsley, mint and other fresh herbs
1 garlic clove
2 oz (50 g) fine 'white' breadcrumbs
2 tbls (30 ml) cider vinegar
salt
freshly ground black pepper
wine vinegar and/or water as needed

Chop the herbs finely. Parsley and mint should predominate. Squeeze the garlic over the herbs in a mortar. Sprinkle the breadcrumbs with the cider vinegar and leave for 10 minutes. Add to the herbs with salt and pepper. Pound until well blended. Then add enough wine vinegar or water, or a mixture, to give you a consistency rather like thickened mint sauce (or green bread sauce). Serve with broiled or poached fish.

Ashmole MS 1439

DRIED PEA PURÉE WITH SPROUTS

The original recipe describes how to hull the dried peas by soaking them in boiling wine lees and water overnight, then rubbing them in a cloth and rinsing. This shortened the boiling time. The recipe below adapts the method for modern hulled peas. Also, since bean sprouts are easier to buy than pea sprouts, they have been used as a substitute for the sprouted peas in the original recipe.

1¼ lb (625 g) white or yellow peas
1 bottle (700 ml) white wine
salt
1 carton bean sprouts
pepper

Soak the peas in the wine overnight, with water to cover if needed. Simmer in the same liquid, with a little salt, for 2-2½ hours or until mushy, adding extra water if needed. (There should be almost no free liquid at the end, and the peas should be reduced to a purée.)
Add the bean sprouts, stir in and simmer until tender. Season with salt and pepper before serving.

Harleian MS 279

BUTTERED VEGETABLES

Buttered wortes: 'Take all maner of good herbes that though may gete, and do bi ham as is forsaid; putte hem on the fire with faire water; put there-to clarified buttur a grete quantite. Whan thei ben boyled ynogh, salt hem; late none otemele come there-in. Dise brede small in disshes, and powre on the wortes, and serue hem forth.'

1½ lb (700 g) mixed fresh vegetables
2 oz (50 g) clarified butter
2 slices 'white' or wholemeal bread, crusts removed
salt
pepper

Prepare the vegetables and chop or slice them neatly, keeping separate any which need only a short cooking time. Put the rest into a saucepan with just enough water to come half-way up the vegetables, and the butter. Bring to the boil, cover, lower the heat and cook gently until tender. Add the short-cooking vegetables partway through the cooking time. Add extra boiling water during cooking if needed to prevent the vegetables drying out. Cut the bread slices into small cubes or dice and put them in a heated vegetable dish. Season vegetables to taste, and turn them into the dish on top of the bread Dot with extra butter if you wish.

Harleian MS 4016

PEAS AND ONIONS WITH SIPPETS

The old recipe suggests green or white peas as alternatives. Other recipes indicate that green peas meant fresh peas as today, and that white peas were dried ones for winter use.

2 lb (900 g) shelled fresh peas
3 medium onions
5 sprigs parsley (leaves only)
2 sage leaves, finely chopped
a good grinding of black pepper
2 tbls (30 ml) white wine
2 tbls (30 ml) white wine vinegar
a pinch of powdered saffron
salt to taste
4 slices 'white' bread, crusts removed and diced

Cook the peas in plenty of water (but no salt) until tender. Strain off ½ pint (275 ml) of the cooking water into a clean pan. Drain the peas and keep warm.
Chop the onions and parsley finely, and add to the reserved cooking liquid, with the sage and pepper. Add the wine. Bring to the boil, and add all the remaining ingredients except the bread. Boil down to half the original quantity, or slightly less. Mix in the peas, then bread dice. Reheat if necessary, then serve.

Ancient Cookery

Sweet dishes

HONEY TOASTS WITH PINE NUTS

'Pokerounce' make a change from the better-known similar dish called Poor Knights and are a lot less rich, being fat free and made with pure honey. The pepper – galingale in the original recipe – just takes off any cloying sweetness the honey may have.

*8 oz (225 g) stiff honey
a pinch of ground ginger
a pinch of cinnamon
a pinch of ground black pepper
4 large square slices white bread, crusts removed, ½ in (10 mm) thick, from tin loaf
½ oz (15 g) pine nut kernels*

Put the honey, spices and pepper in a small saucepan over very low heat. Melt the honey and simmer for not more than 2 minutes. Do not let the honey boil or darken, or it will 'toffee'. Let it cool slightly. Meanwhile, toast the bread lightly on both sides. Cut each slice into four small squares or rectangles. Place on a heated serving plate, and pour the syrupy honey over them. Then stick pine nut kernels upright in each piece, like small stakes. Serve quickly, while still hot, and eat with a knife and fork.

Harleian MS 279

DATE SLICES WITH SPICED WINE

There are several old versions of this favourite medieval recipe – 'leche lumbard'. This one makes an excellent (and healthful) sweetmeat for modern use, because it keeps for 2-3 weeks in a refrigerator if left unsliced.

*1¾ lb (800 g) stoneless block dates
¾ pt (425 ml) medium-dry white wine
3 oz (75 g) light soft brown sugar
½ tsp (2.5 ml) cinnamon
½ tsp (2.5 ml) ground ginger
6 hard-boiled egg yolks
about 6 oz (175 g) soft brown breadcrumbs (not wholemeal)
3-4 tbls (45-60 ml) Madeira heated with a pinch of mixed spice*

Break up the dates and simmer with the wine and sugar until pulpy. Pound or put through a food processor until almost smooth. Mix in the spices and sieve or work in the egg yolks. In a bowl, knead in enough breadcrumbs to make the mixture as stiff as marzipan. Form it into a 2 inch (5 cm) diameter roll, and chill until firm. Cut into ¼ inch (5 mm) slices. Arrange in overlapping lines on a plate, and trickle a drop or two of cooled, spiced wine over each slice.

Harleian MS 4016

PEARS IN WINE SYRUP

This is one of the earliest of many recipes for 'warduns in syruppe'. It suggests mulberries as red fruit, but loganberries make a good modern substitute. It also suggests 'wyn crete or vernage' for the syrup; this usually meant a sweet southern Italian or Cypriot white wine or one from Tuscany. Wardens were a large type of pear.

3 large firm dessert pears
10 oz (298 g) can mulberries or
    loganberries
½ pt (275 ml) full-flavoured red wine
a few drops of red food colouring
¼ pt (150 ml) sweet white Italian wine
1 oz (25 g) white sugar
a good pinch of ground ginger
a small pinch of cinnamon
a small pinch of ground black pepper

Peel the pears but leave them whole. Gouge out the hard cores from the round end if you wish. Drain the berries. Put the pears and berries in a saucepan, and pour the red wine over them with a few drops of colouring. Simmer the fruit until the pears are tender, turning them often to colour them pink evenly. Cool in the liquid, turning them from time to time to deepen the colour. Drain, reserving the liquid. Cut the pears in half or into quarters if you wish. Sieve the soft fruit and return to the pan with the cooking liquid.

Put the white wine, sugar and spices in a clean pan. Boil to 215°F (105°C) or until you have a fairly thick syrup which will glaze the fruit. Add the pears, bring back to the boil, and cook for 2-3 minutes. Serve hot, with the warmed sieved fruit and red wine as a sauce.

Ancient Cookery

● The original recipe specifies powder-douce to flavour the syrup. The sugar, ginger and cinnamon mixture is here based on a Tudor recipe which used 2 oz (50 g) sugar, ¼ oz (7 g) ginger and ⅛ oz (3.5 g) cinnamon.

SWEET CHEESE FLAN

Tart de bry: 'Take a croste ynch depe in trape. Take zolkes of ayren rawe and chese ruayn. Medle it and zolkes togyd and do ther-to poudor, gynger, sugar, saffron and salt. Do it in a trape, bak it and serve it forth.'

shortcrust pastry made with 5 oz (150 g)
    81% flour and 2½ oz (65 g) lard
a pinch of powdered saffron
1 tbls (15 ml) very hot water
12 oz (350 g) Brie cheese, without
    rind, or full fat soft cheese
4 egg yolks
2 oz (50 g) caster sugar
a good pinch of ground ginger
a pinch of salt

Use the pastry to line an 8 inch (20 cm) flan case. Steep the saffron powder in the water until the liquid is deep gold. Meanwhile, beat the cheese until creamy and quite smooth. In a separate bowl, beat the egg yolks and sugar together until thick and pale. Beat in the softened cheese little by little, then the ginger, salt and saffron water. Turn the mixture into the prepared case. Bake at gas mark 5, 375°F (190°C) for 20-25 minutes until just set in the centre. Serve warm or cold the same day.

The Forme of Cury

● The costly medieval sugar came in close-packed 'loaves', whitish outside with treacly residues in the centre. The wealthy had whitish sugar cut or scraped off the loaf but in coarser grains than granulated sugar. Caster sugar is recommended, however, for a lighter cheesecake.
● 'Chese ruayn' meant any rich soft cheese. Brie was well known in England but must have been costly. Anne Wilson therefore suggests that it was almost certainly made up with local Ruayn or Rewain cheese, as the old recipe recommends.

CURD FLAN

Lese fryes: 'Take nessh chese, and pare it clene, and grinde hit in a morter small, and drawe yolkes and white of egges thorgh a streynour, and cast there-to, and grinde hem togidre; then cast thereto Sugur, butter and salt, and put al togidre in a coffyn of faire paast, And lete bake ynowe, and then serue it forthe.'

This is almost the same recipe as the tart de bry except that it is made with 'nessh' (fresh soft curd) cheese and butter without saffron, and both egg whites and yolks are used. Note the neat method of blending and liquifying the egg whites and yolks by straining them.

Use the cheese flan recipe above, using soft smooth curd (not cottage) cheese with 2 tbls (30 ml) butter and 2 large or 3 small eggs. Omit the ginger and saffron.

Harleian MS 4016

Pear-tree

TUDOR BRITAIN

Peter Brears

A cook supervises the work of the kitchen, 1581

The sixteenth century, the colourful flowering of Tudor England, has bequeathed to posterity a whole series of rich and potent images, full of spectacle and a robust *joie de vivre*. In it, we see a largely feudal state boisterously adopting the fashions of Renaissance Europe in all aspects of its courtly life and culture. The paintings of Nicholas Hilliard and his contemporaries show the lavish and colourful dress of men and women who enjoyed the music of Morley, Dowland and Campion, the poetry of Spenser and Sidney, or the plays of Marlowe and Shakespeare. The houses they occupied, from the soaring honey-coloured splendours of Burghley, Hardwick and Longleat to a host of brick and half-timbered country manor houses, similarly evoke the essential spirit of this period. Most potent of all, however, are the portraits of Henry VIII and Elizabeth I, a Renaissance prince and a sacred virgin presiding over a new age of development and increasing trade. The magnificence of their costumes, the fabulous richness of their apartments, and the elaborate ceremonies of their courts were all essential elements in leading and controlling a country still divided into religious factions and under constant threat of insurrection or invasion.

Against this background, cookery may appear to be of trifling importance, but it too reflects the influence of Renaissance Europe, in addition to providing evidence of the sumptuous entertainments held largely for political reasons both at court and in the larger houses. A great variety of documentary sources, ranging from estate papers to plays and poems, refer to the preparation and serving of food, but probably our greatest debt of gratitude is to Edward White and his fellow London publishers of the late sixteenth century. By collecting together and publishing a series of cookery books they have preserved a unique body of information which is still available to us today.

In general terms, the foodstuffs enjoyed in sixteenth-century England were almost identical to those of the medieval period. Roast and boiled meat, poultry, fish, pottages, frumenty, bread, ale, wine and to a much lesser extent, fruit and vegetables, formed the basis of the diet of the upper classes. The range and qualities of these comestibles are best described in Andrew Boorde's *Compendyous Regyment or Dyetary of Health* of 1542, where he writes of venison:

> A lordes dysshe, good for an Englisshe man, for it doth anymate hym to be as he is, whiche is, stronge and hardy...; Beef is a good meate for an Englysshe man, so be it the beest be yonge, & that it be not kowe-fleshe; yf it be moderatly powdered [i.e. salted] that the groose blode by salt may be exhaustyd, it doth make an Englysshe man stronge; Veal is good and easily digested; Brawn [boar's meat] is an usual meate in winter amonges Englisshe men; Bacon is good for carters and plowmen, the whiche be ever labouringe in the earth or dunge... I do say that coloppes [slices of bacon] and egges is as holsome for them as a talowe candell is good for a blereyed mare... Potage is not so moch used in al Crystendom as it is used in Englande. Potage is made of the lyquor in the which fleshe is soden [boiled] in, with puttyng-to chopped herbes and otemel and salt. Fyrmente is made of whete and mylke, in the whiche yf flesshe be soden... it doth nourysshe, and it doth strength a man. Of all nacyons and countres, England is beste servyd of Fysshe, not onely of al maner of see-fysshe, but also of fresshe-water fysshe, and al maner of sortes of salte-fysshe.

He also advised his readers to eat vegetables such as turnips, parsnips, carrots, onions, leeks, garlic and radishes, and fruit in the form of mellow red apples. Even so, raw vegetables and fruit were still regarded with great suspicion by most Tudor diners, who preferred to follow the advice given in the *Boke of Kervynge* of 1500: 'Beware of green sallettes & rawe fruytes for they wyll make your soverayne seke.' It was for this reason that the sale of fruit was banned in the streets during the plague of 1569.

Boiling meat in a cauldron

In addition to the apples, pears, plums, cherries and woodland strawberries which had been grown here for centuries, new fruits from southern Europe were now introduced into the gardens of the wealthy. These included quinces, apricots, raspberries, red and black currants, melons, and even pomegranates, oranges and lemons. The last were never really successful however, and citrus fruits continued to be imported from Portugal, the bitter Seville type of orange now being joined by improved sweet oranges carried from Ceylon into Europe by the Portuguese, and therefore known as Portingales. Dried fruits, such as raisins, currants, prunes, figs and dates, together with almonds and walnuts, were also imported in large quantities to serve the luxury market.

As a result of the mid sixteenth-century Spanish exploitation of their great South American colonies, a number of rare and exotic vegetables slowly began to arrive in Elizabethan England.

A Lady & a Gentleman of the Kitchen

Tomatoes or 'love apples' came from Mexico, and kidney beans from Peru, for example, while the potato originated from Chile and the Andes. Centuries were to pass before the true value of these new foods was fully appreciated, however, and they continued to be served largely as unusual delicacies in the well-to-do households.

A much more popular introduction from the New World was the turkey, a native of Mexico and of Central America, which had already found its way on to English tables by the 1540s. One of Sebastian Cabot's commanders, Sir William Strickland of the East Riding village of Boynton, claimed to have brought the first turkeys into this country, and therefore adopted a white turkey-cock with a black beak and red wattle as his family crest. Birds of this type were available in the London markets of the mid sixteenth century, and from that time onward regularly appeared at important feasts and entertainments.

Of all the changes concerning food in the sixteenth century, the most important and influential was the growing popularity of sugar. Now, in addition to the old-established sources of supply in Morocco and Barbary, increasing quantities were coming into Europe from the new Portuguese and Spanish plantations in the West Indies, some arriving here through the activities of our privateers. From the 1540s a refinery in London was carrying out the final stages of purification, converting the coarse sugar into white crystalline cones weighing up to fourteen pounds. These could then be used to prepare a great variety of sweet-meats, crystallized fruits, preserves and syrups, in addition to being employed in seasoning meat, fish, and vegetable dishes.

The national annual consumption of sugar averaged no more than a pound a head during this period, but the great majority of this was eaten by the aristocracy, who rapidly began to suffer from tooth decay. As Paul Hentzer noted, even Queen Elizabeth's teeth were black, 'a defect the English seem subject to, from their too great use of sugar.' The ashes of rosemary leaves or powdered alabaster rubbed over the teeth with the finger helped to prevent tooth decay, as did the use of elaborate toothpicks of

143

The Wolsey Kitchen, Hampton Court

precious metals, often worn in the hat. In *The Winter's Tale,* Clown was even able to recognize 'A great man... by the picking on's teeth'. Expert barbers might also use metal instruments to scrape the teeth, then apply aqua fortis (nitric acid) to bleach them to whiteness. As Sir Hugh Platt warned, this treatment could be disatrous, for after a few applications a lady may 'be forced to borrow a ranke of teeth to eate her dinner, unless her gums doe help her the better'.

CULINARY ORGANISATION IN THE GREAT HOUSEHOLDS

A s in most aspects of fashionable Tudor life, the sovereign and the courtiers set the required standards of taste in all aspects of cookery and eating habits. At the court itself, based in one of the massive palaces at Whitehall, Richmond, Hampton Court, Nonsuch or Greenwich, vast quantities of high-quality food had to be prepared for perhaps 1,500 or more diners every day. It was therefore essential that each establishment was provided with vast series of domestic buildings, including cellars for the storage of beer and wine, pantries and larders for the storage of food, spacious bake houses, and kitchens lined with wide-arched fireplaces where roasting and boiling could be undertaken.

Similar facilities, albeit on a somewhat smaller scale, were also necessary in the magnificent houses then being erected by the great land-owning families. Mansions such as Burghley, Hardwick, Longleat, Wollaton or Cowdray all incorporated excellent catering facilities capable of dealing with both their own everyday requirements, and also the enormous demands occasioned by the visits of the court during one of its annual progressions through the country. In these houses, the whole of the domestic management was placed in the hands of a senior member of the resident staff, usually the steward. The actual control of the kitchens, provisions, and kitchen staff was then delegated to a clerk to the kitchen. The full extent of this officer's responsibilities, and also the complex workings of a great Tudor establishment are well illustrated in the 'Booke of the Household of Queene Elizabeth' of 1600.

Working under the direction of the Lord Chamberlain, the Clerk to the Kitchen controlled a total staff of 160, his eleven chief officers, either serjeants, chief clerks or master cooks, each contributing the services of their specialist departments. The Serjeant of the Accatry, for example, was responsible for gathering beef and mutton from the queen's pastures, together with veal, pork, lard, sea fish, freshwater fish and salt. These were all passed to the Serjeant of the Larder, whose Yeoman of the Boyling House boiled them as required. It is probable that the actual boilers were large permanent vessels of copper or brass encased within masonry structures and heated by means of their own fireplaces and flues. Smaller quantities of meat would be boiled in metal cauldrons hung from a bar fixed across the chimney in a normal fireplace. Poultry, game birds and lambs were the responsibility of the Serjeant of the Poultry, whose Yeoman of the Scalding House scalded, plucked and drew them ready for the cooks. The Serjeant of the Bakehouse, meanwhile, had a Yeoman Garnetor to maintain supplies of corn and flour, Yeomen Pervayers who carried supplies into the bakehouses, and further yeomen and grooms who baked bread for both the queen's table and the entire household.

The workings of bakehouses at this period are clearly seen in the Ordinances of the York Baker's Company. After measuring and milling the grain, the flour was boulted or sieved to remove the bran. This was done by shaking a quantity of flour through a piece of coarse canvas or linen – probably from Doulas in Brittany – the 'dowlas' which Falstaff gave away to bakers' wives to make boulters of in Shakespeare's *Henry IV, Part I*. The fine flour was then swept up with a small broom and a goosewing, and kneaded with salt, yeast and water in a long wooden dough-trough. After being worked into loaves and carefully weighed, the dough was next pricked or marked, allowed to rise, and slipped into the oven by means of a long oven-slice or peel. The oven itself was of the bee-hive variety, consisting of a large domed masonry structure, entered by way of a small rectangular door. A fire of fast-burning kindling was first lit inside the oven so that its floor, walls and roof were brought up to a high temperature. The fire was then raked out, the bread swiftly

These illustrations from the 1598 Ordinances of the York Baker's Company show: 1 measuring flour

146

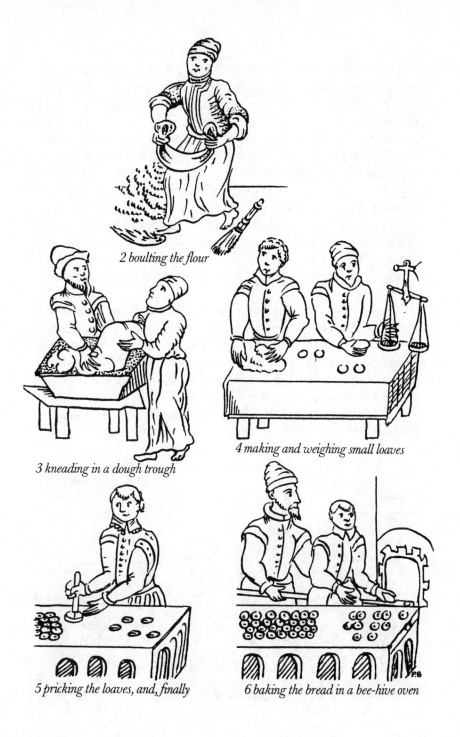

2 *boulting the flour*

3 *kneading in a dough trough*

4 *making and weighing small loaves*

5 *pricking the loaves, and, finally*

6 *baking the bread in a bee-hive oven*

147

inserted, and the oven door sealed in place with mud. After a short while, the oven door was broken open, and the bread, baked by the heat retained by the masonry, withdrawn and allowed to cool. Similar ovens were used by the Serjeant of the Pastry, who prepared all the baked meats, pastries and pies, ensuring that they were 'well seasoned with that proportion of spice which is allowed them, and well-filled, and made according to the rate which is appointed unto them… and see that no waste be made of sauces'. In the Spicery, meanwhile, the Chief Clarke controlled the finer aspects of bakery, with yeomen to beat the spice into powder, using pestle and mortar, yeomen to make wafers for festivals with beautifully decorated iron wafer-tongs, and further yeomen to run the Confectionary which supplied pears, wardens, figs, raisins and other fruit.

The provision of all the equipment used throughout the royal kitchens was the responsibility of the Serjeant of the Scullery. As well as issuing 'chistes, guarde or irons, tubbes, trayes, baskets, flaskets [long shallow baskets], scoopes, broaches [spits], peeles and such like', he had full charge of all the silver and pewter dishes and candlesticks used on the royal tables.

By combining these facilities with those of their own kitchens, the master cooks for the queen and her household were admirably

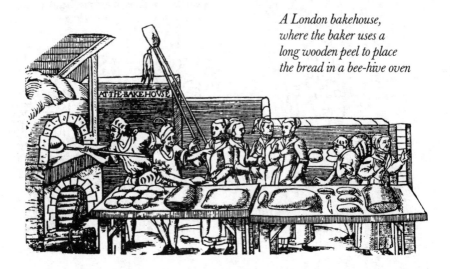

A London bakehouse, where the baker uses a long wooden peel to place the bread in a bee-hive oven

equipped to prepare the elaborate dishes required by the court. In addition to the usual range of utensils, such as knives, spoons, whisks made of bundles of blanched twigs, and a variety of bowls and colanders, the master cook's most useful resource was probably the stove. This was a long masonry bench or worktop, into which was set a number of round firebaskets lined with sheet iron. Fuelled with charcoal, the stove could be used just like one of today's gas or electric stoves, allowing small quantities of food to be heated either fiercely or gently, perhaps in a saucepan or a frying pan, while being stirred or beaten by the cook. Close control of this type was essential when making sauces, egg dishes or many of the sugar-based preserves and confections.

The preparation of fine food was by no means restricted only to the professional cooks employed in the great households, however, for as Lucy Aikin noted:

> Many of the elder sort of courtier ladies were also [in addition to languages, music and needlework] skilfull in surgery and the distilation of waters… each of them cunning in something whereby they keep themselves occupied in the court, there is in manner none of them but when they be at home can help to supply the ordinary want of the kitchen with a number of delicate dishes of their own devising, wherein the portingal [Portuguese] is their chief counsellor; as some of them are most commonly with the clerk of the kitchen.

In this way, the knowledge of the court cooks, exclusively male throughout the Middle Ages, was passed into the hands of the English gentlewomen, who were to develop it to an outstanding degree over the coming centuries.

When a meal was to be served in the royal household, the Serjeant of the Pantrey was responsible for the Yeomen for the Mouthe, the grooms and pages who took the bread, salt, trenchers and cutlery to her majesty's table before carrying up the main courses. The Serjeant of the Seller, meanwhile, took charge of all liquid refreshment. His Yeoman of the Pitcher-house provided the silver drinking vessels, jacks and cups, in which wines from the cellar and other drinks from the buttery were served by further Yeomen for the Mouthe.

The process of laying the royal table was then carried out with great pomp and ceremony, even though the queen was never present. First two gentlemen entered the room, one bearing a rod, and the other a tablecloth, which, after they had both kneeled three times, with the utmost veneration, was spread upon the table. After kneeling again, they then retired to be followed by two others, one with the rod again, the other with a salt-cellar, a plate and bread; when they had kneeled, as the others had done, and placed what was brought upon the table, they too retired, with the same ceremonies performed by the first gentlemen. At last came an unmarried lady, dressed in white silk, along with a married one bearing a tasting knife; the former prostrated herself three times, and in the most graceful manner approached the table where she carefully rubbed the plates with bread and salt. When they had waited there a little time, the yeoman of the guard entered bare-headed, clothed in scarlet with a golden rose upon their backs, bringing in at each turn a course of twenty-four dishes, served in silver plate, most of it gilt. These dishes were received by a gentleman in the same order, who brought them in and placed them upon the table, while the lady taster gave to each of the guard a mouthful to eat, for fear of any poison. During the time that this guard (which consisted of the tallest and stoutest men that could be found in all England) were bringing dinner, twelve trumpets and two kettle-drums made the hall ring for half an hour together. At the end of all this ceremonial, a number of unmarried ladies appeared, who with particular solemnity lifted the meat off the table and conveyed it into the queen's inner and more private chamber, where, after she had chosen for herself, the remainder went to the ladies of the court. On important state occasions, however, the monarch dined in formal state with her courtiers either in the Presence Chamber or some similarly impressive apartment.

*Sir Henry Unton feasting.
Note the symmetrical
arrangement of the dishes
on the table, the square
trenchers and the diners'
habit of folding their
napkins over their forearms*

THE MEALS

In most noble establishments the full medieval ceremonials, menus, courses, and methods of service continued virtually unchanged throughout the sixteenth century, except for one notable detail. Instead of dining at the head of the entire household in the great hall, the lord, his family, and the officers who served him at table now withdrew into their more private great chambers or 'dining chambers'. They still dined in the hall on all major state occasions or feasts, however, including royal visits, Christmastime, weddings or funerals. There was a tendency though to decrease and regulate the number of meals served throughout the day: 'Whereas of old we had breakfasts in the forenoon, beverages or nunchions after dinner, and thereto rear-suppers generally when it was time to go to rest, now these odd repasts, thanked be to God, are very well left, and each one in manner contenteth himself with dinner and supper only.' For the gentry, dinner was served at eleven in the morning and supper between five and six in the evening, but on special occasions these meals could be extended by 'banquets'.

After the main meal had been cleared from the Presence Chamber at York Place (now St James's Palace) a group of masquers disguised as shepherds entered with a flourish of hautboys. As Cardinal Wolsey recognized Henry VIII among this unexpected party, he called to Sir Thomas Lovell, 'Is the banquet ready i'th Privy Chamber?' Here he was referring to the banquet in its original sixteenth-century form, when it was served as an elaborate dessert course of sweetmeats, fruit and wine, either as a meal in itself or as a continuation of dinner or supper, set out in a separate apartment. While Wolsey retired to his Privy Chamber, other noble hosts might go up to the ornate banqueting houses which rose above the leads of their house roofs, as at Longleat, Hardwick, or Lacock Abbey, or perhaps proceed to delightful banqueting houses or lodges erected in some secluded corner of their park. These detached structures might be built in permanent

Rooftop banqueting houses at Longleat, Wiltshire, 1568–9

masonry, but frequently they were 'made with fir poles and decked with birch branches and all manner of flowers both of the field and of the garden, as roses, julyflowers, lavender, marygolds and all manner of strewing herbs and rushes' – such as Elizabeth caused to be erected in Greenwich Park for the reception of the French Embassy in 1560.

The banquet provided the greatest opportunity for the display of wealth, colour, ingenuity and culinary splendour. At Kenilworth, Robert Dudley's entertainment for the queen featured 'a most delicious and an ambrosial banquet; whereof whether I might muse at the daintiness, shapes, and the cost, or else, at the variety and number of the dishes (that were three hundred)'. *The Good Huswifes Closet* gives detailed instructions of how to make all kinds of banqueting stuff, including three-dimensional birds, beasts and fruit in cast sugar, or pies, birds and baskets in marzipan. Even the wine glasses, dishes, playing cards and trenchers were made of a crisp modelled sugar called sugar-plate. This could be elaborately decorated with colourful brush and penwork enriched with bright gilding. Although all the sugar-plate trenchers disappeared centuries ago, we can gain an exact impression of their appearance from their surviving alternatives made of sycamore. Measuring some five inches in diameter, one of their sides was left plain, to provide a surface from which to eat

Elizabeth I takes breakfast before the hunt, 1575

fruit, sweetmeats or cheese, while the other bore floral and strapwork motifs and a suitable inscription. George Puttenham's *Art of English Poesie* of 1589 describes the 'epigrams that were sent usually for New Yeares gifts or to be printed or put upon their banketing dishes of sugar plate or of March paines... they were called "Apophereta" and never contained above one verse or two at the most, but the shorter the better. We call them poesies, and do paint them now a dayes upon the backe sides of our fruit trenchers of wood.'

In addition to taking part in outdoor banquets, the Tudor monarchs also enjoyed the elaborate breakfasts which preceded the hunt. The English were known throughout Europe for their love of field sports, and most of the royal palaces and great houses had a deer park dotted with clumps of trees and enclosed by a high wooden fence. While visiting Viscount Montagu, Elizabeth rode out into the park where a delicate bower had been prepared for her reception. Here a nymph with a sweet song presented her with a cross-bow which she used expertly to despatch three or four deer driven across her view. On these hunting days the preparations for the entertainment of the queen started when the butler set off into the park with a train of waggons, carts and pack-mules carrying all the necessary food and drink to the place of assembly. This location was carefully chosen to ensure adequate shade beneath stately trees, with an array of wild flowers, a nearby spring of clear water, and sweet singing birds to make melody. The butler's first task was to place the bottles and barrels of beer and wine into the spring to cool:

That doone: he spreades his cloth, upon the grassye banke,
And sets to shewe his deintie drinkes, to winne his Princes thanke.
Then commes the captain Cooke, with many a warlike wight,
Which armor bring and weapons both, with hunger for to fight…
For whiles colde loynes of Veale, cold Capon, Beefe and Goose,
With Pygeon pyes, and Mutton colde, are set on hunger loose…
First Neates tongs poudred well, and Gambones of the Hogge,
Then Saulsages and savery knackes, to set mens myndes on gogge…
Then King or comely Queene, then Lorde and Lady looke,
To see which side will bear the bell, the Butler or the Cooke.
At last the Cooke takes flight, the Butlers still abyde,
And sound their Drummes and make retreate, with bottles by their syde.

The assembled hunters then presented the queen with accounts of the various deer they had located, together with samples of the droppings, so that she might select the quarry for the day, and so the hunt commenced.

TABLEWARE

Wherever the meal was to be served, the tableware used in royal and noble households was always of the finest quality. Following the medieval tradition, the great continued to eat from vessels made in gold, silver-gilt or silver. All their magnificent chargers, standing cups and ewers worked in these precious metals were intended for show as much as for use. Henry VIII displayed a cupboard of twelve shelves all filled with plate of gold at his feasts, while George Cavendish, in his *Life of Cardinal Wolsey*, described the proud prelate's 'Cup Board made for the Chamber, in length of the breadth of the nether end of the same Chamber, six desks [i.e. shelves] high, full of gold plate, very sumptuous, and of the newest fashions, and upon the nethermost desk garnished all with gold, most curiously wrought… This Cup Board was barred in round about that no man might come nigh it.' The number of shelves was quite significant, dukes being permitted four or five, lesser noblemen three, knights banneret two, and ordinary gentlemen only one.

On the table, pride of place was still occupied by the great salt, which formed the principal decoration, and was the first vessel to be set in place once the cloth had been laid. In shape it could vary considerably, but it was quite tall, raised on ornate feet, and had its gilt bowl surmounted by a high canopy or cover. Around the table much smaller trencher salts might also be provided for less important diners and members of the household.

Wooden tableware was still in general use. Here is a wooden cup, identical to those used from the Viking period, while the square trencher, with its small hollow for salt, was of recent introduction, replacing earlier trenchers of coarse bread

This tin-glazed plate was probably made by Jacob Jansen at his Aldgate pottery, and shows a stylized view of the nearby Tower of London

The sixteenth century saw the decline of the medieval practice of serving food on square-cut trenchers made of wholemeal bread. These were largely replaced by the sops of bread which were now arranged in the dish beneath boiled or stewed meats before they were brought to table. The trencher continued in a rather different form, however, for it changed into a thin square wooden board, one side of which was turned down to form two shallow recesses. The large central hollow, measuring five or six inches in diameter, contained the meat and gravy, while the smaller one, situated at one corner, held the diner's own supply of salt. As *The Babees Book* advised: 'Do not touch the salt in the salt cellar with any meat, but lay salt honestly on your trencher for that is courtesy.' Further changes in tableware occurred when Jasper Andries and Jacob Jansen came from Antwerp in 1567 to establish tin-glazed earthenware potteries in Norwich and London. Unlike the native English wares, their products had a smooth glossy white surface capable of being painted with metallic oxides to give colourful permanent decoration in the most fashionable Renaissance style.

The sixteenth century saw the general adoption of pottery drinking vessels. This Tudor Green mug from London was probably made in West Surrey, while the dark Cistercian Ware beaker, with the stag's head decoration, comes from Potovens near Wakefield

The materials and design of drinking vessels also made great leaps forward during this period. While silver and gold remained popular with the wealthy, and horn beakers and black leather jacks continued to be used by the poor, important changes were imminent. Already by 1500 the traditional ashwood drinking cups, shallow turned bowls measuring perhaps six inches in diameter, on which Henry VIII expended £20 a year, were starting to be superseded by earthenware cups. In the south-east, they were made in vast quantities in the Surrey kilns, their 'Tudor Green' forms having a brilliant copper-green glaze over a finely-thrown creamy-buff fabric. In the northern counties, the cups were made of a hard-fired dark red fabric, glazed to a glossy dark brown or black, and decorated with flowers, stags' heads or stamped pads of white clay. This type of pottery is now known as Cistercian Ware since it was first discovered during the excavation of Cistercian monasteries in Yorkshire about a century ago.

Glass too was becoming increasingly widespread. As William Harrison noted in his 1577 *Description of England*: 'It is a world to see in these our days how that the gentility do now generally choose rather the Venice glasses, both for our wine and beer. The poorest will also have glass if they may, but, sith the Venetian is somwhat too dear for them, they content themselves with such as are made at home of fern and burned stone.' In 1575 the Venetian Jacomo Verzelini came from the Netherlands to establish a glasshouse in London, where he began to produce bowls and glasses of the highest quality, their surfaces perhaps being elaborately engraved with the customer's coats of arms and initials. In the provinces, meanwhile, in Surrey and Sussex, the Bristol Channel area, Staffordshire, Lancashire, Cheshire and North Yorkshire, further glasshouses were soon employing local materials to make a wide range of goblets, bottles, distillation equipment and beer glasses. The last according to Sir Hugh Platt's *Jewell House of Art and Nature* were 'of six or eight inches in height and being of one equal bigness from the bottom to the top'.

With regard to cutlery, the only significant development was the slow introduction of the fork. Henry VIII had owned 'suckett' forks, with a spoon on one end and a two-pronged fork at the other end of a single shaft, while Elizabeth began to receive New Year gifts of gold, silver and rock-crystal-handled forks from 1582. These were most probably used to eat the sticky sweetmeats served at banquets, for many years were to pass before the fork came into general use in this country.

This silver maiden-head spoon of c.1540 and steel knife of the late sixteenth century both come from London

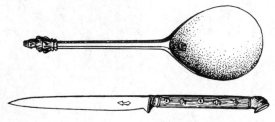

Sixteenth-century cook

160

RECIPES

REAL MINCE PIE

For Pyes of Mutton or Beefe: Shred your meat and Suet togither fine, season it with cloves, mace, Pepper, and some Saffron, great Raisins, Corance and prunes, and so put it into your Pyes.

1½ lb (700g) lean mutton or beef
4 oz (100g) suet
½ tsp (2.5 ml) ground cloves
1 tsp (5 ml) ground mace
½ tsp (2.5 ml) black pepper
a pinch of saffron
2 oz (50g) raisins
2 oz (50g) currants
2 oz (50g) stoned prunes, chopped

For the pastry:
1 lb (450g) plain flour
2 tsps (10 ml) salt
4 oz (100g) lard
¼ pt (150 ml) water
4 tbls (60 ml) milk

For the glaze:
1 tbls (15 ml) each of butter, sugar and rosewater melted together

Mince the meat, and mix in the suet, spices, pepper, saffron and dried fruit. To make the pastry, sift the flour and salt together into a large mixing bowl and make a well in the centre. Heat the lard, water and milk until boiling and pour into the well. Quickly beat the mixture together with a spoon to form a soft dough, and knead until smooth on a lightly floured board. Cut off a quarter of the pastry, and keep covered until required to make the lid. Mould the larger piece of pastry to form the base and sides of the pie within an 8 inch (20 cm) diameter, 2 inch (5 cm) deep loose-bottomed tin. Pack the meat into the pie and dampen the edges of the pie wall. Roll out the remaining pastry to make a lid and firmly press in place. Trim the edges, using the surplus pastry for decoration, and cut a hole in the centre of the lid. Bake in the centre of the oven at gas mark 7, 425°F (220°C) for 15 minutes, then reduce the temperature to gas mark 4, 350°F (180°C) for a further 1¼ hours. Remove the sides of the tin, brush with the glaze, and return to the oven for a further 15 minutes. Serve cold.

A.W.: A Book of Cookrye Very necessary for all such as delight therin

● This pie, with its combination of meat, suet and dried fruit, is the predecessor of today's 'mince pies', in which the meat has been totally replaced by the fruit. It still makes an excellent dish for Christmastime, providing a substantial and finely flavoured dish for a buffet supper.

EGGS IN MUSTARD SAUCE

Sodde Egges: Seeth your Egges almost harde, then peele them and cut them in quarters, then take a little Butter in a frying panne and melt it a little broune, then put to it in to the panne, a little Vinegar, Mustarde, Pepper and Salte, and then put it into a platter upon your Egges.

For each egg take:
1 oz (25g) butter
1 tsp (5 ml) made mustard
1 tsp (5 ml) vinegar
a pinch of salt
pepper to taste

Boil the eggs for 5 minutes. Meanwhile, lightly brown the butter in a small pan and allow it to cool a little before quickly stirring in the remaining ingredients. When the eggs are ready, peel and quarter them, and arrange them on a warm dish. Reheat the sauce, and pour it over the eggs immediately before serving.

J. Partridge: The Widowes Treasure

SPINACH FLAN

To make a tarte of Spinnage: Take three handfull of Spinnage, boile it in faire water, when it is boyled, put away the water from it and put the spinnage in a stone morter, grind it smal with two dishes of butter melted, and foure rawe egges all to beaten, then straine it and season it with suger, Sinamon and ginger, and lay it in your Coffin, when it is hardened in the oven, then bake it, and when it is enough, serve it upon a faire dish, and cast upon it Suger and Biskets.

shortcrust pastry made with 4 oz
    (100g) plain flour, 1 oz (25g) lard
    and 1 oz (25g) margarine
4 oz (100g) fresh spinach or 10 oz
    (275g) can spinach, drained
3 eggs
2 oz (50g) butter, melted
1 tsp (5 ml) cinnamon
1 tsp (5 ml) ground ginger
sugar, to finish (optional)

Line a 6 inch (15cm) flan ring with the pastry, and bake blind for 10-15 minutes at gas mark 7, 425°F (220°C). Wash the fresh spinach and pack into a saucepan with only the water that clings to the leaves, slowly bring to the boil, stirring occasionally, and simmer for 10-15 minutes until tender. Drain the spinach, and allow to cool before blending with the remaining ingredients to produce a smooth dark green mixture. Spread this evenly in the prepared flan, and bake for 30-40 minutes at gas mark 4, 350°F (180°C). Sugar may be sprinkled over the flan just before it is served.

Thomas Dawson: The good huswifes Jewell, pt. 2

CHEESE TART

To make a Tarte of Cheese: Take good fine paste and drive it as thin as you can. Then take cheese, pare it, mince it, and bray it in a morter with the yolks of Egs til it be like paste, then put it in a faire dish with clarified butter and then put it abroad into your paste and cover it with a faire cut cover, and so bake it; that doon, serve it forth.

8 oz (225g) Cheshire or similar cheese
2 oz (50g) butter
3 egg yolks

For the pastry:
3 oz (75g) butter
4 oz (100g) plain flour
1 egg, beaten

To make the pastry, rub the butter into the flour, and slowly add the egg, stirring continuously until the dough can be lightly kneaded with the hands. Roll out rather more than half the pastry and use it to line a shallow ovenproof 10 inch (25 cm) plate. Grate the cheese finely, and blend it with the butter and the egg yolks to form a smooth, moist paste. Fill the pastry-lined plate with this mixture and moisten the pastry edges. Roll.out the remaining pastry to cover, and seal tightly. Press down the edges with the tines of a fork, then trim. Use the surplus pastry to provide any decoration required around the lid of the pie. Pierce the lid with either a fork or a pair of scissors and bake at gas mark 7, 425°F (220°C) for 15 minutes, then reduce the heat to gas mark 4, 350°F (180°C) and bake for a further 30-40 minutes.

The pie is best served hot, for, like most baked cheese dishes, it tends to lose some of its lightness on cooling.

A.W.: A Book of Cookrye Very necessary for all such as delight therin

A bell salt, silver gilt, 1600, with detachable top which serves as a pepper caster

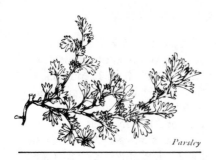

Parsley

SAVOURY TONGUE PIE

To bake a Neatstung: Seeth your Neats tung very tender and slice it in diamond slices, wash it with vergious, season it with Pepper and salt, sinamon and ginger, then lay it into your coffin with Corance, whole Mace, Onions being very small minced, with Marrow or else very sweet butter, some Sugar & some dates being very small minced, and put therein some vergious.

1 small ox tongue, weighing 2½-3 lb
    (1-1.4 kg)
2 tsps (10 ml) salt
1 tsp (5 ml) pepper
1 tsp (5 ml) cinnamon
1 tsp (5 ml) ground ginger
1 tsp (5 ml) blade mace
1 small onion, minced
4 oz (100g) currants
2 oz (50g) dates, stoned and minced
2 oz (50g) butter
2 oz (50g) sugar
2 tbls (30 ml) wine vinegar

For the pastry:
1 lb (450g) plain flour
2 tsps (10 ml) salt
4 oz (100g) lard
¼ pt (150 ml) water
4 tbls (60 ml) milk

For the glaze:
1 tsp (15 ml) each of butter, sugar and
    rosewater, melted together

Place the tongue in a pan, cover with water and bring to the boil, carefully skimming off the frothy scum which rises to the surface. Continue to simmer for a further 2 hours, then drain the tongue, plunge it into cold water, and peel off the skin. Slice the tongue, then cut the slices into long diamond-shaped pieces, and thoroughly mix in a bowl with the remaining pie ingredients.

To make the pastry, sift the flour and salt together into a large mixing bowl and make a well in the centre. Heat the lard, water and milk until boiling and pour into the well. Quickly beat the mixture together with a spoon to form a soft dough, and knead until smooth on a lightly floured board. Cut off a quarter of the pastry and keep covered until required to make the lid. Mould the larger piece of pastry to form the base and sides of the pie within a 7 or 8 inch (18 or 20 cm) cake tin, preferably with a loose bottom, and pack the filling inside. Dampen the edges of the pie wall. Roll out the remaining pastry to make a lid and firmly press in place. Trim the edges, using the surplus for decoration, and cut a hole in centre of lid. Bake in the centre of the oven at gas mark 7, 425°F (220°C) for 15 minutes, then reduce the temperature to gas mark 4, 350°F (180°C) for a further $1^3/4$ hours. Carefully remove the sides of the tin, brush with the glaze, and return to the oven for a further 15 minutes. Serve cold.

A.W.: A Book of Cookrye Very necessary for all such as delight therin

THICK MUTTON STEW

For to make charmerchande: Take coostes of motton chopped and putte theym in a fayre potte and sette it upon the fyre with clene water and boyle it welle; and thanne take percely and sage and bete it in a morter with brede and drawe it uppe with the brothe and put it in the potte withe the fresshe flesshe and lette it boyle welle togyder; and salte it and serve it.

1 lb (450g) lean mutton
1 pt (575 ml) water
4 oz (100g) fresh brown breadcrumbs
1 tsp (5 ml) salt
1 tsp (5 ml) dried parsley
1 tsp (5 ml) dried sage

Cut the mutton into small cubes. Place in a saucepan with the water and simmer gently for $1^1/2$-2 hours until tender, then add the rest of the ingredients and stir until the bread has fully absorbed all the juices to form a thick delicately flavoured stew.

The Boke of Cokery

BOILED ONIONS

To boile Onions: Take a good many onions and cut them in four quarters, set them on the fire in as much water as you think will boyle them tender, and when they be clean skimmed, put in a good many raisons, halfe a spoonefull of grose pepper, a good peece of Suger, and a little Salte, and when the Onions be through boiled, beat the yolke of an Egge with Vergious, and put into your pot and so serve it upon soppes. If you will, poch Egges and lay upon them.

1 lb (450g) onions, peeled and quartered
3 oz (75g) raisins
1 tsp (5 ml) pepper
1 tbls (15 ml) sugar
½ tsp (2.5 ml) salt
½ pt (275 ml) water
1 egg yolk
1 tbls (15 ml) cider vinegar
8 oz (225g) bread, cut into crustless cubes
poached eggs (optional)

Simmer the onions, raisins, pepper, sugar and salt in the water for 10-15 minutes, until the onions are tender. Beat the egg yolk and cider vinegar together, and stir into the onions to thicken the liquid. Serve on a bed of cubes of bread, and top with poached eggs if a more substantial dish is required.

Thomas Dawson: The good huswifes Jewell, pt. 2

CAPON WITH ORANGE OR LEMON SAUCE

*To boile a Capon with Orenges and
Lemmons: Take Orenges or Lemmons
pilled, and cutte them the long way, and
if you can keep your cloves whole and
put them into your best broth of Mutton
or Capon with prunes or currants and
three or fowre dates, and when these
have been well sodden put whole
pepper, great mace, a good piece of
suger, some rose water, and either white
or claret Wine, and let al these seeth
together a while, & so serve it upon
soppes with your capon.*

1 capon or chicken
1 pint (575 ml) chicken stock (see recipe)
2 oz (50g) currants
4 dates
about 8 oz (225g) oranges, mandarins
     or lemons
½ tsp (2.5 ml) black peppercorns
1 tsp (5 ml) blade mace
3 tbls (45 ml) sugar
1 tbls (15 ml) rosewater
¼ pint (150 ml) white wine or claret
8 oz (225g) white bread, cut into large
     crustless cubes

Put the capon or chicken in a pan,
cover with water and boil until
tender, 45 minutes being
sufficient for a tender bird,
although 3-4 hours may be
required for a genuine boiling
fowl. Drain 1 pint (575ml) stock
from bird, and simmer for 5
minutes with the currants, dates,
and fruit, peeled and divided into
individual segments. Then add
the remaining ingredients (white
wine being preferable when using
lemons), simmer for a further 5-10
minutes, and pour over the bird
arranged on a bed of bread cubes
in a large dish.

*Thomas Dawson: The good huswifes
Jewell, pt. 1*

SMOTHERED RABBIT

*How to smeare a Rabbet or a necke of
Mutton: Take a Pipkin, a porrenger of
water, two or three spoonefuls of Vergis,
ten Onions pilled, and if they be great
quarter them, mingle as much Pepper
and salte as will season them, and rub it
upon the meat, if it be a rabbit: put in a
peece of butter in the bellye and a peece
in the broth, and a few Currans if you
wil, stop your pot close and seeth it with
a softe fier but no fier under the
bottome, then when it is sodden serve it
in upon soppes & lay a few Barberies
upon the dishe.*

2 lb (900g) onions
2 oz (50g) currants
1 rabbit, jointed
salt
pepper
½ pt (275 ml) water
3 tbls (45 ml) wine vinegar
2 oz (50g) butter
bread slices, cut into large crustless
   cubes, to serve
barberries or redcurrants, to garnish

Peel and quarter the onions.
Arrange with the currants over
the base of a large saucepan or
casserole. Rub the rabbit joints
with salt and pepper, and embed
them in the onions and currants.
Add the remaining ingredients,
and simmer on a low heat for
1-1½ hours until the rabbit is
cooked. Prepare a deep dish by
lining it with sops – large crustless
cubes of bread – and pour in the
smothered rabbit. Alternatively,
the rabbit meat may be picked
from the bones and returned to the
onions before dishing, as this will
make it much easier to serve and
eat at table. Garnish the dish with
the barberries or redcurrants.

The Good Hous-wives Treasurie

STEWED MUTTON

To boyle a Leg of Mutton with
Lemmons: When your mutton is half
boyled, take it up, cut it in small peeces,
put it into a Pipkin and cover it close,
and put therto the best of the broth, as
much as shall cover your Mutton, your
Lemmons being sliced very thin and
quartered and corance; put in pepper
groce beaten, and so let them boile
together, and when they be well boiled,
seson it with a little vergious, Sugar,
Pepper groce beaten, and a little
sanders, so lay it in fine dishes upon
sops, it will make IV messe for the table.

1 lb (450g) lean lamb or mutton
1 lemon
¾ pt (425 ml) stock
2 oz (50g) currants
¼ tsp (1.5 ml) pepper
1 tsp (5 ml) wine vinegar
1 tbls (15 ml) sugar
red food colouring

Cut the mutton into cubes. Slice
the lemon thinly, then cut each
slice into four quarters. Pour the
stock into a saucepan, then add
the mutton, lemon, currants and
pepper, and simmer for 1½ hours,
until the meat is tender. The
vinegar, sugar and red food
colouring may be stirred in just
before serving. The resulting dish
has a pleasant sharp lemon
flavour, and is extremely palatable.

A.W.: A Book of Cookrye Very
necessary for all such as delight therin

This stag was scratched on the side of the serving hatch in the kitchens at Hampton Court, and probably represents royal venison

BEEF PASTRY, BAKED LIKE VENISON

To make red deere: Take a legge of beef, and cut out all the sinewes clean, then take a roling pin and all to beate it, then perboile it, and when you have so doon lard it very thick, then lay it in wine or Vinegar for two or three howers, or a whole night, then take it out & season it with peper, salt, cloves and maice, then put it into your past, & so bake it.

1½ lb (700g) good-quality steak
½ bottle (350 ml) claret
strips of bacon fat or pork
shortcrust pastry made with 12 oz
    (350g) plain flour and 6 oz (175g)
    butter
2 tsps (10 ml) salt
1 tsp (5 ml) pepper
½ tsp (2.5 ml) ground cloves
1 tsp (5 ml) ground mace
a little gravy or 1 tbls (15 ml) each
    butter, rosewater and sugar
    (optional)

Trim all the fat from the steak, beat it with a rolling pin and soak in the claret for 24 hours. Drain, and use a larding needle to insert numerous small strips of raw bacon or pork fat into one side of the steak. Roll out the pastry into a large rectangle. Arrange the steak on one half, season it with the salt, pepper and spices, fold the remaining pastry over the top, dampen and seal the edges of the pastry, and place on a greased baking sheet. Bake at gas mark 6, 400°F (200°C) for 15 minutes, then reduce the temperature to gas mark 4, 350°F (180°C) for a further 50-60 minutes. Before removing pastry, it may be glazed with either a little gravy or a mixture of butter, rosewater and sugar melted together.
Serve either hot or cold.

Thomas Dawson: The good huswifes Jewell, pt. 1

SWEET CHICKEN PÂTÉ

To make a mortis: Take almonds and blanche them, and beat them in a morter, and boyle a Chicken, and take al the flesh of him, and beate it, and straine them together, with milke and water, and so put them into a pot, and put in Suger, and stirre them still, and when it hath boyled a good while, take it of, and set it a cooling in a payle of water, and straine it againe with Rose water into a dish.

½ chicken
2 oz (50g) blanched almonds
¼ pt (150 ml) milk
1 tbls (15 ml) sugar
1 tbls (15 ml) rosewater

Put the chicken in a saucepan, cover with water and boil until tender – about 45 minutes. Drain, and pick all the meat from the bones. While the chicken is boiling, use either a mortar and pestle or a blender to grind the almonds and milk together to form a smooth paste. Grind the cooked chicken into this paste, then place the mixture in a saucepan with the sugar and cook over a gentle heat for 10-15 minutes, stirring continuously. Cool the saucepan in a bowl of cold water, beat in the rosewater, and finally fork the resulting pâté either down into a deep bowl, or into a symmetrical shape on a plate ready for the table.

Thomas Dawson: The good huswifes Jewell, pt. 1

● This 'mortrews', a survival of the medieval standing pottages, makes a pleasant and interesting addition to any buffet or summer salad.

MUTTON IN BEER

To Stewe Stekes of Mutton: Take a legge of mutton and cot it in small slices, and put it in a chafer, and put therto a pottell of ale, and scome it cleane then putte therto seven or eyghte onions thyn slyced, and after they have boyled one hour, putte therto a dyshe of swete butter, and so lette them boyle tyll they be tender, and then put therto a lyttel peper and salte.

2 lb (900g) leg of lamb or mutton
1 pint (575 ml) brown ale
1 large or 2 small onions, thinly sliced
1 tsp (5 ml) salt
pepper to taste
1 oz (25g) butter
bread slices, cut into crustless cubes, to
  serve

Bone the meat, trim off the skin and excess fat, and cut into thin slices across the grain. Place in a heavy pan with the beer and onions, cover and simmer for an hour before adding the salt, pepper and butter. Simmer for a further 20-30 minutes until tender. Serve on cubes of crustless bread in a deep dish.

A Proper Newe Book of Cokerye

● Stewed steaks later developed into 'Scotch collops', one of the most popular dishes of the seventeenth and eighteenth centuries.

A decorative trencher or roundel for serving sweetmeats

TROUT PASTIES

A Troute baked or minced: Take a Troute and seeth him, then take out all the bones, then mince it fine with three or four dates minced with it, seasoning it with Ginger, and Sinamon, and a quantitie of Suger and Butter, put all these together, working them fast, then take your fine paste, and cut it in three corner waies in a small bignesse, of four or five coffins in a dish, then lay your stuffe in them, close them, and so bake them and in the serving of them baste the covers with a little butter, and then cast a little blaunch pouder on them, and so serve it foorth.

1 trout
3 or 4 dates, chopped
¼ tsp (1.5 ml) ground ginger
¼ tsp (1.5 ml) cinnamon
½ tbls (7.5 ml) sugar
2 oz (50g) butter

For the pastry:
3 oz (75g) butter
4 oz (100g) plain flour
1 egg, beaten

Place the trout in a saucepan, cover with boiling water, and simmer for 10-15 minutes until tender. Drain the trout, remove the flesh from the bones, and blend it with the remaining ingredients to form a soft paste. To make the pastry, rub the butter into the flour, then stir continuously while adding the beaten egg to form a soft dough which can be lightly kneaded with the hands. Turn out on to a floured board, roll out, and cut into four or five large triangles. Place a portion of the trout paste in the centre of each triangle, bringing the corners up over the paste to form triangular envelopes. Moisten the edges, carefully seal them together, place on a baking sheet and bake at gas mark 7, 425°F (220°C) for 15 minutes, then reduce the heat to gas mark 4, 350°F (180°C) and bake for a further 10 minutes. The pasties may then be brushed with melted butter and dusted with caster sugar and cinnamon, although this might be found too sweet for present-day tastes.

Thomas Dawson: The good huswifes Jewell, pt. 2

FRIED WHITING

To fry Whitings: First flay them and wash them clean and seale them, that doon, lap them in floure and fry them in Butter and oyle. Then to serve them, mince apples or onions and fry them, then put them into a vessel with white wine, vergious, salt, pepper, clove & mace, and boile them together on the Coles, and serve it upon the Whitings.

8 oz (225g) apples or onions, minced
butter or oil for frying
½ pt (275 ml) white wine
1 tbls (15 ml) wine vinegar
1 tsp (5 ml) salt
¼ tsp (1.5 ml) pepper
¼ tsp (1.5 ml) ground mace
a pinch of ground cloves
1-1½ lb (450-700g) whiting fillets

Fry the apples or onions in a little butter or oil in a small saucepan until thoroughly cooked, but not browned. Stir in the wine, vinegar, salt, pepper and spices. Allow to cook for a few minutes, then keep hot ready for use. Remove any skin from the fillets, dust them with flour, fry in butter or oil for 5-10 minutes, and serve with the sauce.

A.W.: A Book of Cookrye Very necessary for all such as delight therin

THICK PEA POTTAGE

To boyle yong Peason or Beanes: First shale them and seethe them in faire water, then take them out of the water and put them into boyling milk, then take the yolks of Egs with crums of bread, and ginger, and straine them thorow a strainer with the said milk, then take chopped percely, Saffron and Salt, and serve it foorth for Pottage.

1 oz (25g) fresh breadcrumbs
1 egg yolk
1 tsp (5 ml) chopped parsley
1 tsp (5 ml) salt
½ tsp (2.5 ml) ground ginger
a pinch of saffron
½ pt (275 ml) milk
12 oz (350g) cooked peas, or 19 oz (525g) can peas

Beat together the breadcrumbs, egg yolk, parsley, salt, ginger and saffron. Bring the milk almost to the boil, pour in the peas and the breadcrumb mixture, then bring to the boil over a low heat, stirring continuously. This thick pottage can be used as a quickly made and very substantial warming soup, or it may be served as a vegetable, making an excellent accompaniment to fish dishes.

A.W.: A Book of Cookrye Very necessary for all such as delight therin

APPLE MOUSSE

To make Apple Moyse: Take a dozen apples and ether rooste or boyle them and drawe them thorowe a streyner, and the yolkes of three or foure egges withal, and, as ye strayne them, temper them wyth three or foure sponefull of damaske water yf ye wyll, than take and season it wyth suger and halfe a dysche of swete butter, and boyle them upon a chaffyngdysche in a platter, and caste byskettes or synamon and gynger upon them and so serve them forth.

1½ lb (700g) apples
3 tbls (45 ml) water
2 egg yolks
2 tbls (30 ml) rosewater
2 tbls (30 ml) sugar
1 oz (25g) butter
ground ginger and cinnamon, to finish

Peel, core and slice the apples, and stew them with the water until soft in a heavy covered saucepan. Make the apples into a smooth purée by either rubbing through a sieve or using a blender. Return the purée to the saucepan, stir in the egg yolks beaten with the rosewater, then the sugar and the butter, and slowly heat to boiling point, stirring continuously. Pour the purée into a dish and allow to cool before serving. To finish, spinkle with a little ground ginger and cinnamon.

A Proper Newe Book of Cokerye

PRUNE TART

To make a Tarte of Prunes: Take Prunes and wash them, then boil them with faire water, cut in halfe a peny loaf of white bread, and take them out and strain them with Claret wine, season it with sinamon, Ginger and Sugar, and a little Rosewater, make the paste as fine as you can, and dry it, and fill it, and let it drie in the oven, take it out and cast on it Biskets and Carawaies.

12 oz (350g) prunes
4 oz (100g) fresh white breadcrumbs
½ pt (275 ml) red wine
1 tsp (5 ml) cinnamon
1 tsp (5 ml) ground ginger
4 oz (100g) sugar
1 tbls (15 ml) rosewater

For the pastry:
3 oz (75g) butter
4 oz (100g) plain flour
1 tsp (5 ml) caster sugar
1 egg, beaten

Soak the prunes overnight, then simmer in a little water for 10-15 minutes until tender. To make the pastry, rub the butter into the flour, mix in the sugar, and slowly stir in the egg until it forms a soft dough which can be lightly kneaded with the hands. Roll out the pastry, and use it to line an 8 inch (20 cm) diameter, 2 inch (5 cm) deep flan ring. Line the pastry with greaseproof paper, fill with uncooked haricot beans or crusts, and bake blind at gas mark

7, 425°F (220°C) for 15 minutes. Remove the beans and greaseproof paper.

To make the filling, drain and stone the prunes, then blend them with the remaining ingredients to form a smooth thick paste. Spoon the filling into the pastry case, and return to the oven to bake at gas mark 4, 350°F (180°C) for 1½ hours. Serve either hot or cold.

A.W.: A Book of Cookrye Very necessary for all such as delight therin

SWEET CUBES OF JELLIED MILK

A white leach: Take a quart of newe milke, and three ounces weight of Isinglasse, half a pounde of beaten suger, and stirre them together, and let it boile half a quarter of an hower till it be thicke, stirring them al the while: then straine it with three sponfull of Rosewater, then put it into a platter and let it coole, and cut it in squares. Lay it faire in dishes, and lay golde upon it.

5 tsps (25 ml) gelatine
1 pt (575 ml) milk
4 oz (100g) sugar
1½ tbls (25 ml) rosewater

Sprinkle the gelatine on to 4 tablespoons (60 ml) of the milk in a cup. Leave for 5 minutes before standing the cup in hot water and stirring the gelatine until it is completely dissolved. Warm the remaining milk, stir in the gelatine and the sugar, and simmer, stirring continuously, for 5 minutes. Remove from the heat, stir in the rosewater, and pour into a shallow baking dish about 7 inches (15 cm) square which has been freshly rinsed in cold water. Allow to set firmly in a cool place before cutting into squares with a sharp knife. The squares may then be either arranged in a regular pattern or stacked as a pyramid on a flat plate ready for the table.

Thomas Dawson: The good huswifes Jewell, pt.2

● This unusual dish has a delicious, cool sweet flavour and a translucent ivory-white appearance similar to Turkish delight, but is much less cloying to the palate. A coat of pure gold leaf would certainly transform it into a magnificent edible centrepiece, but at considerable expense.

PEARS IN SYRUP

To conserve wardens all the yeere in sirrop: Take your wardens and put them into a great Earthen pot, and cover them close, set them in an Oven when you have set in your white bread, & when you have drawne your white bread, and your pot, & that they be so colde as you may handle them, then pill the thin skinne from them over a pewter dish, that you may save all the sirroppe that falleth from them: put to them a quarte of the same sirroppe, and a pinte of Rosewater, and boile them together with a fewe Cloves and Sinnamon, and when it is reasonable thick and cold, put your wardens and Sirroppe into a Galley pot and see alwaies that the Syrrop bee above the Wardens, or any other thing that you conserve.

3 lb (1.4 kg) pears
1½ pt (850 ml) water
8 oz (225g) sugar
¼ pt (150 ml) rosewater
1 tsp (5 ml) whole cloves
2 sticks cinnamon

Place the pears in a casserole and bake at gas mark 4, 350°F (180°C) for 1-1½ hours until soft to the touch. Cool, then peel. Simmer any liquor which runs from them with a syrup made from the remaining ingredients, add the pears, and simmer for a few minutes before cooling.

Thomas Dawson: The good huswifes Jewell, pt. 2

JUMBLES OR KNOTTED BISCUITS

To make Iombils a hundred: Take twenty Egges and put them into a pot both the yolkes & the white, beat them wel, then take a pound of beaten suger and put to them, and stirre them wel together, then put to it a quarter of a peck of flower, and make a hard paste thereof, and then with Anniseeds moulde it well, ane make it in little rowles beeing long, and tye them in knots, and wet the ends in Rosewater, then put them into a pan of seething water, but even in one waum, then take them out with a Skimmer and lay them in a cloth to drie, this being don lay them in a tart panne, the bottome beeing oyled, then put them into a temperat Oven for one howre, turning them often in the Oven.

2 eggs
4 oz (100g) sugar
1 tbls (15 ml) aniseed or caraway
6 oz (175g) plain flour

Beat the eggs in a 2 pint (1.1 litre) basin, then beat in the sugar, the aniseed or caraway, and finally the flour, thus forming a stiff dough. Knead the dough on a lightly floured board, and form into rolls approximately $3/8$ inch (1 cm) in diameter by 4 inches (10 cm) in length. Tie each of these in a simple knot and plunge them, five or six at a time, into a pan of boiling water, where they will immediately sink to the bottom. After a short time dislodge the knots from the bottom of the pan with a spoon so that they float and swell for a minute or two. Then lift the knots out with a perforated spoon, and allow them to drain on a clean tea-towel laid over a wire rack. Arrange the knots on lightly buttered baking sheets and bake for 15 minutes at gas mark 4, 350°F (180°C), then turn the knots over and return to the oven for 10-15 minutes until golden.

Thomas Dawson: The good huswifes Jewell, pt. 2

POSSET

To make a good Possett Curde: First take the Milke and seeth it on the fire, and before it seeth put in your Egges according to the quantitye of your Milke, but see that your Egges be tempered with some of your milke that standeth on the fire, and you must stirre it still untill it seeth, and beginning to rise, then take it from the fire, and have your drinke ready in a fair Bason on a chafing dishe of coles, and put your Milke in to the bason as it standeth, and cover it, and let it stand a while, then take it up, and cast on ginger and synomon.

3 eggs
1 pt (575 ml) milk
½ pt (275 ml) strong brown ale
cinnamon and ground ginger, to finish

Beat the eggs into the milk, and heat gently, stirring continuously, until the mixture has thickened and is about to rise to the boil. Meanwhile, heat the ale almost to boiling point and pour into a large warmed bowl. Quickly pour the hot egg and milk mixture into the ale from a good height, cover the bowl, and leave in a warm place for 5 minutes to allow the curd to set. Sprinkle a little cinnamon and ginger over the posset, which is now ready to be served.

J. Partridge: The Widowes treasure

● Simple possets of this type became much richer and sweeter as they grew in popularity in the later seventeenth century.

Pear-tree

PRUNES IN SYRUP

To make Prunes in sirrope: Take Prunes, and put Claret Wine to them, and Sugar, as much as you thinke will make them pleasant, let all these seeth together till yee thinke the Liquor looke like a sirrope, and that your Prunes be well swollen: and so keepe them in a vessell as yee doe greene Ginger.

8 oz (225g) prunes
¾ pt (425 ml) claret
4 oz (100g) sugar

Soak the prunes overnight in the claret, then simmer the prunes, claret and sugar for 10-15 minutes until the prunes are fully swollen and tender. They may then be eaten directly, or sealed into sterilized jars for use at a future time.

J. Partridge: The Treasurie of Commodious Conceites and Hidden Secrets

● This rich but simple dish provides a convenient example of the suckets eaten with a fork during the banquet course.

SUGAR PLATES AND WINE GLASSES

To make a paste of Suger, whereof a man may make al manner of fruits, and other fine thinges with their forme, as Plates, Dishes, Cuppes, and such like thinges, wherewith you may furnish a Table: Take Gumme and dragant asmuch as you wil, and steep it in Rosewater till it be mollified, and for foure ounces of suger take of it the bignes of a beane, the juyce of Lemons, a walnut shel ful, and a little of the white of an eg. But you must first take the gumme, and beat it so much with a pestell in a brasen morter, till it be come like water, then put to it the juyce with the white of an egge, incorporating al these wel together, this don take foure ounces of fine white suger well beaten to powder, and cast it into ye morter by a little and little until they be turned into ye form of paste, then take it out of the said morter, and bray it upon the powder of suger, as it were meale or flower, untill it be like soft paste, to the end you may turn it, and fashion it which way you wil. When you have brought your paste to this fourme spread it abroad upon great or smal leaves as you shall thinke it good, and so shal you form or make what things you wil, as is aforesaid, with such fine knackes as may serve a Table taking heede there stand no hotte thing nigh it. At the ende of the Banket they may eat all, and breake the Platters, Dishes, Glasses, Cuppes, and all other things, for this paste is very delicate and saverous.

½ tsp (2.5 ml) gelatine
1 tsp (5 ml) lemon juice
2 tsps (10 ml) rosewater
½ egg white, lightly beaten
12-16 oz (350-450g) icing sugar

Stir the gelatine into the lemon
juice and rosewater in a basin and
place over a bowl of hot water
until melted. Stir in the lightly
beaten egg white, and work in the
icing sugar, little by little, until a
dough is formed. It can then be
turned out on a board dusted
with icing sugar, and kneaded
until completely smooth. Having
dusted the board with a little
cornflour, the mixture is then
rolled out thinly and pressed into
saucers, plates or the bowls of
wine glasses to mould it into the
required shapes. The surplus
trimmed from the rims may then
be modelled in the form of
baluster stems and bases, either
for the glasses or to convert the
saucers into standing tazzas for
the better display of sweetmeats.
A little royal icing can be used to
join the various sections together
after they have been allowed to
dry and harden for a few hours.
Glasses and dishes made in this
porcelain-like translucent material
can provide an interesting range
of vessels for the presentation of
any cold dry sweetmeats on the
banqueting table. Sugar wine
glasses filled with crystallized
flowers make a particularly
elegant display, the contrast of
textures and colours bringing a
rare beauty to the table.

*Thomas Dawson: The good huswifes
Jewell, pt. 2*

*One of the finely engraved
wine glasses made by
Jacomo Verzelini in his
London glasshouse in 1581*

SEVENTEENTH-
CENTURY BRITAIN

Peter Brears

THE
LAMENTABLE
COMPLAINTS
OF
NICK FROTH the Tapſter, and
RVLEROST the Cooke.

Concerning the reſtraint lately ſet forth,
againſt drinking, potting, and piping on the Sab-
bath day, and againſt ſelling meate.

In this broadside of 1641,
the tapster and the cook complain of
the new regulations which prevent them from trading on Sundays.
Note the cook's 'lusty surloins of roast Beefe'
turning in front of the fire

he seventeenth century was a period of tremendous upheaval and change in this country, a period in which virtually every aspect of our national and domestic life was transformed as England cast off many of her medieval traditions to emerge as a new, forward-looking state. As a result of the dissolution of the monasteries in the 1530s, vast areas of land and previously untapped economic resources had passed into lay hands. As they were enthusiastically developed over the succeeding century, their growing productivity financed the rise of what was to be a new, prosperous and influential class – the landed gentry.

In an age when the sovereign sturdily maintained his Divine Right to govern as he wished, it was impossible for the gentry to obtain the political power they now sought, the friction generated between these opposing views flaring up into the Civil Wars which terminated in the execution of Charles I in 1649. After just a decade of puritanical Commonwealth government, England returned to monarchy with Charles II in 1660. Now it was a constitutional monarchy, however, one which recognized the right of Parliament to play a leading role in managing the country's affairs.

These upheavals had a considerable effect on domestic life. From the early 1600s the increasing affluence of the gentry had enabled them to spend much more on recreation, travel and luxury goods. Instead of living throughout the year on their quiet estates, they now spent long periods in the towns, visits to London allowing them to acquire all manner of social graces. Here they might participate in advantageous parliamentary, commercial or legal business, perhaps take fencing or dancing lessons, use the services of fine tailors and wig-makers, or enjoy excursions to the theatre, musical events, great houses, or the court. In the 1620s, proclamations ordered the gentry to return to their estates to prevent the neglect of public duties, avoidance of tax and the heavy expenditure on foreign luxuries and expensive foods. These were largely ignored, however, and lavish entertainment flourished during the London season, as the city continued to develop as the finest food market in the kingdom.

Up to this time the fare of the country gentleman had been relatively plain and simple, largely based on home-produced meat, game and grain, roasted, boiled or baked as required. Plenty had been preferred to variety, but now there was an increasing demand for new delicacies, with new flavours and new methods of cookery. As in all aspects of social life, the royal household set the required fashions and standards of culinary taste, drawing both on its own centuries-old traditions and on new developments from France. Dishes which appeared at court would be imitated in lesser households, and thus proceed on down the social scale, their recipes probably being passed on at dinner or supper parties. At these functions the ladies would also exchange recipes for their own specialities, together with those culled from the ever-increasing range of cookery books. Between 1600 and 1700 a new volume appeared almost every other year, the most popular of these often running into a number of editions. With titles such as *The English Hus-wife, The Accomplish'd Lady's Delight,* or *The Genteel House-Keeper's Pastime,* they appear to have been primarily intended for use in prosperous families, where the lady of the house was responsible for all aspects of housekeeping. Many of the recipes were individually attributed to the royal kitchens, or to ladies of the court, which presumably gave them a certain socially prestigious cachet. These volumes contained many items from overseas, such as 'a Persian Dish', 'a Turkish Dish', 'a Portugal Dish', or even 'an Outlandish Dish', but France provided the most fertile source of new recipes. In the late sixteenth century Sir Hugh Platt had published some 'after the French fashion', while John Murrell's *New Booke of Cookerie* of 1617 was 'all set forth according to the now new English and French Fashion'. F.P. de La Varenne's *Cuisinier françois,* published in Paris in 1651, was to have the greatest influence, particularly after it was 'English'd by J.G.D.' and appeared as *The French Cook* in London in 1653. It included recipes for hash, and for dishes both 'a la daube' and 'a la mode'. By 1688

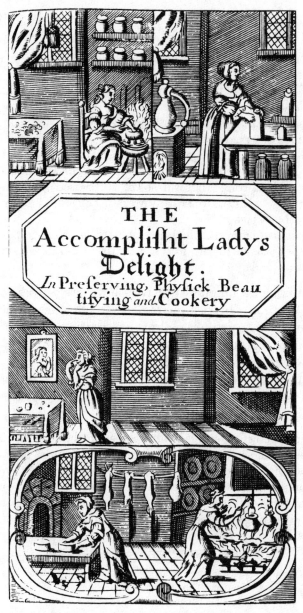

The frontispiece of The Accomplisht Lady's Delight *of 1677 shows ladies busily preserving, distilling, making cosmetics, and working in the kitchen*

cooks' glossaries included a wide range of newly introduced French terms, including:

> *A-la-Sauces* Sauce made after the French Almaigne or German fashion.
> *A-la-Doode* is a French way of ordering any large Fowl or Leg of Mutton.
> *A-la-Mode way* is the new, or French way of dressing all manner of boiled or baked Meat.
> *Bouillon* is a kind of Broth or boiled meat made of several things.
> *Hash* is a Dish-meat made of any kind flesh minced or in Gobbets stewed in strong broth with spices, and served up in a Dish with Sippets: to Hash is to stew any Meat that is cold. The French call it Hach or Hachee.
> *Hautgoust* a thing that hath an high taste, viz. a Ho-goo.
> *Salmagundi* an Italian dish [actually from France] made of cold turkey and other Ingredients.

Although a number of new dishes were introduced from other European countries, such as Italy's macaroni, vermicelli and 'tortelleti', and Spain's olla podrida (an amazing variety of stewed meats and vegetables, anglicized to 'hotch-potch'), the French influence was predominant. Even so, it did not overwhelm the native English taste for good plain cooking. Many still preferred substantial, solid, wholesome roast and boiled meats, to the highly priced Frenchified

> Hogg-podg Dish-meats, neither pleasing to the Pallet, or of credit to the Masters ... But let Cooks study new Dish-meats and work out their Brains, when they have done all they can, there are but four sorts of Meat which they can properly, and with safety, work upon, viz. Flesh of Beasts, Flesh of Fowle, Flesh of Fish and Field Fruits; and these again are according to their kinds either Stewed, Boiled, Parboiled, Fryed, Broiled, Roasted, Baked, Hashed, Pickled, Souced, or made into Sweet-Meats. Nil Ultra.

INGREDIENTS

By the opening of the seventeenth century, most of our present-day foodstuffs had already been introduced. The English countryside, parks and farms were producing venison and all other kinds of game, mutton, pork, and beef, while increasing quantities of beef were also being imported from Scotland. Ever since the Union of the Crowns in 1603, great herds of black cattle had been driven south over the border, slowly working their way down to London, beasts being sold off at fairs en route. On all but the poorest tables, meat often formed some three-quarters of every meal. Much of this was freshly killed, but various techniques of salting and potting enabled it to be preserved for use throughout the winter months.

Most vegetables grown today were already known, ranging from cabbages, savoy, kale, cauliflower and broccoli, to carrots, turnips, parsnips and beetroot, artichokes, onions, peas and beans. Common (or sweet), Virginian and Canadian potatoes were grown here too, but they were still regarded as a novelty. The interest in gardening which had started in the later sixteenth century continued to expand; orchards and gardens now yielded a wealth of fruit, in addition to lettuce, chicory, celery, cucumbers and radishes. The medieval suspicion of raw vegetables and fruit was slowly subsiding, and salads were beginning to appear on the table with increasing frequency. In 1699 John Evelyn even published a whole book on the subject, *Acetaria, a Discourse of Sallets,* in which he suggested a dressing made of three parts of olive oil, one part vinegar, lemon or orange juice, dry mustard, and mashed hard-boiled egg yolks.

New foodstuffs imported from overseas during this period included allspice or Jamaica pepper from the West Indies, cochineal from Mexico, and sago from Malaya. From the 1640s, when the English colonists in Barbados turned their land over to sugar cane, sugar became much more plentiful, leading to a great increase in the production of homemade preserves, confectionery and syrups. The most significant group of new foods, however, were all beverages. By the 1660s it was possible to purchase in London: 'That excellent and by all Physitians approved China drink called by the Chineans Tcha, by other nations Tay alias Tee', 'Coffa, which is a blacke kind of drinke made of a kind of Pulse like Pease, called Coaus', which came from Arabia and Turkey, and chocolate, from the West Indies. Despite complaints that these novel drinks would damage the trade in home-grown barley and malt, in addition to making men 'as unfruitful as the deserts', they all enjoyed a popularity which has continued unabated up to the present day.

In addition to these new and exotic dishes, great strides were being made in the use of traditional home-grown produce. This was most clearly seen in bakery, where a whole host of significant developments were taking place. The 'great cakes' of the medieval period, enriched with butter, cream, eggs and sugar, heavily fruited and spiced, raised with yeast, and weighing twenty pounds or more, continued to be popular for important occasions. Now they were contained within a tinplate hoop, however, thus making them much more convenient both to bake and to serve. One new variety was the Banbury cake. Specially baked for wedding feasts, its outer layer of plain dough concealed a rich filling of dough mingled with currants. It was in this period too that the modern baked gingerbread appeared, this somewhat sticky sponge, flavoured with ginger and cinnamon, replacing the earlier solid paste of highly spiced breadcrumbs and wine.

Biscuits went through a similar transformation. The medieval biscuit had been made by dusting slices of an enriched bread roll with sugar and spices before returning them to the oven where they hardened into a kind of sweet rusk. By baking the biscuit-bread in the form of a single light, finely-textured loaf, it changed into sponge cake. This was often entitled 'fine cake' in contemporary recipe books. Other new varieties of biscuit included both jumbals, where caraway-flavoured dough was worked up into interlaced rings, knots, or plaits, and Shrewsbury cakes whose rounds of shortcake were perhaps spiced with ginger or cinnamon.

As baking skills developed throughout England, some areas acquired a reputation for their own local specialities. This was particularly true of a number of northern towns, Chorley, Eccles, Dewsbury and Halifax giving their names to distinct variations of the currant pasty.

'BLESSED BE HE THAT INVENTED PUDDING', wrote M Misson in the 1690s; 'Ah, what an excellent thing is an English pudding!' Savoury black and white puddings forced into animal guts had been made for generations, but the early seventeenth century saw the development of that great English invention, the pudding cloth. Utilizing this simple device, it was possible to convert flour, milk, eggs, butter, sugar, suet, marrow and raisins, etc. into a whole series of hot, filling and nutritious dishes with minimal time, trouble and cost. Having securely tied the ingredients within the cloth, the pudding had only to be plunged into a boiling pot, perhaps along with the meat and vegetables, where it could simmer for hours without further attention. Varying in texture and quality from light, moist custards to substantial masses of heavily fruited oatmeal, the boiled pudding soon became a main-stay of English cookery, being adopted by all sections of society.

Further puddings or 'pudding pies' were poured into dishes and baked in the oven. Rice puddings were readily made in this way, as were whitepots, the luxurious predecessors of bread-and-butter pudding.

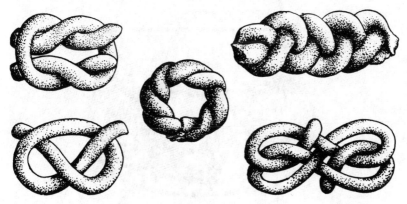

Designs for 'Knotts or Gumballs'

187

EQUIPMENT

I n the kitchens of the seventeeth century, activity centred around broad-arched fireplaces recessed into the walls, each measuring at least six feet wide by a yard in depth. Here great log fires supported on firedogs, or coal fires raised within elevated wrought-iron baskets, provided all the heat necessary for boiling and roasting. Boiling was one of the most economical ways of cooking, cauldrons of iron or brass suspended over the fire being employed to heat whole meals in a single operation. Joints of meat could be plunged into the boiling water, together with vegetables contained in net bags, or puddings either tied up in cloths or floating in wooden bowls, there to remain until thoroughly cooked. As an alternative, poultry, game or small quantities of meat could be placed in an earthenware vessel, with butter, herbs and spices, a lid sealed in place with a strip of pastry, and the vessel immersed in the cauldron for a few hours. In this

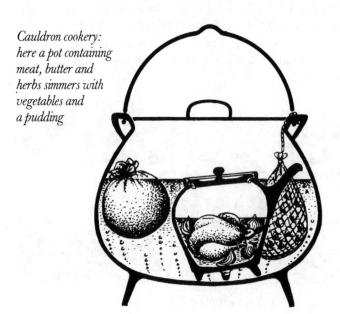

Cauldron cookery: here a pot containing meat, butter and herbs simmers with vegetables and a pudding

Roasting a pig

way, richly flavoured and tender dishes were produced, including jugged hare, in which the jointed animal was cooked within a jug.

A similar principle was employed in one of the most ingenious culinary inventions of this period, the pressure-cooker or 'digester'. Denys Papin, a French physicist and mathematician living in London, discovered that most foodstuffs could be efficiently cooked in a totally sealed vessel, thus making considerable savings in time, fuel and flavour. To demonstrate the advantages of this method, he invited a number of fellow-members of the Royal Society to join him for a supper in April 1682, at which 'all was dressed, both fish and flesh, in digesters, by which the hardest bones were made as soft as cheese, without water or other liquor, and with less than eight ounces of coals, producing an incredible quantity of gravy, but nothing exceeded the pigeons, which tasted just as if baked in a pie, all these being stewed in their own juice, without any addition of water save what swam about the digester.' As with so many other improvements, centuries were to pass before these advantages were fully appreciated, and pressure-cooking finally became an everyday method of preparing meat, fish and vegetables for the table.

For roasting, meat was mounted on long iron spits or 'broaches' supported on spit dogs or cobirons. Here it could be rotated before the fire, probably for four or five hours in the case of a large joint. For the turnspit, the youth employed to turn the spit, it was a laborious, boring and uncomfortable job, his front being roasted by the heat of the fire while his back was chilled by the cold draughts which rushed forward to fan the flames. It is not surprising that this was the first domestic process to be fully mechanized. From the early seventeenth century weight-driven clockwork jacks mounted on the sides of the fireplaces were increasingly used to turn the spits at a slow and uniform rate. In some kitchens dog-power was preferred. Doctor Caius, founder of Caius College, Cambridge, stated that: 'There is comprehended under the curs of the coarsest kind a certain dog in kitchen service excellent. For when any meat is to be roasted, they go into a wheel, which they turning about with the weight of their bodies, so diligently look to their business, that no drudge or scullion can do the meat more cunningly, whom the popular sort hereupon term turnspits.'

Turning the meat was only one of the tasks involved in roasting. Even before it was secured on to the spit, game and poultry had to be cleaned and trussed, while sucking pigs required more detailed attention. Having made sure that the mouth was wedged open before rigor mortis set in, this most succulent of roasts was mounted on the spit, stuffed with bread and herbs such as sage, sewn up, and then placed before the fire. As roasting proceeded, the drops of fat issuing from the meat were caught in a long shallow dripping pan whose sloping base conducted them into a central well. From here they could be taken up with a basting ladle and poured back over the meat, to keep it moist and tender.

For heating smaller quantities of food, saucepans were made of iron, bronze, tinned copper, or silver. As they were difficult to use over the open fires, they were supported either on a brigg, a horizontal framework bridging the topmost firebars, or on a trivet, a tall three-legged iron stand which stood in front of the fire to take advantage of the radiant heat. Alternatively, a shorter version of the trivet, called a brandreth, could hold a pan just a few inches above the gentle heat of a small fire burning on the hearth. Skillets and posnets were also used in this position, their pan-like bodies being raised on three integral legs.

In large establishments, where entertainment was provided on a lavish scale, the kitchen usually housed a stove in addition to the normal fireplace. This took the form of a long masonry bench built against a wall, usually being placed close to a window to ensure adequate ventilation. Its working surface was pierced by a number of iron-sheathed fire baskets, their bases being separated from open flues below by series of closely spaced firebars. Once filled with

A weight-driven clockwork jack, used to turn the spit before the fire

glowing charcoal, the stove provided a clean and easily controlled heat, ideal for making sauces, preserves or many made dishes.

The only other cooking facility to be found in the seventeenth-century kitchen was the bee-hive oven. This was a circular domed construction, measuring perhaps three feet or more in diameter, built into the thickness of one of the walls and entered by way of a small square doorway. The equipment and methods used in baking bread, one of the major tasks in any household, are clearly described in Randle Holme's *Academy of Armory* of 1688. Using a meal shovel *(1)* the baker first transferred a batch of flour from a large storage chest or ark into a plank-built kneading trough *(2)*. Here it was blended with warm water, salt or spices, and yeast which had been made by dissolving a piece of old sour dough in water. The soft dough was then removed from the trough, using a dough scraper *(3)*, and transferred to the brake *(4)*, a strong table fitted with a long hinged roller with which the dough was kneaded and beaten until ready for moulding. On the moulding table *(5)* a dough knife *(6)* measuring about two feet in length was used to divide the dough so that it could be weighed and moulded into loaves or rolls. After the loaf had been cut, by

Illustrated in Randle Holme's Academy of Armory *of 1688,*
these bakers' tools include 1 a meal shovel, 2 a kneading trough,
3 a dough scraper, 4 a brake, 5 a moulding table, 6 a dough knife, 7 an oven,
8 a kid of gorse on a pitchfork, 9 a peel, and 10 a custard filler

running the knife around the sides, and pricked across the top with a sharp bodkin, it was stamped with the baker's name or mark so that it could be readily identified if found faulty or short in weight.

It was now ready for the oven *(7)*. This had been fired to a high temperature by thrusting a burning kid of gorse into its chamber, using a short pitch fork *(8)*. When the oven was up to temperature, the fire and ashes were swept out, and the loaves slipped inside using a long-handled peel *(9)*. Once the oven had been sealed with a slab of stone, set in place with clay or dirt out of the street, the heat remaining in the masonry slowly baked the bread to perfection. Having broken away the mud which sealed the door, the oven was opened and the bread drawn out on the peel. As there was still a considerable quantity of heat left in the oven, further items of bakery, such as puddings, pasties and pies which required longer low-temperature cooking, were then inserted. If custards were being made, their blind pastry cases were now put in and filled almost to the brim with a sweet egg and milk mixture poured from a long-handled wooden custard filler *(10)*. The door was then sealed in place again and the contents left to bake for the required time. If further baking was required, the whole process had to be repeated, reheating the oven with more gorse, cleaning out the hot embers, etc. It is not surprising that the first iron ovens which were able to provide a constant source of heat proved to be so successful when introduced in the eighteenth century.

In the kitchens of the royal household, and in those of leading members of the court, the cooks had to develop new skills from the early 1660s, when ice-cream began to be made in this country. By constructing straw-thatched ice-houses or snow-pits, dug deep into the ground, it was now possible to keep stocks of winter ice throughout the year. When ice-cream was required, blocks of ice were brought into the kitchen, broken into lumps, and packed around a small metal pan containing sweetened cream, perhaps flavoured with orange flower water. Having been left to freeze for a couple of hours, it was then turned out on to a salver and sent up to the table, where it formed an interesting delicacy for the banquet course.

Table setting, c.1660

TABLEWARE

U p to the opening decades of the seventeenth century the gentry had lived within large households, usually thirty or more in number, including relations, chaplains, tutors, porters and a large number of servants. In all but the grandest houses, they all dined together in the great hall. The master and his chief guests sat at the top table, probably raised on a dais surmounted by a tall canopy, while the remainder occupied tables below, in the body of the hall. When the gentry started to spend more time in town, and more money on personal pleasures, the old-fashioned extended household proved to be an expensive encumbrance, and soon became a thing of the past.

Imitating the Elizabethan nobility, the gentry now abandoned the great hall for all but the largest social events, and began to take their meals in a completely new setting – the dining room. In older houses, the parlour, a private bed-sitting room, was often transformed into a dining room, with new decorations and furniture, while in new houses a good-quality purpose-built dining room was of the greatest importance. With its walls lined with elegant timber panelling or embossed, painted and gilded Cordovan goatskin, its plaster ceiling enriched with mouldings and robustly-modelled ornament, its impressive fireplace and curtained windows, the dining room provided an ideal setting in which to entertain guests, and make a powerful display of wealth and taste.

From the middle of the century, dining rooms were being furnished with a dining table, often of the oval gate-legged variety, surrounded by a matching set of chairs for the most important diners. There might also be a long table and a set of stools for other members of the household, while livery cupboards or sideboards would be provided both to hold dishes of food and to display vessels of gold, silver or fine pottery.

When preparing the table, it was first covered with a fine linen cloth, probably woven with a damask design. Over this, the table was laid with all the required plates, salts, casters and saucers. These were made of silver or silver-gilt in the larger houses, for they provided a convenient and ostentatious means of storing one's wealth in a period when modern banking systems were still in their infancy. Much early plate was melted down during the Civil War, but from the Restoration there was a great revival in the use of silver tableware, which now appeared in a whole range of new and robustly elegant designs. In 1670, for example, Prince Rupert purchased five dozen silver plates from Alderman Blackwell, each plate weighing 17¾ ounces at 5s 8d per ounce, the whole set costing almost £300. This gives some indication of the high costs involved in furnishing a table with good-quality silverware. Much of this domestic plate was made in London, where it found a ready market among the nobility and gentry who came up to town for the winter season, but major regional centres such as Newcastle, York, Chester, Norwich and Exeter also produced silverware of the highest standard.

Since solid silver was extremely expensive, many households used pewter as a substitute. Composed of tin, with a small percentage of lead and copper, this metal cost only 1s to 1s 2d a pound, and therefore could be used in much greater quantities by

Earthenware drinking vessels in 'jewelled' and feathered Staffordshire slipware, 1690, in black-glazed redware from Potovens near Wakefield c.1680, in tin-glaze decorated with blue brushwork, made in Southwark in 1633, and a brown salt-glazed stoneware mug probably made in Nottingham by James Morley, c.1700

On this fine Staffordshire charger by Thomas Toft, Charles II makes an appropriately loyal image for the multi-coloured slipware decoration

a far wider section of the community. When brightly polished, it closely resembled silver, but it was much softer. Even a moderately hard cut with a knife would score its surface quite deeply, so that it was in need of constant maintenance, the marks received at table either burnished over, or polished out using fine abrasive sand.

This troublesome operation could be avoided by using delftware made of a light biscuit-coloured pottery covered in a smooth and glossy opaque white glaze. Having been made in England from the 1560s, it now enjoyed great popularity, its production being centred in the London parishes of Aldgate and Southwark and, from the mid-seventeenth century, at Brislington near Bristol. Many pieces were decorated with blue brushwork in the Chinese manner, imitating Ming or 'Transitional' porcelain, while others, particularly the large 'blue-dash chargers' (so-called from the decoration around their rims), were painted with brightly coloured flowers, portraits, or pictures of Adam and Eve. English lead-glazed earthenware also made great advances from the mid-seventeenth century, particularly in the manufacture of tableware. By the 1660s, the supremacy of the Staffordshire potters had already become fully established, their slipwares decorated in coloured liquid clays being particularly attractive. The great dishes of Thomas Toft, with their lively royal portraits or coats of arms, provided appropriately loyal images for the dining room.

In many households, wooden tableware was still in use, the square wooden trencher, with a large hollow for meat and a small hollow for salt, now being replaced by circular wooden plates or platters. Large communal drinking bowls still survived too, but from the end of Elizabeth's reign glassware had become much more common, appearing in the form of wine glasses, tumblers, and an excellent range of sweetmeat, jelly and syllabub glasses.

The most significant change in tableware was the introduction of the fork. Forks had been used for eating sweetmeats on royal and noble tables since the fourteenth century, but they only emerged as a major item of cutlery from the early seventeenth century, when they were popularized by Thomas Coryat. He published an account of their use in Italy in 1611, while in 1616 Ben Jonson asked

'Forks! what be they?'
'The laudable use of forks,
Brought into custom here, as they are in Italy,
To the sparing of napkins.'

Half a century was to pass before they were generally accepted, however, but by the 1660s sets of knives and forks were being made, the knife now adopting a rounded end, in contrast to its earlier pointed form which had been necessary when it had to spear meat from the dishes.

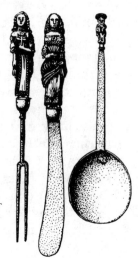

Dating from the 1660s, the knife and fork are of steel with carved ivory handles, while the spoon is of solid silver, with a gilt knop

THE MEALS

At this period the day was punctuated by three main meals; breakfast, taken shortly after rising, dinner, taken at midday, and supper, taken in the early evening. The first of these was a relatively light meal by the standards of the day, probably having a selection of cold meats, bread and butter, and cakes served with tea, coffee or chocolate by the end of the century. Then as now, there were great contrasts in breakfast preferences, however, the Cromwells taking rich broth or caudle, followed by a cup of small ale with toast and sugar at mid-morning.

Unlike today's dinners, in which the frequent courses follow each other in a set sequence from soup to dessert, the seventeenth-century dinner was only of two or, at most, three courses. Each course comprised a number of diverse dishes, including both sweets and savouries, so that the diner could help himself to whatever he liked in the manner of a modern buffet, thus giving each individual a much greater freedom of choice. The first course would be placed on the table in a neat, symmetrical arrangement, and include most of the major meat dishes, together with soups which would be removed and their place taken by a further dish once everyone had been served. In the second course there would be a range of lighter meats, game and sweet stuff laid in a similar symmetrical pattern, but this division of the dishes was only a general rule, leaving plenty of scope to include whatever might be available at any particular time.

The third course was composed of fruit, sweets and cheese, but the manner in which it was served changed as the century progressed. In the earlier decades, it continued the popular Elizabethan practice of banqueting; the 'banquet' in this case being an elaborate dessert course of sweetmeats etc. served either as a meal in itself or as a continuation of dinner or supper, usually set out in a separate apartment. It presented an opportunity for the cooks and the gardeners to make a great show of their skills, with elaborate confections and rare fruits displayed in new and exciting

James I and the young Prince Henry entertaining the Spanish Ambassador.
Note the plate, knife and manchet bread-roll set before each diner,
the arrangement of the dishes on the table, and the two standing salts

ways. For important functions, cardboard galleons sailing on seas
of salt could startle guests with their cannon, fired with real
gunpowder, while pastry deer bled red wine when arrows were
pulled from their sides.

John Evelyn gives the following colourful account of
William and Mary's entertainment for the Venetian ambassadors,
when 'the banquet was twelve vast chargers piled up so high that
those that sat one against another could hardly see each other. Of
these sweetmeats, which doubtless took some days piling up in this
exquisite manner, the Ambassadors touched not, but left them to
the spectators… in a moment of time all that curious work was
demolished, the confitures voided, and the tables cleared.' This
appears to have been the fate of many royal banquets. Even when
the Garter knights held their great dinner in the magnificent
Banqueting House in Whitehall, 'the banqueting-stuff was flung

around the room profusely.' In most households, however, particularly from the Restoration, the third course began to be served at the dining table, in the manner of a modern dessert.

At supper, early in the evening, only a single course was laid, but it could be made up of numerous dishes, or be extended by a banquet whenever necessary. Then, after a few hours of good conversation, music, singing or cards, accompanied by much alcohol and perhaps tobacco, the company would be served with a light meal to prepare them either for their homeward journey or for the chill of the bedroom – Pepys, for example, having 'a good sack-posset and cold meat and sent my guests away about 10 a-clock at night'. The sack posset certainly provided the ideal close to the day. Made of eggs, wine and spices scalded with sweetened cream, spooned from the most beautifully decorated silverware, or sipped from voluminous earthenware vessels, its rich smooth warmth and alcoholic potency soon lulled the diners into total oblivion: 'And so to bed.'

This London silver posset pot was purchased by John Hutton of Marske in 1669 to celebrate the birth of his son and heir

In this broadside of 1641, Mistress Abel
fixes a chicken on the spit in her kitchen at
'The Ship', Old Fish Street, in London

RECIPES

The recipes have been chosen to demonstrate a typical range of seventeenth-century dishes, and to give some impression of their diverse flavours. They include some of the newly introduced varieties of pudding and bakery, in addition to contemporary versions of well-established foods.

First and second courses for a meal may be made up from a combination of any of the meat dishes with a pudding and either hot or cold roasts; while the various sweets, cakes and biscuits, with fresh fruit and cheese, can form a banquet or third course. As an alternative, any of the recipes can be used individually as part of an otherwise modern meal.

DIET BREAD

The receypte of the Dyett bread: Take halfe a pecke of Fyne Wheaten Flower, three handfull of sage shredd small, An ounce and a halfe of ordinary Fennell seede lightly bruised, strawe the sage and the Fennell seede amongst the Flower, and so with barme kneade and bake ytt as you do other breade, and eate ytt nott untill ytt be a day old.

14 oz (400 g) plain flour
2 tbls (30 ml) dried sage
½ oz (15 g) fennel seed, bruised
½ oz (15 g) dried yeast mixed with 1 tsp (5ml) sugar and ½ pt (275 ml) warm water

Mix the dry ingredients in a warm bowl, make a well in the centre, work in the liquid, knead, and leave to rise in a warm place for 1 hour. Knead the dough on a floured board, shape into a round cob or a number of small cakes, and allow to prove for 15 minutes before baking at gas mark 8, 450°F (230°C) for 15 minutes, and then for a further 40 minutes at gas mark 6, 400°F (200°C). This bread has a delicate aniseed flavour, and makes an interesting accompaniment to soups, fish or cheese.

A Temple Newsam recipe quoted in The Gentlewoman's Kitchen

DUTCH PUDDING

Take a pound and a halfe of Fresh Beef, all lean, take a pound and a quarter of Beef Suet, sliced both very small, then take a half-penny stale Loaf and grate it, a handfull of Sage and a little Winter Savory, a little Time, shred these very small; take four Eggs, half a pint of Cream, a few Cloves, Nutmegs, Mace and Pepper, finely beaten, mingle them all together very well, with a little Salt; roll it all up together in a green Colwort Leaf, and then tye it up hard in a Linnen-Cloth, garnish your Dish with grated bread and serve it up with mustard in Sawcers.

12 oz (350 g) coarsely minced lean beef
8 oz (225 g) suet
4 oz (125 g) dry breadcrumbs
2 tsps (10 ml) dried sage
1 tsp (5 ml) dried savory
1 tsp (5 ml) dried thyme
2 eggs
¼ tsp (1.5 ml) ground cloves
¼ tsp (1.5 ml) grated nutmeg
¼ tsp (1.5 ml) ground mace
¼ tsp (1.5 ml) pepper
2 tsps (10 ml) salt
1-2 large cabbage leaves
fresh breadcrumbs, to garnish
made English mustard, to serve

Mix all the ingredients together and form into a round ball. Wrap in a large cabbage leaf, and tie up tightly in a linen cloth. Plunge into boiling water, and simmer for 2 hours. To serve, turn out of the cloth on to a bed of fresh breadcrumbs, accompanied by a saucer of English mustard. The dish looks just like a cabbage at this stage, but may be carved with ease.

Elizabeth Cromwell: The Court and Kitchen of Mrs Elizabeth Commonly called Joan Cromwell

SCOTCH COLLOPS

To Make Scotch Collops: R. a legge of Mutton, cutt itt in round pieces as broad as you can, & the thickness of a thin halfe-crowne, fry them in sweet butter very browne, but not too hard, then take four or five spoonfull of Clarett-wine, two spoonfull of vinegar, an onion slit, halfe a nuttmegge grated, Lemon-pill, an Anchovee, a little horse-radish, & oysters if you have them, putt all into the Frying-pan together with the meat, & a quarter of a pound of butter beaten thick, tosse them in the Pan a while over the fire, but do not let them boyle, then heat your dish, rubb it with Shallot or garlick, & send them upp quick.

1 lb (450 g) lean lamb or mutton
6 oz (175 g) butter
5 tbls (75 ml) claret
2 tbls (30 ml) vinegar
1 onion
2 anchovy fillets
1 tbls (15 ml) horseradish sauce
1 garlic clove

Thinly slice the meat, and stir fry gently with half the butter for 5-10 minutes until browned. Remove from the heat, and add all the remaining ingredients, except for the garlic. Heat gently for a few minutes, stirring the pan continuously, until almost at boiling point. Slice the garlic, and rub it around the inside of the serving dish before pouring in the collops. Serve immediately. This is an excellent way of making a rich and full-flavoured meat dish in a very short time.

The Savile Recipe Book, 1683, quoted in The Gentlewoman's Kitchen

---

SALAD

For the salad:
young leaves of lettuce, sorrel, mustard, cress, dandelion, spinach, radishes
8 oz (225 g) capers
12 dates, sliced lengthways
2 oz (50 g) raisins
2 oz (50 g) currants
2 oz (50 g) blanched almonds
6 figs, sliced
6 mandarin oranges, peeled and divided into segments

For the decoration:
5 small branches of rosemary
4 lemons
8 oz (225 g) fresh or glacé cherries
6 hard-boiled eggs

Mix the contents of the salad together (reserving half the capers, dates, almonds and oranges for decoration) and spread evenly across a wide shallow dish. Spike each branch of rosemary into the pointed end of five half-lemons, and hang with the cherries before placing one in the centre of the salad, and the remaining four equidistant around it. Prick four half-eggs with the reserved almonds and dates, both sliced lengthways, and place these between the four half-lemons. Quarter the remaining eggs, and alternate with slices of lemon just within the brim of the dish. Then decorate the brim with alternating orange segments and small piles of capers.

The Second Book of Cookery

A 'Grand Sallet' of 1641

205

BRAWN

To bake Brawne: Take two Buttocks and hang them up two or three dayes, then take them down and dip them into hot-water, and pluck off the skin, dry them very well with a clean Cloth, when you have so done, take Lard, cut it in pieces as big as your little finger, and season it very well with Pepper, Cloves, Mace, Nutmeg, and Salt, put each of them into an earthen Pot, put in a pint of Claret-wine, a pound of Mutton Suet. So close it with paste, let the Oven be well heated, and so bake them, you must give them time for the baking according to the bigness of the Haunches and the thickness of the Pots, they commonly allot seven hours for the baking of them; let them stand three days, then take off the Covers, and pour away all the liquor, then have clarified butter, and fill up both the Pots to keep it for use, it will very well keep two or three months.

2-3 lb (900 g–1.4 kg) joint of lean
   pork
½ bottle (350 ml) claret
2 oz (50 g) suet
2 tsps (10 ml) salt
½ tsp (2.5 ml) ground mace
¼ tsp (1.5 ml) pepper
¼ tsp (1.5 ml) ground cloves
¼ tsp (1.5 ml) grated nutmeg
shortcrust pastry made with
   4 oz (125 g) plain flour and
   2 oz (50 g) lard

Trim any fat or rind from the joint, and cut into strips. Truss the joint tightly, place in a deep casserole, then add the strips of fat and the remaining ingredients except for the pastry. Roll out the pastry, and use it to cover the casserole, carefully sealing the edges. Bake at gas mark 4, 350°F (180°C) for 2½ hours, then leave in a cool place overnight. Remove the crust, lift out the joint, wipe clean, and carve as required. The remaining stock can be used to provide a highly-flavoured basis for soups etc.

Rebecca Price: The Compleat Cook

A cast bronze skillet of 1684

CHICKEN CULLIS

To make a cullis as white as snowe and in the nature of gelly: Take a cocke, scalde, wash and draw him clene, seeth it in white wine or rhenish wine, skum it cleane, clarifie the broth after it is strained, then take a pinte of thicke & sweet creame, straine that to your clarified broth, and your broth will become exceeding faire and white; then take powdred ginger, fine white sugar and Rosewater, seething your cullis when you season it, to make it take the colour the better.

1 chicken
1½ pt (850 ml) white wine or white
    wine and water
1 egg white, lightly beaten
1 pt (575 ml) single cream
½ tsp (2.5 ml) ground ginger
2 tbls (30 ml) sugar
1 tbls (15 ml) rosewater

Simmer the chicken in the wine, or wine and water, until tender – about 45-50 minutes. Remove the chicken from the pan and keep it hot, ready for the table. Beat the egg white into the stock, and continue to whisk over a moderate heat until it comes to the boil. Stop whisking immediately and allow the liquid to rise to the top of the pan before removing it from the heat for a few minutes to allow the fine particles to form a soft curd with the egg white. Pour the liquid through a fine cloth into a clean pan, place on a gentle heat, and stir slowly while pouring in the cream. Heat the cullis almost to boiling point, stirring continuously, and finally add the ginger, sugar and rosewater just before serving.

The cullis may be poured over the chicken resting on crustless cubes of white bread, in a deep dish. Alternatively, it can be served separately as a soup, when its smooth texture and rich, delicate flavour can be enjoyed to the full.

Sir Hugh Platt: Delightes for Ladies

KNOT BISCUITS

*To make Knotts or Gumballs: Take 12
Yolkes of Egges, & 5 Whites, a pound
of searced Sugar, half a pound of
Butter washed in Rose Water, 3
quarters of an ounce of Mace finely
beaten, a little Salt dissolved in Rose
Water, half an ounce of Caroway-seeds,
Mingle all theise together with as much
Flower as will worke it up in paste, &
soe make it Knotts or Rings or What
fashion you please. Bake them as
Bisket-bread, but upon Pye-plates.*

1½ oz *(40 g) butter*
1 tbls *(15 ml) rosewater*
4 oz *(100 g) sugar*
2 *eggs, beaten*
1 tsp *(5 ml) ground mace*
1 tsp *(5 ml) aniseed*
1 tsp *(5 ml) caraway seed*
8 oz *(225 g) flour*

Beat the butter with the
rosewater, then cream with the
sugar. Mix in the beaten eggs and
spices, then work in the flour to
make a stiff dough. Make into
long rolls about ¼ inch (5 mm) in
diameter, and form into knots,
rings, or plaited strips before
baking on lightly greased baking
sheets for 15-20 minutes at gas
mark 4, 350°F (180°C).

Henry Fairfax: Arcana Fairfaxiana

MARZIPAN BACON

*To make Collops like Bacon of
Marchpane: Take some of your
Marchpane Paste and work it in red
Saunders till it be red: then rowl a
broad sheet of white Paste, and a sheet
of red Paste, three of the white, and
four of the red, and so one upon another
in mingled sorts, every red between,
then cut it overthwart, till it look like
Collops of Bacon, then dry it.*

8 oz *(225 g) ground almonds*
4 oz *(100 g) caster sugar*
2 tbls *(30 ml) rosewater*
red food colouring
cornflour or icing sugar for dusting

Beat the almonds and sugar with
the rosewater to form a stiff paste.
Divide in two, and knead a few
drops of the red food colour into
one half. Using either cornflour or
icing sugar to dust the paste, roll
out half the white mixture into a
rectangle about ⅜ inch (10 mm) in
thickness, and the remainder into
three thinner rectangles of the
same size. Divide the red paste
into four, and roll each piece out
into similar rectangles. Starting
with the thick white slab ('the fat')
build up alternate red and white
layers to form a miniature piece
of streaky bacon, from which thin
slices or 'collops' can then be cut
and allowed to dry.

*W.M.: The Compleat Cook and
Queen's Delight, 1671 edition*

SHROPSHIRE CAKES

To make a Shropsheere cake: Take two pound of dryed flour after it has been searced fine, one pound of good sugar dried and searced, also a little beaten sinamon or some nottmegg greeted and steeped in rose water; so straine two eggs, whites and all, not beaten to it, as much unmelted butter as will work it to a paste: so mould it & roule it into longe rouses, and cutt off as much at a time as will make a cake, two ounces is enough for one cake: then roule it in a ball between your hands; so flat it on a little white paper cut for a cake, and with your hand beat it about as big as a cheese trancher and a little thicker than a past board: then prick them with a comb not too deep in squares like diamons and prick the cake in every diamon to the bottom; so take them in a oven not too hot: when they rise up white let them soake a little, then draw. If the sugar be dry enough you need not dry it but searce it: you must brake in your eggs after you have wroat in some of your butter into your flower: prick and mark them when they are cold: this quantity will make a dozen and two or three, which is enough for my own at a time: take off the paper when they are cold.

8 oz (225 g) butter
1 lb (450 g) flour
8 oz (225 g) caster sugar
¼ tsp (1.5 ml) grated nutmeg
1 egg
1 tsp (5 ml) rosewater

Rub the butter into the dry ingredients, then work in the egg and rosewater to form a very stiff dough. Cut off lumps of dough, and work into ¼ inch (5 mm) thick cakes, 4 inches (10 cm) in diameter. Using a comb, mark the top surface into diamonds, cutting half-way through the cake, then use a broad skewer to prick through the centre of each diamond. Transfer to baking sheets, and bake for 20 minutes at gas mark 4, 350°F (180°C). Remove from the sheets with a metal spatula, and place on a wire tray to cool.

Madam Susanne Avery: A Plain Plantain

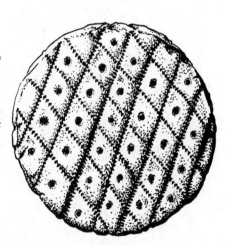

A Shropshire cake, marked with a comb and a skewer

SPICE CAKE

To make an Extraordinary Good Cake: Take half a bushel of the best flour you can get, very finely searced, and lay it on a large pastry board, make a hold in the middle thereof, put to it three pounds of the best butter you can get; with 14 pounds of currants finely picked and rubbed, three quarts of good new thick cream, 2 pounds of fine sugar beaten, 3 pints of new ale barm or yeast, 4 ounces of cinnamon beaten fine and searced,also an ounce of beaten ginger, 2 ounces of nutmegs beaten fine and searced; put in all these material together, and work them up to an indifferent stiff paste. Keep it warm till the oven be hot, then make it up and bake it, being baked an hour and a half ice it, then take 4 pounds of double refined sugar, beat it and searce it, and put it in a clean scowered skillet the quantity of a gallon, and boil it to a candy height with a little rosewater, then draw the cake, run it all over, and set it in the oven till it be candied.

3 oz (75 g) butter
1 lb (450 g) plain flour
12 oz (350 g) currants
2 oz (50 g) sugar
½ tsp (2.5 ml) ground cinnamon
½ tsp (2.5 ml) ground ginger
¼ tsp (1.5 ml) grated nutmeg
½ pt (275 ml) cream
½ oz (15 g) dried yeast mixed with
   1 tsp (5 ml) sugar and ¼ pt
   (150 ml) warm water

For glazing:
1 tbls (15 ml) sugar
1 tbls (15 ml) rosewater

Rub the butter into the flour, add the remainder of the dry ingredients, and mix in the cream and yeast to form a soft dough. Leave to rise in a warm place for about an hour, when it will double in size, then knead and place in a greased 8 inch (20 cm) cake tin. Leave to prove for 20 minutes, then bake at gas mark 7, 425°F (220°C) for 20 minutes, then for 1 hour at gas mark 5, 375°F (190°C). Melt the sugar in the rosewater over a low heat, and brush this glaze over the cake immediately after removing it from the oven.

Robert May: The Accomplisht Cook

One of a set of six plates made in white tin-glazed earthenware decorated with purple and yellow brushwork. It was made in London in the 1680s

GINGERBREAD

To make Gingerbread: Take three stale Manchets and grate them, drie them, and sift them through a fine sieve, then adde unto them one ounce of ginger beeing beaten, and as much Cinamon, one ounce of liquorice and aniseedes being beaten together and searced, halfe a pound of sugar, then boile all these together in a posnet, with a quart of claret wine till they come to a stiffe paste with often stirring of it; and when it is stiffe, mold it on a table and so drive it thin, and print it in your moldes: dust your moldes with Cinamon, Ginger, and liquorice, beeing mixed together in fine powder. This is your gingerbread used at the Court, and in all gentlemens houses at festival times. It is otherwise called drie Leach.

8 oz (225 g) fresh white breadcrumbs
1 tsp (5 ml) ground ginger
1 tsp (5 ml) cinnamon
1 tsp (5 ml) aniseed
1 tsp (5 ml) ground liquorice (if
    available)
1 oz (25 g) sugar
¼ pt (150 ml) claret

Dry the breadcrumbs under the grill or in the oven (but without browning), and add to the remaining ingredients in a saucepan. Work the mixture over a gentle heat with a wooden spoon, until it forms a stiff dough. Turn the dough out on to a wooden board dusted with ground ginger and cinnamon and roll it out to about ¼ inch (5 mm) in thickness. It may then be impressed with a small stamp, a 1 inch (2.5 cm) diameter butter print being ideal for this purpose, and cut into small circles, using a pastry cutter. If antique gingerbread moulds are available, then they should be dusted with the ground spices before the slab of dough is firmly impressed into their designs. Then, after the surplus has been trimmed off with a knife, the gingerbread can be removed by inverting the moulds, and gently knocking their edges down on to the table.

Sir Hugh Platt: Delightes for Ladies

● Like most early gingerbreads, this version releases its flavours gradually, the gentle aniseed being slowly overwhelmed by the fiery ginger.

DEVONSHIRE WHITE POT

Take a pint of Cream and strain four Eggs into it, and put a little salt and a little sliced Nutmeg, and season it with sugar somewhat sweet, then take almost a penny Loaf of fine bread sliced very thin, and put it into a dish that will hold it, the Cream and the Eggs being put to it, then take a handfull of Raisins of the Sun being boiled, and a little sweet Butter, so bake it.

2 oz (50 g) raisins
1 lb (450 g) white bread, crusts
    removed and thinly sliced
1 oz (25 g) butter
3 eggs
1 pt (575 ml) single cream
¼ tsp (1.5 ml) grated nutmeg
¼ tsp salt
3 oz (75 g) sugar

Soak the raisins in hot water for 10 minutes. Line a 2 pint (1.1 litre) ovenproof dish with some of the the remainder, mixing in the raisins and knobs of the butter. Beat the eggs with the cream and stir in the nutmeg, salt and sugar. Pour over the bread, and allow it to stand for 15 minutes. Bake at gas mark 4, 350°F (180°C), for 40-50 minutes.

Rebecca Price: The Compleat Cook

QUAKING PUDDING

To make a quaking Pudding: Take a pint and somewhat more of thick Cream, ten Eggs, put the whites of three, beat them very well with two spoonfuls of Rose-water: mingle with your cream three spoonfuls of fine flour: mingle it so well, that there be no lumps in it, put it altogether, and season it according to your Tast: butter a Cloth very well, and let it be thick that it may not run out, and let it boyl for half an hour as fast as you can, then take it up and make Sauce with Butter, Rosewater and Sugar, and serve it up. You may stick some blanched Almonds upon it if you please.

4 egg yolks
2 egg whites
½ pt (275 ml) double cream
1½ tbls (25 ml) flour
1 tbls (15 ml) rosewater
butter
1 oz (25 g) blanched almonds, to
    decorate
For the sauce:
2 tbls (30 ml) rosewater
2 tbls (30 ml) sugar
2 oz (50 g) butter
2 tbls (30 ml) water

Beat the egg yolks and whites into the cream, then beat in the flour and rosewater to form a thick batter. Rub a piece of butter into a thick pudding cloth to help it to retain the batter. Support the cloth in a 1 pint (575 ml) basin, pour in the batter, tie the cloth securely, and plunge the pudding into a pan of boiling water. Simmer for 30 minutes, then remove from the pan, swiftly plunge in cold water, turn the pudding out on to a warm plate, and decorate with almonds. Make the sauce by melting the ingredients together, stirring constantly, and pour over the pudding.

Rebecca Price: The Compleat Cook

SYLLABUB

My Lady Middlesex makes Syllabubs for little Glasses with spouts, thus Take 3 pints of sweet Cream, one of quick white wine (or Rhenish), and a good wine glassful (better the ¼ of a pint) of Sack; mingle them with about three quarters of a pound of fine Sugar in Powder. Beat all these together with a whisk, till all appeareth converted into froth. Then pour it into your little Syllabub-glasses, and let them stand all night. The next day the Curd will be thick and firm above, and the drink clear under it. I conceive it may do well, to put into each glass (when you pour your liquor into it) a sprig of Rosemary a little bruised, or a little Lemon-peel, or some such thing to quicken the taste… or Nutmegs, or Mace, or Cloves, a very little.

1 pt (575 ml) double cream
7 fl oz (200 ml) Rhenish white wine
2 tbls (30 ml) dry sherry
4 oz (125 g) caster sugar
sprigs of rosemary or the peeled zest of a
    lemon

Beat the cream, wines and sugar together to form a thick froth, and spoon into large wine glasses. Insert the rosemary or lemon as desired, and allow to stand in a cool place for at least 12 hours before serving. The resulting syllabub is one of the most delicately flavoured, smooth and delicious of all seventeenth-century dishes.

Sir Kenelm Digby: The Closet of Sir Kenelm Digby Opened

Made by George Ravenscroft, this glass spouted vessel of 1677 was used for serving syllabub, the spout allowing the clear wine which collected beneath the creamy curd to be drunk separately

ORANGE BUTTER

R. a quarter of a Pint of cleared juice of Oranges, a quarter of a Pint of white wine, pare the Peel of your Oranges thinne, steep itt in the juice & white-wine halfe an hour, then put in when you have taken out the pill a little fine Sugar, to take away the sharpnesse. Then beat the yolks of six eggs very well, & put them into the liquor, & sett them over the fire, & keep itt continually stirring till you find it almost as thick as Butter then throw itt about the dish or bason, & let itt stand all night, in the morning take itt off lightlie with a spoon, & serve itt as other Butter.

¼ pt (150 ml) fresh orange juice, and
*   thinly-peeled zest of the oranges*
¼ pt (150 ml) white wine
6 egg yolks
2 tbls (30 ml) sugar

Soak the zest in the orange juice and white wine for 30 minutes, to enrich the flavour, and then remove. Beat the egg yolks and sugar and add to the orange juice. Pour the mixture into a saucepan, and stir continuously over a low heat until thick and creamy, but do not allow to boil. Allow the butter to cool and serve with wafers as a rich full-flavoured fruit dip.

The Savile Recipe Book, 1683, quoted in The Gentlewoman's Kitchen

MARMALADE

To make marmelade of Lemmons or Oranges: Take ten Lemmons or Oranges and boyle them with halfe a dozen pippins, and so drawe them through a strainer, then take so much sugar as the pulp dooth weigh, and bottle it as you doe Marmelade of Quinces, and boxe it up.

For 2 lb (900 g) marmalade use:
5 large lemons (or oranges)
3 apples (Cox's pippins, for example)
¼ pt (150 ml) water
about 1 lb (450 g) sugar

Cut the pointed ends off the lemons, quarter them, and take out the pips while holding them over a stainless steel pan. Peel, core, and quarter the apples, then place them in the pan with the lemons and water, cover and simmer gently until tender – about 45-60 minutes. Remove the fruit from the heat and convert it into a stiff pulp either by rubbing it through a sieve with the back of a wooden spoon, or by blending it until smooth. Weigh the pulp, transfer it into a clean saucepan with its own weight of sugar, and stir over a low heat until it boils to setting point (221°F/105°C). If it is to be stored for some time, the marmalade may be packed into glass jars and sealed in the usual way, but if it is to be served within the next day or so, it may be either spooned into small waxed paper baking cases, or spread as a ½ inch (12 mm) thick slab on a sheet of waxed paper. It can then be cut into small cubes, sprinkled with caster sugar, and eaten with a fork.

Sir Hugh Platt: Delightes for Ladies

SACK POSSET

My Lord of Carlile's Sack-possett: Take a Pottle of Cream, and boil in it a little whole Cinnamon, and three or four flakes of Mace. To this proportion of Cream put in eighteen yolkes of Eggs, and eight of the whites; a pint of Sack. Beat your Eggs very well, and mingle them with your Sack, Put in three quarters of a pound of Sugar into the Wine and Eggs with a Nutmeg grated, and a little beaten Cinnamon; set the basin on the fire with the wine and Eggs, and let it be hot. Then put in the Cream boyling from the fire, pour it on high, but stir it not; cover it with a dish, and when it is settled, strew on the top a little fine Sugar mingled with three grains of Ambergreece and one grain of Musk and serve it up.

9 egg yolks
4 egg whites
½ pt (275 ml) dry sherry
¼ tsp (1.5 ml) cinnamon
¼ tsp (1.5 ml) ground mace
½ tsp (2.5 ml) grated nutmeg
2 pt (1.1/L) single cream
6 oz (175g) sugar

Beat together the egg yolks, egg whites, sherry and spices, and gently heat in a large pan, stirring constantly, until warm, but still not thickened. Heat the cream and sugar together and as it rises to the full boil pour from a good height into the warm eggs and sherry mixture. Allow the posset to stand in a warm place for a few minutes, sprinkle a little sugar across its surface, and serve.

Sir Kenelm Digby: The Closet of Sir Kenelm Digby Opened

The hollow stem of this 1690 wine glass contains a silver 6d. of William III

" Fresh Oysters ! penny a lot !"

GEORGIAN
BRITAIN

Jennifer Stead

A first course for six; first half of the eighteenth century

I n 1700 the English still lived and ate in a way which would have seemed familiar to their medieval ancestors: agricultural, self-sufficient, killing cattle in winter, eating thick pottages. By 1800 England was on the brink of the modern era, seeing a widespread move off the land into the towns, the rise of a prosperous middle class, the development of newspapers, advertising, and the birth of a consumer society.

In 1700 most kitchen equipment was simple, made locally by blacksmith, whitesmith or potter. By 1800 there was on the market a huge variety of kitchen equipment, tools, pots, dishes and glasses, for the consumer to choose. At the beginning of the century a housewife might buy one pan. By the end, she might purchase a whole set. Technological discoveries in one field were often applied to others. For example, improvements in rolling sheet iron, which produced better kitchen utensils, also produced finer flour when the rolling process was seized upon by millers. And new eating and drinking habits were a spur to new design in the metal and pottery industries – habits such as the eating of soup, or the drinking of tea and coffee.

This rapid development of scientific and technological discoveries affected nearly every area of life, including both the preparation of food, and the quality of food itself.

Punch bowl

A kitchen range of the first half of the eighteenth century. Note the iron oven on the left, the clockwork spitjack, the two salamanders to the right, and pudding cloth drying above

CULINARY METHODS

Originally, cooking was done over a wood fire built on the floor of an open hearth. When coal was adopted as a fuel in the sixteenth century, however, the wrought-iron fire basket was developed, called in the seventeenth century the 'grate' or 'range'.

By 1700 the usual form of grate was a large oblong basket on four legs, fastened to the chimney back with tie bars, ideal for roasting large joints of meat. The spits were rested on hooks on the two front legs and were usually turned mechanically by a clockwork spitjack, then later in the century, by a smokejack sited inside the chimney and operated by the heat of the fire. The fire could be made smaller by winding adjustable sides or 'cheeks' inwards by a rack and pinion mechanism. Supports for pans, called trivets, fastened to the cheek tops, could swing out over the fire. Sometimes the top front bar let down, a 'fall bar', into a further ledge for pans. By the middle of the century in fashionable town houses, panels of cast iron were added to the front on each side, with flat iron plates on top to provide hobs.

Roasting was the most important facility, as it was the most favoured method of cooking meat. Boiling came second, done in large pots hung over the fire. Stewing and sauce-making, where a gentle heat was required, had been done over little chafing dishes of charcoal on the floor of the hearth. From the late seventeenth century fashionable houses had a brick stove built into a corner of the kitchen, under a window for ventilation. Let into the top were small round fire baskets, about the size of chafing dishes, in which charcoal was burnt. This arrangement was much more convenient and comfortable for the cook than having to bend down to the hearth, though fumes were more of a

A clockwork mechanism for turning a spit

221

problem than they had been in the draught of a chimney. As late as 1800, James Woodforde recorded in his diary on 22 July when his niece Nancy was making jam, 'she became giddy, too long at the stove where charcoal was burning, though the outward door was open all the time.'

Ovens were of masonry, and generally of beehive shape built into the thickness of the wall. They had to be laboriously heated by building a fire inside the oven itself, then the hot ashes swept out and the food to be baked put in. It was impossible to regulate the heat of the oven once the food was in. The development in mid-century of the iron oven with grate underneath, a 'perpetual oven', was of enormous benefit. One of the earliest recorded was the perpetual oven installed in Shibden Hall, Halifax, in 1750 for the Rev. John Lister, for which he paid over 4 guineas.

Since the perpetual oven was often sited near the fireplace so that it could share the flue and chimney, it was a short step to combine oven and main fire. Accordingly, about 1770, in the north of England, one of the iron panels at the side of the grate was replaced by an iron oven, directly heated from the side of the fire. However, this tended to cook unevenly. A more expensive type was developed with flues running all round the oven and thence up the chimney. Then the iron panel at the other side of the grate was replaced by a water boiler, which was filled and emptied through

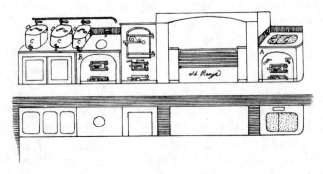

Kitchen and scullery plans of the 1780s, Bretton Hall, West Yorkshire. The new boiler at the back of the range was to supply kitchen and scullery with hot water and steam for the warm closet and steam table (both of iron: extreme right.

the aperture in the hob top, and soon a tap was fitted to the front for even more convenience. On larger ranges, L-shaped boilers made use of the space at the side and behind the grate and very large boilers were put at the back, fed from a cistern with a ball-cock.

The fire was still open to the chimney, however, and a great deal of heat was lost. The criticism of Count Rumford who came from Bavaria in 1775 may have helped speed up the covering of the fire by a further iron plate, creating another useful simmering hob (and making the charcoal stove redundant), all the smoke being drawn through flues and up the chimney. The first patent for such a closed range was taken out in 1802.

Those without ovens sent their pies, stamped with the owner's initials, to the local bakery ('Pat it and prick it and mark it with D'). Alternatively they could use screens or hasteners put close to the fire for meats, puddings and some breads and cakes. In the metal Dutch oven with a polished tin interior to reflect the heat it was possible to roast meat and bake a batter pudding at the same time (this came to be called Yorkshire pudding). Thomas Turner, a Sussex shopkeeper, records that on Christmas day 1756 they had among other things 'a sirloin of beef roasted in the oven with a batter pudding under it'. Meanwhile the cauldron hanging on the reckon hook over the fire could efficiently boil joints of meat, puddings and nets of vegetables all in the same water.

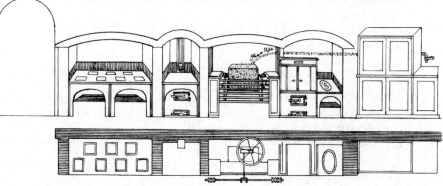

The pipe passes over the oven). It also supplied steam for the three kettles with taps (C) in the scullery. A is a double boiler with cast front and hob. B is a cast hot plate. The old oven and range were to be left intact. Note the new smokejack in chimney

A Dutch oven lined with polished tin Smaller houses of the period did not have a spit and irons for roasting meat. The poor man's spit was a danglespit suspended from the mantelpiece; this was nothing but a hook on a piece of string, from which the piece of meat spun before the fire. This was superseded by the clockwork bottlejack with a cast-iron balance wheel. On it were four hooks to spit four small birds or pieces of meat. The danglespit or bottlejack could also be mounted inside the Dutch oven, which had a door at the back for basting.

The majority of English people preferred plain food, roasted and boiled meat, puddings and pies, and so a large variety of kitchen utensils was not necessary. Those who wished to be fashionable, however, and could afford it, employed French cooks to make French dishes, and these required a more extensive *batterie de cuisine*. William Verral, who worked for M de Clouet, the chef of the Duke of Newcastle in Sussex, wrote a very readable and entertaining cookery book *(A Complete System of Cookery,* 1759). While purporting to be French in emphasis, in reality it sets out the solid English fare of the type he was producing for his customers at the White Hart in Lewes. He lists the utensils which every well-equipped kitchen of the well-to-do should have:

Stoves
2 Boilers, one to hold a leg of Mutton, the other two fowls
A Soup-pot
Eight small Stew-pans, of different sizes, and their covers
Two very large [Stew-pans], and covers
A neat Frying-Pan
Two copper Ladles, tinned
3 large copper Spoons, tinned
2 Slices, tinned
An Egg-Spoon, tinned
A Pewter Cullendar
4 Sieves – one of Lawn
5 Copper-cups, to hold above ¼ of a Pint
6 Do. smaller
2 Etamines [for straining thick soup]
3 large wooden Spoons
Sauce-Pans, Several

Among other utensils he could have mentioned are: rolling pins, baking tins, cake hoops or tins, earthenware pans, bowls, knives, forks, graters, coffee mills, pestle and mortar, whisks, slotted spoons, mashers, syringes for icing, or making biscuits and fritters, cabbage nets, pastry brush and jagging iron (marker), skimmer, salamander, fish kettle, lemon squeezer, writing paper, pudding cloths, weighing scales, spice and peppermills, patty pans, mustard bullet, jugs, dredgers, sugar cutters, baking spittle, toasting forks, dripping pans, larkspits, and preserving pots.

Verral gives an amusing account of going to cook at a house in Sussex where the old gentleman typified many of his class in preferring his meat plain roast and boiled, and very little else. Although he was quite well-off, his kitchen had hardly anything but one frying pan and one sieve, and that had been used for sanding the floor.

The inventory of a Sussex farmer would bear out Verral's comment on the plainness of fare: the farmer had only 3 spits, 1 large iron skillet and a small brass one, an old iron kettle, 3 old iron porridge pots, 2 iron dripping pans, 1 old gridiron, 1 chopping knife, 1 old cleaver and 9 pewter dishes.

A dripping pan, salamander
and basting spoon

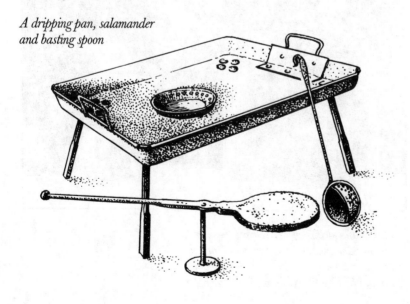

*A gentleman's kitchen of 1727. Note the open
hearth and the chicken being turned on the spit by
the clockwork spitjack. After the engraving in
Eliza Smith,* The Compleat Housewife

COOKERY BOOKS

From the late seventeenth century the increase of literacy, and the independence of mind which that gave, created a thirst for knowledge. Didactic books on every topic from health to geography, philosophy to gardening, were eagerly snapped up. Cookery books, which often included medical recipes and also directions for brewing and winemaking, were enormously popular. Between the years 1700 and 1800 over 300 titles on food and cookery alone were published, many of these going into several editions. It can be seen that as countless thousands were produced, it was possible for every middle-class household to own at least one.

At the start of the century these books were mainly royal or court cookery, written by men who had served apprenticeships with a French chef who had worked at court or for the aristocracy. Many of the recipes in these books are French and elaborate, involving the use of expensive ingredients like truffles and morels, and the recipes are expressed in old-fashioned chef's jargon, difficult to understand.

The attitude to French cooking was ambivalent. It was considered very fashionable to hire a French chef (whose skill consisted largely in elaborate 'made dishes' using an extravagant special gravy called 'cullis'), and yet they, and French food, were scoffed at. 'So much is the blind Folly of this Age', writes Hannah Glasse, 'that [people] would rather be impos'd on by a French Booby, than give Encouragement to a good *English* Cook!' It must be remembered that Britain was at war with the French for a large part of the eighteenth century, and patriotism and the idea of true-born Englishmen, were important. It was thought that the plain roast beef of old England made plain stalwart Englishmen.

Perhaps the preference for plainness is one reason why it is the cookery books written by women which succeeded so spectacularly; notably those by Eliza Smith (1st edition 1727), Hannah Glasse (1st edition 1747) and Elizabeth Raffald (1st edition 1769).

Mrs Glasse's *The Art of Cookery made Plain and Easy* went into no less than seventeen editions between 1747 and 1803, all other cookbooks pirating her recipes (as she herself had pirated from Eliza Smith and others). Mrs Glasse's recipes are more detailed in measures and method than those of her predecessors. She wrote out her recipes very clearly and precisely, so that even an untutored cook-maid could understand them: 'I have attempted a Branch of Cookery which Nobody has yet thought worth their while to write upon... My Intention is to instruct the lower Sort [so that] every servant who can read will be capable of making a tolerable good Cook.'

Mrs Glasse reflects the preferred simplicity in cooking and also the new standards of hygiene, due in part to piped water in some parts of towns. The cleanliness of London servants was remarked on by foreign visitors. She gives instructions on how to clean spits, gridirons, wooden bowls and other cooking utensils with sand and hot water only (soap would leave a flavour).

Thomas Bewick, A cook in the kitchen, c. 1790

MEALS

The new recipe books were for the gentry, the professional middle classes and richer tradesman class, and were an encouragement to aspire to a higher standard of living.

The times of dinner gradually began to change. In the early eighteenth century the middle classes and the higher orders might breakfast at 9 or 10 am, and have nothing else before dinner, which was usually at 2 or 3 pm. As the century progressed, dinner time got later, so that by the late eighteenth century dinner was generally at 6 or 7 pm. This left a long gap before dinner, which was filled by the new development of afternoon tea. The less fashionable classes who continued to have dinner in the middle of the day had a dish of tea in the afternoon, then had a supper in the evening of cold meats, cold pies, bread and cheese.

Many cookery books have diagrams of dinner-table layouts, which vary from the modest to the lavish (royal or aristocratic layouts on a massive scale appear in only a few, early books, all by men). The dishes for each course were to be placed very correctly and symmetrically on the table.

The first course to be arranged on the table always consisted mainly of meats, roasted, boiled, stewed and fried; some with sauces. Vegetables do not generally appear except as garnish to the meat. Bread was handed round. Soup, if it was on the bill of fayre, was served and eaten first, then removed, and a fish dish put in its place. After fish, the meat, which must have by then cooled considerably, was served. One writer, John Trusler, advises removing the cold fat that swims upon the gravy in cold weather.

The first course was removed, and the second put in its place. This consisted of lighter dishes of meat and fish, with the addition of sweet pies, puddings and tarts. Little side dishes of biscuits and pickles stayed on the table throughout the meal. After the second course, the cloth was removed and dessert followed, of jellies, sweetmeats, fruit, nuts and cheese (though jellies and sweetmeats

An elegant dinner of 7 and 9 dishes, using the recipes in this book

were sometimes placed in the centre of the second course). After the dessert had been removed, and a glass or two of wine drunk, the ladies withdrew, leaving the men to their drinking. Then the men would join the ladies for conversation or card games.

Rules for behaviour during the meals were set out by John Trusler in *The Honours of the Table*, 1788, which gives us a glimpse of the current etiquette among the upper middle classes, gentry and aristocracy. Guests were to walk into the dining room in strict order of rank, ladies first. The mistress sat at the top end of the table amongst all the women, with the most important female guests next to her. The master sat among the men in order of rank at the bottom end of the table. At the time Trusler was writing, however, a new mode of seating was gaining in preference, whereby the ladies and gentlemen sat alternately, though still in order of rank. As the old segregated arrangement went out, so did the boisterous drinking of healths and bumpers and loyal toasts. Male joviality became tempered with female sensibility.

At the beginning of the century the English hostess did all the carving and serving, thereby missing food and conversation herself. By mid-century, a new 'French ease' became fashionable whereby the master and mistress carved the dishes that were before them at each end of the table, and helped guests to these. Then the guests helped themselves and each other to the rest. By the turn of the nineteenth century when Mrs Rundell was writing, even this fashion had declined, guests had ceased to help themselves, and food was now served by the servants.

Trusler instructs the guests to behave properly. It is vulgar to eat too quickly or too slowly, which shows you are either too hungry, or you don't like the food. It is also vulgar to eat your soup with your nose in the plate. You must avoid 'smelling to the meat whilst on the fork'–it shows you suspect the meat is tainted. 'It is exceedingly rude to scratch any part of your body, to spit, or blow your nose… to lean your elbows on the table, to sit too far from it, to pick your teeth before the dishes are removed.' If the necessity of nature obliged you to leave the table, you had to steal away unobserved, and return without announcing where you'd been. Chamberpots had been kept in or just outside the dining room, but the new delicacy of feelings shrank from such crudeness.

Jonathan Swift wrote a satirical handbook (*Directions to Servants*, 1745) in which he 'recommends' bad, slovenly practices. From these we may infer that servants had subtle ways of getting even with their masters and mistresses. For instance he tells the cook, if her mistress does not allow her the usual prerequisite of the dripping, to use it now and then along with expensive butter to enliven the fire; to take half the meat and share it with the butler in exchange for the butler's wine; if a lump of soot falls in the soup, to stir it well in to give the soup a high *French* taste; if dinner is late, to put the clock back; to comb her hair over the cooking, so she can keep her eye on it while grooming herself – if the master complains about hair in the food, to say it's the footman's; if a chicken leg disappears (into the butler) to say a dog got it.

A banquet course: the table laid with pyramids of sweetmeats 1702, from F. Massialot, The Court and Country Cook

232

INGREDIENTS

How did eighteenth-century food differ from that of the preceding century? Because of the increasing use of sugar, which made food more palatable, many of the old spices, flavourings and colourings, such as ambergris and musk, saffron and sanders (red), went out of fashion, as also did native potherbs like daisies and violets. Raw green sauces and mashed herbs and vinegar were replaced by pickles, ketchups and, later in the century, bottled sauces. Other concoctions were disappearing; spiced wines like hippocras, and the wilder gothic mixtures of Stuart cookery, where there might be twenty or thirty ingredients, elaborately mixed up, such as battalia pie with crenellated turrets filled with exotica.

Food became simplified; for example there were new simple sauces, tasting of one thing only: parsley or mustard or anchovy. But the universal sauce for vegetables was melted butter sauce (see p.41) usually served in over-generous amounts. Thomas Turner, dining at his uncle's on 17 October 1756, had roasted pig and very good turnips, 'but spoiled by almost swimming in butter and also a butter pond pudding and that justly called, for there was almost but enough in it to have drowned the pig, had it been alive.' Butter, in spite of its expense, was used lavishly in almost every dish.

One of the biggest changes was brought about by the advances and discoveries in agriculture. At the beginning of the century, cattle had to be killed at the start of winter because there was no fodder, and so salt meat was eaten until the following spring or summer. Now winter feeding practices were copied from Dutch farmers, and cattle could be kept through the winter. Enclosure of land and improved breeding with superior strains from Holland meant that the quality of meat improved dramatically, though this did not happen on a wide scale until the end of the century. Farm animals began to replace wild in the nation's diet, especially as game became more and more the prerogative of the landowner, through enclosures and severe game laws.

Foreign visitors were amazed at English meat-eating, What M Misson said in the 1690s held true (except for the poorer people) for the whole of the eighteenth century:

> I always heard that they [the English] were great flesh-eaters, and I found it true. I have known people in England that never eat any bread, and universally they eat very little; they nibble a few crumbs, while they chew meat by whole mouthfuls... Among the middling sort of people they had ten or twelve sorts of common meats which infallibly takes their turns at their tables, and two dishes are their dinners: a pudding, for instance, and a piece of roast beef.

Habits in fish-eating changed. Improved transport by the end of the century meant that sea fish could be carried to the towns in barrels of sea water comparatively quickly, and so many fresh-water fish, with their muddier taste, went out of favour, only the better species such as carp, pike, and eel, remaining popular. Fish ponds gradually became redundant and were turned into ornamental ponds. Oysters were plentiful and were eaten in large numbers.

Pudding was an English phenomenon. It took the place of cereal pottage as a starchy filler, and by the 1740s roast beef and plum pudding had become a national dish. At one time puddings were boiled only in the clean guts of newly slaughtered animals, but the increased use of the pudding cloth meant that pudding could be made at any time and the varieties proliferated so that foreign visitors were astonished. M Misson wrote: 'They bake them in the oven, they boil them with the meat, they make them fifty several ways: BLESSED BE HE THAT INVENTED PUDDING, for it is a manna that hits the palates of all sorts of people... [and they] are never weary of it.' The wonderfully versatile suet pudding could be filled with beefsteak, giblets, pigeon, duck, raw fruit, currants and great ponds of butter. Boiled and baked puddings could be of rice, oatmeal, vermicelli, sago, custard. Sweet baked puddings, often cooked in puff pastry crust, were somewhat more elegant, and could be made with such things as curds, fruit, potatoes, carrots, spinach, custard, bread and butter, dried fruit and almonds.

Thomas Turner has as many as three puddings at once. On 15 November 1759 his dinner is 'a fine piece of beef roasted, a currant pond pudding, a currant suet pudding, and a butter pudding cake' (all boiled).

The other filler, bread, as noticed by Misson, was eaten sparingly by the well-off, but it was eaten increasingly by the poor. In the Midlands and south white bread became available for the first time to the poor, who then scorned rougher bread when bad harvests struck in the later eighteenth century. Cake was eaten at breakfast and afternoon tea. The traditional raising agent was wet ale yeast, then eggs were added, but eggs alone were soon found to be effective in raising a cake.

The most common vegetables were cabbage, turnips and carrots, along with parsnips and onions. Potatoes were not eaten every day, except in Ireland and parts of the north-west. Green vegetables, which had once been eaten in cereal pottages, were now simply plain boiled with melted butter sauce. Garden peas, French beans, asparagus and artichokes, cauliflower and celery were enjoyed by the well-off as were green salad things in summer: lettuce, cress, cucumber, spring onions. Tomatoes began to appear in recipes in the late eighteenth century, but were not eaten raw until the end of the nineteenth.

Improved seed from Holland meant better varieties of vegetables and fruit. Hothouses permitted the growing of grapes and peaches and even pineapples for the privileged. Raw fruit was at last acknowledged by medical opinion to be safe; at one time it was thought to cause colic and spread plague, now it was eaten as a healthy food. Garden rhubarb, introduced from Italy in the seventeenth century, was put into English tarts in the late eighteenth. Raw fruit was made into wine, with the help of cheaper sugar. Fruit was bottled and made into jam, which was cheaper than butter as a spread for bread. Favourite fruits were damsons and gooseberries, and the favourite garnish was lemons.

Chocolate mill

Coffee, chocolate and tea had been introduced in the late seventeenth century. Chocolate was at first mixed with wine, then water. It came in a cake or roll, and had to be grated into hot liquid, then swizzled with a notched stick called a chocolate mill (it was not made into chocolate bars until the end of the century). All three beverages were drunk sweetened, as people were used to sugaring their wine. Coffee was drunk mainly by the well-to-do; it was expensive and could not be faked. Tea, from China, was so very expensive it was kept in a locked caddy. Consequently it was drunk very weak, sweetened and at first without milk. However, both tea and coffee were recognized as stimulant drugs, and it was thought the addition of milk would lessen the deleterious effects. Because of the high customs duties on tea, smuggling was carried out on a large scale. Parson Woodforde records in his diary, 29 March 1777, 'Andrews the Smuggler brought me this night about 11 o'clock a bag of Hyson tea 6 pound weight. He frightened us a little by whistling under the parlour window just as we were going to bed. I gave him some Geneva and paid him for the tea 10s. 6d. per pound.'

Coffee, chocolate and tea necessitated new special cups and pots, kettles and urns, which stimulated the pottery and metalware industries. Making and taking tea became an elegant ceremony at which the mistress of the house could show off her pretty china. In 1717 Thomas Twining opened the first Tea Shop for Ladies (in imitation of coffee shops for men) and in the 1720s the first tea garden was opened in the old Vauxhall Gardens, and this soon became a fashion which spread.

Taking tea 1720. Notice the delicate china tea dishes without handles, sugar bowl with cover, plate for finger biscuits, caddy, hot water jug, sugar tongs, spoons on a spoon tray, slop bowl, and tea pot on a stand over a spirit lamp

Because of improved transport, regional specialities, such as Scotch salmon, Newcastle salted haddock, Cheddar, Gloucester, Cheshire and Stilton cheeses, came to be widely known. Foreign food included sea turtles from the West Indies (those who could not afford it made mock turtle dishes); sago from Malaya; vermicelli, macaroni and Parmesan from Italy; piccalilli, punch, curry, rice pilau and pickled mangoes from India and ketchups from the Far East (China and Malaya). Ketchups were imitated, and bottled sauces were produced commercially at the end of the century, the first being Lazenby's anchovy essence and Harvey's sauce. Ready-mixed curry powder was on sale from the 1780s.

Butcher's meat was cheap, but butter was double the price of meat (which would make it £3 a pound today). The prices recorded by the Rev. J. Ismay in 1755 in Mirfield, West Yorkshire, are typical: beef, mutton and veal were 2½d to 3d a lb, butter 5d to 6d, cheese 3d to 4d a lb, a roasting pig was 2/-, a Christmas goose or turkey 2/6, a hen 7d and ducks 8d. In 1756 Thomas Turner in Sussex was paying ½d more for these things, saying they were dear. Cheshire cheese was as much as 5½d a lb. In 1759 Turner pays 9/3 for a pound of green tea, in 1777 Parson Woodforde pays 10/6, though tea could fetch as much as 3 guineas a lb. A bottle of ordinary wine was 2/-. Truffles for the privileged cost in the 1730s £1 to 30/- a lb. It was the price of wheat which fluctuated most and had most effect on the poor.

If one compares the prices with wages it may be seen that working men could not afford to eat well; weavers earned only 5d a day, tailors only 6d plus food, farm labourers 7d, day labourers 1/-, carpenters and masons 1/3. Shopkeepers, tradesmen and master-craftsmen might get £1 a week and could afford to eat meat every day. Wages in London were higher but then so were prices.

A coffee mill, grinder and nutmeg grater of the late eighteenth century

237

In 1786 John Trusler in *The London Adviser and Guide* reports that fowl and game were extremely expensive; ducks were 3/-each, chickens 3/10, geese 5/-, hare 4/6, pheasants 5/- and a brace of partridge 3/6. Mackerel which you could buy in Billingsgate for 4d or 5d a pound was 1/3 in town and even 2/6 when sold to houses in fashionable squares.

Certain members of the aristocracy still found it important to display their wealth and power on a massive scale, one instance being the Earl of Warwick's outdoor banquet for 6,000 in 1746, described by Horace Walpole. The court was not so ostentatious. In view of the patriotism attached to the roast beef of old England it is perhaps not surprising to discover that the king and his court at St James's Palace, when not entertaining, ate rather plain food. Stephen Mennell has discovered that the daily royal menus as set down in the papers of Lord Stewart of the Royal Household were not so different from the company menus of the country gentlemen, consisting mainly of meats roast and boiled. In 1740 when Paris was getting *'nouvelle cuisine'*, George II and his household were eating good plain English fare (though a few French names for dishes were thrown in for effect).

A gentleman now had for breakfast–instead of ale and cereal pottage–tea, coffee, chocolate (the last going out of fashion as the century advanced), whigs (rich bread rolls) or buttered toast or cake. Sometimes he had broth or water gruel.

Supper was taken by those who had dined at midday. It usually consisted, at least among the tradesman class, of cold meats, cold pies and tarts. A typical company supper in February 1758, enjoyed with his neighbours by Turner, consisted of cold roast beef, cold giblet pasty, cold roast goose, cold neat's tongue, cold apple pasty, bread and cheese. After these suppers, Turner and his wife usually play at cards, winning or losing as much as 5 shillings, and drink into the early hours of the morning. He is frequently drunk, and his over-indulgence typifies the widespread drunkenness which affected all classes in the eighteenth century.

Strong drink was cheap, and widely available. Because of the troubles with France which started in the late seventeenth century, French wines and brandy became scarce and expensive (and widely smuggled) and Portuguese and Spanish wines were drunk instead. However, the government, in the hopes of reducing smuggling, encouraged the production of homemade wines and brandy. This was so successful, and spirits were so cheap, that scenes were common such as that depicted by Hogarth in 'Gin Lane' where the gin shop notice declared 'drunk for a penny, dead drunk for twopence, clean straw for nothing'. In Scotland even the poor drank neat whisky with their meals.

Gambling too was common. It was at the gaming table that the sandwich was invented, when in 1760 John Montague, 4th Earl of Sandwich, called for his meat to be put between two pieces of bread so that he could carry on playing uninterrupted.

In all classes, drunkenness and gambling went together, along with rough or cruel sports, bespeaking a callousness which was reflected in the cruel treatment of creatures intended for food. Living fish were slashed to make the flesh contract. This was called 'crimping'. Eels were skinned alive, lobsters roasted alive, crammed poultry were sewn up in the guts, turkeys were suspended by the feet and bled to death from the mouth, bulls were

Dogspit in use

239

baited before slaughter to make the meat more tender, pigs and calves were lashed for the same reason. One of William Kitchiner's recipes begins 'Take a red cock that is not too old and beat him to death.' Towards the end of the century the new sensibility and humanitarian principles caused a growing revulsion against these cruel practices.

A century of unbridled appetite took its toll on health. Such massive amounts of protein, animal fat and alchohol, in the absence of fibrous vegetables or coarse bread, coupled with a sedentary existence (and smoking) caused problems. The high proportion of salt meat eaten in Scotland helped cause heart disease there. The degenerative diseases gout, diabetes, apoplexy (heart attack) and cirrhosis of the liver were common. Health hydros and spas became fashionable. At Bath, many people took the waters during the day, only to debauch themselves in the gay social whirl of dinners, balls and theatres at night.

Parson Woodforde is one of those who indulge themselves. His diet is a heavy one with too much meat, too few vegetables, too many puddings, cakes and pies, so that he suffers from the common complaints of heartburn, colic, bleeding piles and gout. When his gout gets unbearable, he takes water gruel for supper.

The labouring classes in the Midlands and south fared badly. They lived on bought bread and cheese, enlivened with a few potatoes and washed down with tea, which by the end of the century had become a necessity to them, beer being expensive. Beer had once supplied them with both calories and vitamins. Deficiency diseases such as scurvy and rickets actually increased towards the end of the century, especially in towns. In Wales and the north the diet was much healthier, the staple being barley or oats. Nutritionists have recently discovered the enormous benefits of fibrous foods and of oats in particular in protecting against degenerative diseases.

There were also certain hazards in eighteenth-century kitchens. Apart from the ever-present danger from fire, scalding and fumes, there were dangers in the very utensils. Brass and copper pans if used with acid food could create verdigris which

240

was poisonous. 'A whole family died', writes Hannah Glasse, 'owing to verdigrease.' Even so, some fruits and pickles were deliberately cooked in these vessels in order to achieve a bright green colour. Alum and boiling vinegar were used to make apples green–too much could upset the stomach. Peach-laurel leaves were used to impart a bitter almond flavour–safe only if the food was brought to a boil. Used tea leaves were sold by servants to dealers who recoloured them, often with poisonous materials, and then resold them. Bad meat and stale fish, rancid butter and spoiled fruit and vegetables were traps that lay in wait for the unwary shopper, and many cookery books have an important section on how to choose the best market stuff. (They also have recipes on how to rescue bad meat with vinegar and spices–a rather dangerous practice–for example, Hannah Glasse's recipe on how 'to save potted birds, that begin to be bad'.)

Fresh food was kept in cellars or larders, but it could not be kept long–less than a week. A great deal of preserving took place. Jams and pickles, fruit and vegetables were put up in glass or earthenware jars sealed with paper or leather, though there was always the possibility of botulism since the jars were not then boiled. Meat, fish and shellfish were potted or baked in a crust and kept several weeks airtight under a sealing layer of clarified fat. Hams and bacon were cured, beef and mutton were salted. Meats, fish, sausages and puddings were smoked, hung in the chimney over a wood or peat fire (coal smoke was not suitable). The Scots had fresh meat for only five months of the year, August to December, living off salt beef and mutton the rest of the time.

The idea of ice as a preserving agent had been introduced from the Continent in the late seventeenth century. Fashionable people built ice-houses in their grounds, where ice lasted most of the year. Ice-creams were a speciality of those with ice-houses.

Modern readers of eighteenth-century recipes may well be mystified by some of the weights and measures. It soon becomes clear when making these recipes that a 'spoonful': is roughly equivalent to a modern standard tablespoon, and that 'a teaspoon' is bigger than a modern teaspoon, that is, one used for measuring tea, not for stirring. 'A glass' is roughly 4 fluid ounces. 'A pint' is a wine pint, that is 16 fluid ounces, and not 20 fluid ounces as today (the pint changed to Imperial in the nineteenth century; America has kept the old measure). The pound avoirdupois in most districts was the same as today, but a stone, when referring to meat, was 8lb. A peck of flour was 2 gallons, or 14lb, and a peck loaf was 17lb 6oz (!); the half peck loaf 8lb 11oz and the most usual size, the quartern loaf, was 4lb 5oz (the modern 'large loaf' is 1¾lb). A penny white loaf, according to Elizabeth David, was 6oz in the early eighteenth century, though this varied with the price of wheat – it could be as little as 3-4oz. The penny brown loaf was about three times heavier. It is evident from shorter cooking times that fowl were generally smaller, and eggs were equivalent to our smallest modern eggs (size 4).

I have tried to choose only those eighteenth-century recipes capable of being made today without changes or substitutions of ingredients. Some of them do taste unfamiliar, but no less enjoyable for that. The overwhelming impression on the taste buds is one of butter, wine and nutmeg – nutmeg seemed to be the national flavouring as cinnamon was in other countries. Many of the recipes were for very large amounts, which I have reduced.

I hope this glimpse into the tastes of our eighteenth-century ancestors will whet readers' appetites to experiment further.

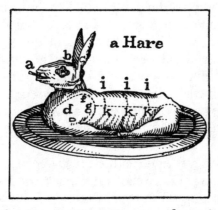

Carving diagram for a hare. Rabbits and hares were frequently served with the heads on, which some considered a delicacy

RECIPES
Dishes made by all classes

PLAIN PUDDING

Puddings boiled or baked, sweet, plain or savoury, formed a major part of eighteenth-century fare. Plain pudding is simply pancake batter boiled in a cloth (plain and suet puddings are actually lighter when boiled in a cloth, because they can expand in all directions). The same batter baked in a tin under roasting meat becomes Yorkshire pudding. On 13 February 1757 Thomas Turner dines on hog's cheek and vegetables with a 'plain batter pudding', all boiled. Parson Woodforde regaled his parishioners on Tithe Audit-day 1799 with boiled and roast meat and plenty of plum and plain puddings. Mrs Raffald's pudding is simple to make, and very good.

2 oz (50 g) plain flour
¼ tsp (1.5 ml) salt
3 eggs
8 fl oz (225 ml) milk or single cream

For this size of pudding make an 18 inch (45.5 cm) square pudding cloth of white cotton or doubled muslin. Boil a large pan of water and put an old plate in the bottom. Drop the pudding cloth in briefly, lift it out with a wooden spoon and let it drape over the spoon handle placed across a pan to drip. Have ready a piece of string. Sift the flour and salt into a bowl. In another bowl beat the eggs well. Add the flour, salt and milk and beat to make a thin batter. Squeeze out the pudding cloth, lay it on the table, and sprinkle well with flour. Gently shake off the excess. To support the cloth while filling it, lay it in a basin with the floured side up, pour in the batter, gather up the corners and all the edges (leaving room for the pudding to expand), tie securely with string and place in a pan of boiling water, which must cover the pudding at all times. Cover the pan, leaving a small gap, and boil for 30 minutes. Lift the pudding out and dip briefly into cold water to loosen the cloth. Place in a colander, untie the string and peel back the cloth. Place a heated dish over the pudding, reverse the colander, and gently peel away the rest of the cloth. Serve at once with meat, or as a dessert with hot wine sauce (p. 45).

Elizabeth Raffald: The experienced English housekeeper

243

BARLEY GRUEL

Barley gruel, or 'plumb porridge', was a common dish and tastes very good. It is similar to frumenty but less rich. (Frumenty or furmity was usually made with hulled wheat, enriched with milk, cream and egg yolks, and in many areas remained to this century a special Christmas dish.)

2 pt (1.1 L) water
2 oz (50 g) pearl barley
1 oz (25 g) raisins
1 oz (25 g) currants
½ tsp (2.5 ml) ground mace
2 tbls (30 ml) sugar
2 fl oz (50 ml) white wine

Put the water in a saucepan with the barley, raisins, currants and mace, and boil until the water is reduced by half and the barley is tender. Stir in the sugar and white wine, and serve.

Hannah Glasse: The art of cookery made plain and easy

● This dish can be made in advance and reheated when required.

WATER GRUEL

To make water gruel: 'Take a Pint of Water, and a large Spoonful of Oatmeal, stir it together, let it boil up three or four times, stirring it often. Don't let it boil over, then strain it through a sieve, salt it to your Palate, put in a good Piece of fresh Butter, brue [stir] it with a Spoon till the Butter is all melted, and it will be fine and smooth, and very good. Some love a little Pepper in it.'

This light but sustaining dish was eaten by all classes. The well-off ate it with wine sauce and buttered toast, added plumped currants and raisins, sugar, mace and sack (sherry) or took it plain for breakfast or as an invalid food. Although water gruel was eaten hot, when allowed to go cold it sets into an oatmeal flummery, which is equally good eaten with sugar and light cream.

16 fl oz (450 ml) water
1 heaped tbls (20 ml) oatmeal
½ oz (15 g) butter
a pinch of salt

Put the water and oatmeal in a saucepan and bring to the boil, stirring. Boil for 2 minutes, stirring occasionally. Strain through a sieve into an individual bowl or mug, add butter and salt, and eat with a spoon.

Hannah Glasse: The art of cookery made plain and easy

OATMEAL
HASTY PUDDING

*To make an oatmeal hasty pudding:
'Take a Quart of Water, set it on to
boil, put in a Piece of Butter, some
Salt, when it boils, stir in the
Oatmeal… till it is of good Thickness;
let it boil a few Minutes, pour it in your
Dish, and stick Pieces of Butter in it; or
eat with Wine and sugar, or Ale and
Sugar, or Cream, or new Milk. This is
best made with Scotch Oatmeal.'*

*Oatmeal hasty pudding was an instant,
comforting hot meal. Served with wine
sauce it was a middle-class dish, but to
the majority of the labouring classes in
the Welsh and northern hilly districts it
was a staple food, often being eaten for
breakfast, dinner and supper with milk,
beer or treacle. When supplemented
with vegetables and a little meat, this
made a healthy diet.*

*1 pint (575 ml) water
¼ tsp (1.5 ml) salt
1½ oz (40 g) butter
8 oz (225 g) oatmeal*

Put the water in a saucepan and
bring to the boil with the salt and
½ oz (15 g) butter. Then, stirring
briskly all the time, slowly add
the oatmeal. Cook, stirring, 3 or 4
minutes longer. Serve hot, with
the remaining butter or with wine
sauce (p. 45), cream or milk.

*Hannah Glasse: The art of cookery
made plain and easy*

BUTTERED WHEAT
OR BARLEY

Dishes of this convenient food were still being sold on the streets of London in the mid-eighteenth century. The hulled wheat or barley was preboiled to a jelly, then reheated on the spot with butter, sugar and spice, usually nutmeg. The buttering of cereals had been common since Tudor times.

2 oz (50 g) pearl barley
2 pt (1.1 L) water
2 oz (50 g) butter
1 tbls (15 ml) sugar
a pinch of nutmeg

Simmer the barley and water together in a saucepan until the barley is very tender. Drain. Reheat the drained barley with the butter, sugar and nutmeg, then serve.

Hannah Glasse: The art of cookery made plain and easy

WHEY

Curds and whey was still eaten in the early eighteenth century. It was junket, made from milk with rennet, and eaten in a dish with sugar, cream and flavourings such as nutmeg and rosewater. But during the century this gradually lost favour as unrenneted fresh cream confections became more and more fashionable. Curds and whey (junket) is easily made today using rennet essence, following the instructions on the bottle. It is especially good made with rich Jersey milk.
Whey as a drink (sometimes called whig) was a popular everyday drink in many dairying districts, and it was also sold in the streets of large towns. Many people made whey at home by curdling blue (skimmed) milk with cream of tartar or other acids, such as old verjuice (a condiment made from sour apples) or juice of scurvy grass.

¼ pint (150 ml) skimmed milk
1 tbls (15 ml) fresh lemon juice or
*   2 tbls (30 ml) fresh orange juice*

Reconstituted dried skimmed milk can be used for this recipe. Heat the milk until tepid (70°F/ 21°C), then add the lemon or orange juice. Leave in a warm place for at least 10 minutes to curdle. Strain through a fine sieve or muslin, or 'pour the Whey clear off, and sweeten to your Palate.'

Hannah Glasse: The art of cookery made plain and easy

● Whey makes a refreshing drink, especially when chilled. You may eat the *curds,* mixed with sugar, cream and nutmeg, with fresh soft fruit. Or use the curds for a tart filling (see p. 43).

PLUM POTTAGE

The old traditional rich plum pottage, which had been made especially at feasts and festivals, came to be associated in the later seventeenth century principally with Christmas. This continued to be made well into the eighteenth century (and as late as the nineteenth in Scotland). Hannah Glasse calls it 'plum-porridge' which indicates its thick consistency. By now, the actual meat was not used in the dish, only the broth, and the mixture was beginning to resemble a rather sloppy plum pudding. The modern very rich Christmas pudding developed from this liquor-laced porridge only in the nineteenth century. The 'plum puddings' eaten on Christmas Day in the eighteenth century (for example by Thomas Turner and Parson Woodforde) are just ordinary plum puddings. Hannah Glasse comments that the beef broth may be thickened with sago instead of breadcrumbs. Lady Grisell Baillie used the newly fashionable sago in Scotland on Christmas Day 1715 to thicken her Christmas plum pottage, which was served as part of the first course. (You may do this using 3 oz (75 g) sago to 1½ pints (850 ml) broth and simmering for 15 minutes.)

2–3 lb (1–1.4 kg) shin of beef
2–2½ pt (1.1–1.4 L) water
4 oz (125 g) fresh white breadcrumbs
7 oz (200 g) mixed dried fruit (currants, raisins, dates, cooked prunes)

1 tsp (5 ml) grated nutmeg
¼ tsp (1.5 ml) ground mace
¼ tsp (1.5 ml) ground cloves
½ tsp (2.5 ml) cinnamon
a pinch of salt
3 fl oz (75 ml) sherry
3 fl oz (75 ml) port
juice of 1 Seville orange or lemon, to serve

Simmer the beef in the water, covered, for about 2 hours until tender. Strain it and keep the meat for another dish. Add the breadcrumbs to 1½ pints (850 ml) of the broth and soak for 1 hour. Then stir in the fruit, spices and salt and bring to the boil. Add the sherry and port and simmer, uncovered, until the fruit is plump (about 15 minutes). Serve hot in individual bowls, with the juice of the Seville orange or lemon.

John Nott: The cook's and confectioner's dictionary

Dishes made by the tradesman class and above

GREEN PEA SOUP

Peas pottage, or peas pudding, made with field peas, had once been a national dish. At the turn of the eighteenth century the gentry and middle classes began to scorn thick pottages as labourers' food, preferring the new elegant French dish called soup. Soup was a 'remove' dish – always set at the head of the table and eaten first, then removed to make way for fish.

This typical recipe was a way of using over-mature garden peas. If you have none, use split peas.

1 pt (575 ml) old garden peas or
    8 oz (225 g) split peas
1½ pt (850 ml) water
a little celery, chopped
a little onion, chopped
a pinch of ground mace
a pinch of ground cloves
a pinch of black pepper
2½ pt (1.4 L) good meat or
    vegetable stock
12 oz (350 g) fresh or frozen young peas
6 slices French bread and clarified
    butter (p. 45), to serve

If using split peas, soak them in 1½ pints (850 ml) water overnight. Then simmer the split peas or old garden peas in the water with the celery and onion, mace, cloves and black pepper, covered, until tender. Mash, sieve or blend, then add this pulp to the stock. Just before serving, heat the soup, add the fresh young peas and simmer until tender. If using frozen peas, simmer no longer than 3 minutes. Serve with slices of French bread fried in clarified butter floating in each bowl, or as Mrs Glasse puts it: 'Let a fried French roll swim in it.'

Hannah Glasse: The art of cookery made plain and easy

● If time is short, a 15.2 oz (430 g) can of pease pudding may be used instead of the cooked old or split peas.

POTTED VENISON

Potted meats and fish were popular during the seventeenth and eighteenth centuries as side dishes for a second course. Potting is a good way to preserve these foods for several weeks. Game and particularly venison was highly prized, because, through enclosures and harsh game laws, it had become scarce. Game could be bought in

London markets, but much of it was probably poached. The venison in shops today has not usually been hung till 'gamey'. Many large country houses had outdoor game larders, where game could be hung for as long as several weeks before being eaten.

1¾–2 lb (800–900 g) piece of rolled venison shoulder with fat
3 oz (75 g) butter
3 tbls (45 ml) flour
½ tsp (2.5 ml) salt
½ tsp (2.5 ml) black pepper
1 tsp (5 ml) ground mace
½ tsp (2.5 ml) ground cloves
2 tsps (10 ml) grated nutmeg
6 anchovy fillets

Put the meat in an ovenproof lidded pot that is only just big enough to hold it. Cut the butter in pieces and lay on the meat. To seal the lid, make a huff paste by mixing the flour with enough water to make a dough that can be moulded round the lid edge. Bake at gas mark 1, 275°F (140°C) for 3–4 hours, or until a sharp fork goes in easily. Leave until cool.

Lift the meat clear of the juices into a large bowl, and tear the meat to fine shreds with the fingers, discarding any gristle, bone and fat. Then mash the meat finely in a pestle and mortar (or use a blender) until light and dry. Add seasoning and spices. Mash the anchovies finely in 5–6 tbls (75–90 ml) melted fat from the cooking pot, or use freshly melted clarified butter (p. 45), and incorporate with the meat. (Do not include any meat juices as the meat would not then keep.) Press the meat well down in a clean dry pot, to exclude all the air. Pour more melted fat on top to completely seal. Serve in slices, with pickles.

Hannah Glasse: The art of cookery made plain and easy

PRUNE SAUCE FOR LAND FOWL

---

1 lb (450 g) prunes
21 fl oz (600 ml) water
½ tsp (2.5 ml) ground ginger
½ tsp (2.5 ml) cinnamon
2 oz (50 g) sugar

Simmer the prunes in the water for about 1 hour until tender. Cool, then remove the stones. Boil the prunes and the juice, about ¼ pint (150 ml), with the ginger, cinnamon and sugar for about 2–3 minutes, until thick, stirring constantly. Serve with chicken, turkey, duck or goose. Nott's recipe includes a little blood of the fowl.

John Nott: The cook's and confectioner's dictionary

● This rich sauce may also be used as a black tartstuff (see p. 42).

STEWED VENISON

To stew venison in claret: 'Cut your Venison into Slices, put it into a Stew-pan, with a little Claret, a Sprig or two of Rosemary, half a dozen cloves, a little Vinegar, Sugar and grated Bread; when these have stew'd some time, grate in some Nutmeg, and serve it up.'

John Nott would have cooked his stew in a stew-pan or 'casserole' (a French utensil) on a brick-built stewing stove. Those without stoves would use a chafing-dish of charcoal on the hearth, or would cook their stew in a covered jar inside a cauldron of boiling water.

2 lb (900 g) stewing venison or beef
6 whole cloves
1 tsp (5 ml) rosemary
1 tsp (5 ml) salt
1 tsp (5 ml) black pepper
4 tsps (20 ml) wine vinegar
16 fl oz (450 ml) red wine
2 tsps (10 ml) sugar
½ pt (275 ml) good stock
2 oz (50 g) fresh white breadcrumbs
a little grated nutmeg
orange slices, to garnish

Cut the meat into 1½ inch (4 cm) pieces. Then stew all the ingredients, except the nutmeg, together, covered, *very* gently for 2 hours. About 15 minutes before serving, stir in a grating of nutmeg. Garnish with sliced oranges.

John Nott: The cook's and confectioner's dictionary

JUGGED PIGEONS

Pigeons were plentiful, many large houses having their own dovecots, and were valuable fresh meat in winter. The process of jugging goes back to medieval times when several pots and puddings would be economically cooked together in a large cauldron of boiling water. Cooked in a tall closed pot, without gravy, jugged meat does not 'stew', but cooks moist and even. There would be just enough liquid when cooked to moisten the meat.

6 pigeons
1 head of celery, sliced
lemon slices, to garnish

For the stuffing:
8 oz (225 g) fresh white breadcrumbs
8 oz (225 g) suet, chopped
½ tsp (2.5 ml) salt
½ tsp (2.5 ml) pepper
½ tsp (2.5 ml) grated nutmeg
zest of 1 lemon
4 tbls (60 ml) chopped parsley
2 hard-boiled egg yolks, mashed
2 oz (50 g) butter, grated
1 egg, beaten

For the beurre manié:
1 oz (25 g) butter
1 oz (25 g) flour

Wash the pigeons and dry on absorbent paper. If you feel any lead shot in the skin, remove it. Mix the stuffing ingredients together, binding with the beaten egg. Divide into six and stuff each pigeon, sewing up the vents with needle and thread. Place in a very large jug with pieces of celery on top. Make the top of the jug airtight, using huff paste if necessary (see potted venison, p. 34). Place the jug in a deep pan or metal pail, fill with boiling water to a point above the pigeons, and boil for 3 hours. To thicken the juices, make a beurre manié. Knead the butter and flour together with the fingers. Lay the birds on a heated dish. Pour the juices into a small pan and boil, adding little pieces of beurre manié. Pour the gravy over the birds, and garnish with slices of lemon.

Hannah Glasse: The art of cookery made plain and easy

OYSTER LOAVES

Oysters were a favourite food in the eighteenth century, and were often served as a garnish or sauce with meat. (A common way of cooking them was to dip them in batter and deep-fry in lard.) Oyster loaves make a pretty side dish for a first course.

4 underdone French rolls, each
  weighing about 2 oz (50 g)
4 oz (100 g) butter, melted
12 small fresh oysters
2 tbls (30 ml) white wine
a pinch of grated nutmeg
a pinch of ground mace

Preheat the oven to gas mark 7, 425°F (220°C). Cut the tops off the rolls and scoop out most of the middles. Brush the undersides of the lids and the hollows of the rolls with melted butter. Toast in the oven until lightly golden. Sauté the oysters in the remaining hot butter for 2–3 minutes or until the edges curl. Add the wine and spices to the pan. Put 3 oysters and a little sauce in each hot roll, replace the lids, and serve at once.

Hannah Glasse: The art of cookery made plain and easy

ANCHOVIES WITH PARMESAN CHEESE

'To make a nice whet before dinner, or a side dish for a second course. Fry some bits of bread about the length of an anchovy in good oil or butter, lay the half of an anchovy, with the bone upon each bit, and strew over them some Parmesan cheese grated fine, and colour them nicely in an oven, or with a salamander, squeeze the juice of an orange or lemon, and pile them up in your dish and send to table. This seems to be but a trifling thing but I never saw it come whole from the table.'

Brown your anchovies in the oven, or under the grill. 'The half of an anchovy' means half a fish, or two modern tinned 'fillets'.

William Verral: The cook's paradise

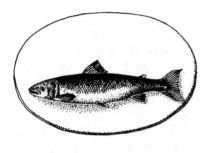

How to do fish in pastry

WHOLE FISH
IN PASTRY

'*Scale the Salmon, wash and dry him,
chine him, and season him with Salt,
Pepper, Ginger, Cloves, and Mace; lay
him on a Sheet of Paste, and form it in
the Shape of a Salmon, lay in Slices of
Ginger, large Mace, and Butter upon
the Fish, and turn up the other half of
your Sheet of Paste on the Back, closing
them on the Belly-side, from Head to
Tail, bringing him into Proportion with
Head, Fins, Gills, and Tail: Scale him,
leave a Funnel to pour in Butter, and
when it is bak'd, set it by to cool.*'

*1 whole fish, gutted and boned, but
    with head and tail left on, weighing
    about 1 lb (450 g)*
salt
pepper
¼ tsp (1.5 ml) ground mace
*½ tsp (2.5 ml) ground ginger or grated
    fresh ginger root*
1½ oz (40 g) butter, cut into slivers
1 lb (450 g) shortcrust or puff pastry
1 raisin
1 egg white
1 tbls (15 ml) top of the milk

Wash the fish and dry with
absorbent paper. Season it inside
with the salt, pepper, mace and
ginger, and insert the slivers of
butter.
Roll out the pastry into a long
oval, 2 inches (5 cm) longer at
each end than the fish, making
sure it is wide enough to fold over

the fish, with a spare 1–2 inches (2.5–5 cm) to seal it. Transfer the fish carefully on to the pastry and place on the bottom half of the oval, its belly towards you. Fold the pastry over, and trim off the excess. Seal with water and crimp the edge. Adjust the shape of the tail and head if necessary. Transfer the fish to a foil-covered baking sheet. To make scales: bring the pastry trimmings to the edge of the work surface, and cut out oval scales by pressing on the back of a teaspoon. Beginning at the tail end, stick them on with water in an overlapping design. Make a gill and fins, and stick in a raisin for an eye. Beat the egg white and milk together, then drizzle it over the pastry from a brush (brushing would flatten the scales too much).

Bake in the top part of the oven at gas mark 6, 400°F (200°C) for 10 minutes until beginning to colour, then move it to the middle for 10 minutes, after which reduce the heat to gas mark 4, 350°F (180°C) and bake for a further 20 minutes. (If the fish was short and thick, give it 10 minutes longer.) Serve hot or cold with pickled or sliced lemons. It may be decorated with sprigs of flowers.

John Nott: The cook's and confectioner's dictionary

FRIED CELERY

Most vegetables were plain boiled and served with melted butter. The original of this recipe calls for several whole heads of celery, which were probably smaller than today.

5 oz (150 g) plain flour
½ tsp (2.5 ml) salt
¼ tsp (1.5 ml) grated nutmeg
2 egg yolks
4 fl oz (125 ml) white wine
1 head of celery, weighing about
*   12 oz (350 g)*
clarified butter (p. 45).

First make the batter: mix the flour, salt and nutmeg in a bowl, make a well in the centre and drop in the egg yolks with 1 tbls (15 ml) of the wine. Mix, stirring in the flour, then gradually add the remaining wine. Leave to stand. Cut the celery into 5 inch (12.5 cm) lengths and simmer in boiling water until *almost* tender. Drain well and pat dry. Dip each piece in the batter to completely coat, then fry in hot clarified butter (or deep-fry in lard) for about 2 minutes on each side until golden.

Mrs Glasse adds 'pour melted Butter over them'!

Hannah Glasse: The art of cookery made plain and easy

POTATO PUDDING

Vegetables such as potatoes, carrots, spinach and artichokes were often used in place of a cereal thickener in sweet dishes, pies and puddings. Puddings could be boiled in a cloth, or baked. If baked, most often the dish was lined with puff pastry first. This recipe makes a rich yet delicate pudding-pie, which is rather like a curd tart.

12 oz (350 g) puff pastry
1 lb (450 g) potatoes, cooked and
    mashed
4 oz (125 g) unsalted butter, softened
4 oz (125 g) caster sugar
2 eggs, beaten
2 egg yolks, beaten
4 tbls (60 ml) sherry or brandy
1 rounded tsp (7 ml) grated nutmeg
4 fl oz (125 ml) double cream
4 oz (125 g) currants

Roll out the pastry and use to line a 9½ inch (24 cm) diameter, 2 inch (5 cm) deep pie dish with a rim. Use the pastry trimmings to make a decorative border. Beat the remaining ingredients to a smooth batter and pour in. Place the dish above the middle of the oven and bake at gas mark 4, 350°F (180°C) for about 1 hour, or until risen and golden. Serve with hot wine sauce (see p. 45). This is good hot or cold.

Hannah Glasse: The art of cookery made plain and easy

● Mrs Glasse advises that a stiffer mixture may be made with only 2 oz (50 g) butter, 3 egg yolks, 2 tbls (30 ml) liquor, formed into small cakes and fried in clarified butter. These pancakes should be served as a side dish with the wine sauce poured over.

BEETROOT PANCAKES

'A pretty corner dish for dinner or supper'

6 oz (175 g) peeled cooked beetroot
2 tbls (30 ml) brandy
3 tbls (45 ml) double cream
4 egg yolks
2 tbls (30 ml) plain flour
2 tsps (10 ml) caster sugar
1 tsp (5 ml) grated nutmeg
clarified butter (p. 45)

Mash the beetroot as finely as possible and mix with the other ingredients (or put all into a blender). Heat a shallow layer of clarified butter in a frying pan. Drop the beetroot mixture from the point of a tablespoon into the butter and shake the pan to flatten if necessary. Turn down the heat, as these burn very easily. Turn the pancakes over – they will cook quickly. Wipe out the pan if necessary between batches. These unusual delicate pancakes are good hot or cold. 'Garnish with green sweetmeats, preserved apricots, or green sprigs of myrtle.'

Elizabeth Raffald: The experienced English housekeeper

Hannah Glasse's
Salamangundy
1747

MELTED BUTTER SAUCE

This was the most usual sauce for vegetables.

2 tsps (10 ml) plain flour
¼ pt (150 ml) water
a pinch of salt
2–3 oz (50–75g) butter

In a small pan mix the flour, water and salt. Stir over gentle heat, *without allowing it to boil.* When hot, add the butter, cut into bits. Stir well until smooth. This sauce will not reheat, and if allowed to boil will taste raw. Sometimes a drop or two of lemon juice was added.

SALAMANGUNDY

This magnificent salad is an opportunity for the cook to show her expertise in choosing a good balance of bland soft meats, sharp pickles, crisp vegetables and colourful leaves and flowers. Traditionally the ingredients were chopped small, and layered and heaped into a sugar-loaf shape, which mixed them all up together. This 1747 recipe reflects the new 'clean' taste in food: Mrs Glasse keeps each ingredient separate and recognizable in its own saucer, arranged on a large tray or platter, around a raised central dish. The spaces between the saucers are filled with watercress and nasturtium flowers. The central raised dish is of chopped pickled herring. For the others you may choose a good balanced selection from the following:

cucumber, sliced very thin
apples, chopped small
onions, chopped small
celery, chopped small
crisp lettuce, finely shredded
peeled grapes
cooked French beans

pickled herring, chopped small
pickled gherkins, chopped small
pickled red cabbage
capers
lemons, sliced or chopped
anchovies

hard-boiled egg yolks
hard-boiled egg whites
cooked fowl, cut in fine strips or chopped

Hannah Glasse: The art of cookery made plain and easy

HERALDIC DEVICES
MADE OF TARTS

A courtly seventeenth-century dish of the kind which continued in the eighteenth century on grand occasions. In 1702 the great French chef Massialot published in English his influential The Court and Country Cook. *Of 'Marmelades' (very thick jams) he writes: 'These Marmelades are of great Use . . for the making of Pan-pies, or Tarts; or else, by the Mixture and Distribution of their Colours, the Coats of Arms of Several Families may be represented; as also; Flower-de-luces, Crosses and many other Devices.'*

You may make a large coat of arms all on one tin, or an assemblage of smaller shapes. Make sure the tin you want to bake and serve it on will go in your oven without touching the sides (don't use pewter – it will melt). For a huge heraldic tart in one piece, a local baker may lend you a tin and bake it for you. Or at home, you may bake each quartered field separately and assemble later. One pound (450 g) of pastry is sufficient for a simple design on a 12 inch (30 cm) square tin.

1 lb (450 g) shortcrust pastry

For the fillings:
jams of different colours, red, purple, green, yellow, orange
black tartstuff (see p. 35)
curds (see p. 32)

Roll out the pastry to make the base of your shield or shape, cut into the desired shape and place on the baking tin. Roll the edges into ramparts ½ inch (1.2 cm) high. Using pastry trimmings, make 'walls' at least ½ inch (1.2 cm) high to divide the various compartments. This is easiest if you make 'Swiss roll' shapes by rolling with the fingers. Stick these into place with water, making sure there are no gaps. Fill the compartments (not too full) with the appropriate coloured filling. Bake stars, crescents, etc. separately, baking them pallid if they are to go on dark jam, and brown if they are

to go on a curd compartment.
Bake at gas mark 8, 450°F
(230°C) for about 20-25 minutes,
inspecting frequently for burning.

Curd filling:
4 oz (100 g) curds, finely sieved
  (see p. 32)
2 egg whites
2 tbls (30 ml) cream
1 tbls (15 ml) sugar

Blend all the ingredients together
and use to fill the pastry before
cooking.

STRAWBERRY FRITTERS

*Plain fritters, made of ale, flour and
eggs, were eaten commonly, but
especially at Easter. These strawberry
fritters are rather special.*

1 lb (450 g) large dry strawberries
6 oz (175 g) plain flour
2 oz (50 g) caster sugar
2 tsps (10 ml) grated nutmeg
2 eggs, well beaten
8 fl oz (225 ml) single cream
lard for deep-frying
sugar, to finish

The strawberries must be dry.
Leave the stalks on for easier
handling. Sift the flour into a
bowl and add the caster sugar and
nutmeg. Make a well and drop in
the eggs and cream. Then stir
until all the flour and sugar are
gradually assimilated. Let the
batter stand an hour or two. Dip
each strawberry in batter until it
is completely coated, and fry a
few at a time in hot lard. Your
lard must be hot enough to puff
them, but not so hot as to brown
them too quickly. Drain on
absorbent paper and keep hot.
Pile them up in a pyramid in a hot
dish and sprinkle sugar over.
Decorate with leaves.

William Verral: The cook's paradise

● Fresh pineapple and apple is
also very good done this way.
Any leftover batter may be
dropped by the teaspoonful in
lard to make delicious fritters.

FAIRY BUTTER

*This delicious, finely extruded
confection would be eaten with wafers –
'a pretty Thing to set off a Table at
Supper'.*

2 hard-boiled egg yolks, mashed
1 tsp (5 ml) orange flower water
1 oz (25 g) caster sugar
3 oz (75 g) unsalted butter, softened

Mix all the ingredients together
with a fork, and 'force it thro' a
fine Strainer full of little Holes
into a Plate'. You may have to
chill it a little first. Keep it chilled
until serving time.

*Hannah Glasse: The art of cookery
made plain and easy*

*A whipt syllabub cup of glass.
The whipped cream rested in the top
bowl over the sweetened wine,
whey or fruit juice below*

WHIPPED SYLLABUB

*To make a fine syllabub from the cow:
'Make your Syllabub of either Cyder or
Wine, sweeten it pretty sweet, and
grate Nutmeg in, then milk the Milk
into the Liquor; when this is done, pour
over the Top half a Pint or Pint of
Cream, according to the Quantity of
Syllabub you make. You may make this
Syllabub at Home, only have new
Milk; make it as hot as Milk from the
Cow, and out of a Tea-pot or any such
Thing, pour it in, holding your Hand
very high.'*

*Traditionally, syllabub was made by
milking a cow into a bowl of ale or
cider, which gave a frothy top to the
liquor, and so it was partly eaten, partly
drunk. Gradually, in the seventeenth
century, milk and ale were replaced by
cream and wine, whipped together,
which produced a creamy froth on a
liquor base. During the eighteenth
century, a new development was to
increase the proportion of cream, so that
no separation took place, and this
'everlasting syllabub' as it was called
(really a modern whipped cream)
existed side by side with the separated
version throughout the eighteenth
century. Thomas Turner of Hoathley
near Lewes writes in his diary for
Sunday 28 May 1758, 'Tho. Durrant,
Tho. Davy and Mr. Elless at our house
in the even a-drinking of syllabub,
Tho. Durrant finding milk, and we
cider etc.' And so it is clear that the
original traditional milk syllabub was
still enjoyed also. Special wooden cows
were sold, from which to pour milk from
a height, in order to make a froth in the
ale or cider.
Whipped syllabub is the separated
version made with cream.*

*6 tbls (90 ml) sherry, wine, cider, lemon
    or orange whey (see p. 32), all sweet
    or sweetened*
juice and finely grated rind of 1 lemon
4 tbls (60 ml) sherry or white wine
2 oz (50 g) caster sugar
½ pt (275 ml) double cream

Put 1 tbls (15 ml) of the liquor or
whey into each of six conical

wine glasses. In a deep bowl, mix the lemon rind, juice, sherry or wine and sugar. Now, whisking all the time, with a hand whisk *only,* slowly add the cream. Keep whisking until soft peaks form. *Do not overbeat.* Just before serving, spoon into the glasses, laying the cream mixture carefully on top of the liquor.

Hannah Glasse: The art of cookery made plain and easy

● John Nott uses for the liquor in his glasses, white wine plus the juice of raspberries, mulberries or black cherries.
● To make everlasting syllabub, use the same whipped cream mixture as above, adding 1 tsp (5 ml) orange flower water. Put into glasses without any liquor at the bottom.

CLARIFIED BUTTER

This is well worth doing. You will find it invaluable in modern cooking too. Once the buttermilk sediment has been removed from butter, it will keep indefinitely.

Melt 1 lb (450 g) of unsalted butter gently in a saucepan and let the first foam subside. Pour it through a coffee filter paper, or simply let it stand, then pour off the clear into a keeping basin. When cold, remove any buttermilk from the bottom.

WINE SAUCE

This was the most usual sauce for puddings.

8 fl oz (225 ml) wine
2 oz (50 g) butter
1¼ oz (30 g) caster sugar

Mix the ingredients together and heat. Serve in a hot sauceboat. Lemon juice can be substituted for the wine.

POTTED CHESHIRE CHEESE

This was a good way of improving a hard cheese, and of preserving one that was about to go 'off'. It actually improves with keeping.

8 oz (225 g) mature Cheshire cheese
2–3 oz (50–75 g) unsalted butter
2 tbls (30 ml) good sweet sherry
1 rounded tsp (7 ml) ground mace
clarified butter (see above)

Grate the cheese finely, and mix with the butter, which should be soft but not melted. Add the sherry and mace, and mix well. Press well down in a pot, and cover with clarified butter.

Hannah Glasse: The art of cookery made plain and easy

● Port may be used in place of sherry. Eat sliced with walnuts and pears at the end of dinner.

A silver tea-kettle with spirit lamp

TEA CAUDLE

'Elegant enough for a supper table.'

*Ale or wine caudles were traditional hot
drinks, still taken at breakfast or supper
until well into the eighteenth century.
Tea caudle seems to be an innovation in
the late seventeenth century when tea
was first introduced from China.
(Indian tea did not arrive until the
1830s.) Green China tea may be
bought from specialist shops.*

*½ pt (275 ml) strong green China tea
3 tsps (15 ml) caster sugar
1 tsp (5 ml) grated nutmeg
1 egg yolk
4 fl oz (125 ml) white wine*

Strain the tea into a small
saucepan. Add the sugar and
nutmeg and heat. Meanwhile in a
small basin beat the egg yolk, add

the wine, and pour these into the
hot tea, stirring continuously over
gentle heat until very hot. Pour
into a warmed caudle pot or
china tea dishes.

*Eliza Smith: The compleat housewife,
1736 edition*

● Posset is a similar hot drink, but
richer, being made with cream or
milk.
● Use the green tea leaves over
again to make weak tea, for drinking with slices of rich seed cake.
Tea was so expensive, the leaves
were often used twice. Servants
would sell them to dealers, who
recoloured them, often with
poisonous materials, and passed
them off as genuine tea.

RICH SEED CAKE

*Caraway seeds were enormously
popular in the later eighteenth century.
This rich cake would be eaten at
breakfast or afternoon tea among the
gentry and middle classes. It was
thought the longer cakes were beaten
the better – Mrs Raffald recommends
beating this cake for 2 hours. Modern
baking powder was not invented until
the mid-nineteenth century, so the
success of a cake like this lies in its very
careful technique. All ingredients and
bowls must be slightly warmer than
room temperature. Assemble all the
ingredients before you begin, prepare
the tin and preheat the oven.*

8 oz (225 g) plain flour
1 tsp (5 ml) grated nutmeg
1 tsp (5 ml) cinnamon
1 oz (25 g) caraway seeds
8 oz (225 g) unsalted butter, softened
8 oz (225 g) caster sugar
4 eggs, separated, tepid

Line and grease an 8 inch (20 cm) diameter; 3 inch (7.5 cm) deep cake tin. Sift the flour and spices into a bowl, and add the caraway seeds. Make sure your mixing bowl is big enough, and slightly warm. Cream the butter and sugar in it very thoroughly, scraping the sides of the bowl. In a warm jug, beat the tepid yolks very well, then add to the creamed mixture gradually, beating very well after each addition. With a scrupulously clean beater, beat the whites stiff but not dry. Using a metal tablespoon fold the beaten whites and the flour into the creamed mixture, about a fifth at a time; fold in by slicing the spoon edge gently down the middle, lifting and turning as lightly as possible, at the same time turning the bowl slowly with your other hand. The flour should be shaken in gently from a height. Stop as soon as the mixture appears amalgamated. Empty gently into the prepared tin and fork roughly level. Bake in the middle of the oven at gas mark 3, 325°F (170°C) for 1½ hours. Cool in the tin for 10 minutes, then turn on to a wire rack and remove the papers. The cake will be delicately crisp on the outside, and inside will have a light crumbly texture.

Elizabeth Raffald: The experienced English housekeeper

PUNCH

A favourite eighteenth-century drink, brought from India in the late seventeenth century by merchants of the East India Company.

2 pt (1.1 L) claret
½ pt (275 ml) brandy
grated nutmeg, sugar and lemon juice
    to taste
toast, to serve

Mix the ingredients and serve in a punchbowl with toasted bread floating on the top. A variation of this was milk punch, where milk replaces the wine.

261

VICTORIAN
BRITAIN

Maggie Black

Mid nineteenth-century Westmorland kitchen showing cast-iron range with oven and, above, a movable pot-hook

How Our
Foodstuffs Changed

1800-1845: The foods which ordinary people ate in 1800 were limited, more or less, to what they could get locally at the time, or what they had preserved at home by pickling and smoking or making into sweet preserves. Almost all our essential foodstuffs were still grown or raised on our own farmland and were mostly sold in local markets because the roads were slow, difficult and sometimes dangerous. There were no railways yet. Only London, a few other city ports, and towns on a navigable river or canal could get supplies from other parts of Britain brought round the coast by sea, and imported foods.

Since most people still depended on local supplies for staple foods, especially grain, prices varied greatly from place to place. If the harvest failed in the north, corn was scarce and expensive there, even if a good harvest had made it cheap further south.

Bread was everyone's staple food. From about 1800, wheat largely replaced other grains for bread-making, and so became, literally, the basic vital commodity. It had to be bought, from abroad if necessary, and milled when needed because the flour was perishable; it still contained all the wheat germ nowadays removed from white flour. Even the whitest bread which affluent people ate was yellowish and bun-like because of this. The 'hard' wheat which makes spongy modern white loaves was not imported until the 1840s.

We get a good idea of what else middle-class people ate at the start of the nineteenth century by reading about the home life of the author Jane Austen. Her father was a modest country clergyman, fairly typical of his class. He farmed enough land to grow wheat for home bread-making, and kept cows, pigs, and sheep for mutton, a favourite standard joint. (Lamb, then, meant baby lamb, a delicate dinner-party meat.) Mrs Austen kept poultry. She had a varied vegetable garden, and fruit trees, and taught her daughters how to supervise their maids in making butter and cheese, preserves, pickles and homemade wines, and in brewing beer and curing bacons and hams. The only foods she had to buy were game and fish, and imported goods such as tea, coffee and sugar. When they moved into the town, prices loomed much larger in the family's thinking, and the cost of meat, especially, seemed frighteningly high. But they still ate well, if more simply than their grand neighbours.

The rich lived lavishly, indeed grossly, catered for by French-trained chefs; but the only differences between the actual products which they and their lesser country neighbours ate and drank were that they had various costly luxuries and more imported foods and wines. Although we were at war with France for most of the period up to 1815, the wealthy, who profited from the high war-time prices, could well afford to pay for smuggled wines, tea and sweetmeats. They could also afford exotic foods brought in with the imported staples: sugar, tea, coffee and rice.

For the poor, things were very different. Thousands of country labourers had lost their small homes and vegetable plots as a result of the eighteenth-century enclosing of land. They were

now reduced almost to paupers by having to buy food at war-time prices. Yet peace brought them no relief. The farmers persuaded the government to keep the price of corn (and therefore bread) high, and wages did not rise but un-employment did. Bad harvests followed, and there were wide-spread food riots. In desperation, thou-sands of men, with wives and

Sugar came in large loaves and had to be broken down with a cleaver and sugar nippers

266

children trekked to the squalid slums of the growing cities to work in the factories now being set up. A rural cottager who kept his job might still afford a bit of bacon on Sundays although on other days his family lived largely on bread with a little flavoured lard and potatoes. In the cities, bread and potatoes or porridge were almost the only foods of slum-dwellers. Strong tea, giving an illusion of warmth and fullness, was the main comfort of both rural and urban poor.

Things went from bad to worse in the thirties and forties because wages fell, and this was made more bitter for the poor because the middle classes, especially the growing numbers in the cities, were prospering. The new cheap labour pool there was helping to create an industrial and commercial boom, in new food industries among others; while macadamized roads and long-distance railways made it possible to transport factory-made and processed goods in bulk quickly and easily. The gap between even the modestly well-paid and the workers widened.

As J.C. Drummond has written in *The Englishman's Food:* 'Things came to a head in 1845 when with wages at the lowest level they had touched for over a century, the food situation became desperate for the very poor as the result of a widespread invasion of "potato disease"... with a poor corn harvest. England has never been nearer to revolution.' The potato fungus brought famine and starvation to Ireland and to parts of Scotland and England where potatoes now were the poor family's main or only food. The government was forced, at last, to bring down the price of bread.

The famine also brought home to some of the better-off how many of the working people they called 'the poor' actually were destitute, and made them want to do something for the starving. For instance, two renowned London chefs, Alexis Soyer and Charles Francatelli, more used to handling delicacies such as ortolans and truffles, designed new soup recipes for cheap mass feeding. The soups had little or no nourishment value, but the gesture marked the start of a new humanitarian movement.

1848-1890: After 1848, the variety, quality and freshness of food in the cities began to improve for all, largely because the railways distributed both fresh foods, such as milk, and the new bulk-processed foods efficiently and quickly.

The urban middle classes benefited most. They were getting more and more prosperous, and conscious of their rising social status. They ate well to show it off, and since they did not grow or preserve their own foods, they bought lavishly the new, better-quality meat and vegetables, and the mass-produced and mass-preserved foods which now came to the shops.

However poor people, too, began to eat slightly better. By 1864 a country labourer with a job could afford one hot meal a week and some vegetables. Better-off artisans might have a cheap knuckle joint now and then, cooked at the baker's, or get a midday meal of meat and root vegetables, bread, cheese and beer at a tavern or basement cookshop.

Even the very poor who still subsisted mostly on bread and potatoes were catered for by manufacturers and importers of the cheapest new mass-market foods. For instance, when cattle disease sent meat (and dairy food) prices sky-high in 1865, importers brought in cheap fatty American bacon and Australian canned meats. Poor folk could now get dark, cheap treacle to flavour their bread too. Then, towards the end of the century, cheap jam made of coloured, sweetened vegetable or fruit pulp offered them a sweeter, if less nourishing, alternative.

The poor shared, too, in another development. In 1861, roller mills came into use in Britain, and by the seventies gave everyone the refined white flour without wheatgerm which we eat today.

However, most of the new processed, packeted, bottled and canned foods which came in during the second half-century were only for the people who lived 'above stairs'. The poor could neither afford them nor make use of them.

Those foods were legion: it would be impossible to list them all. Here are some which changed the look and taste of the dishes on middle-class tables:

Quick-acting compressed yeast, self-raising flour, baking powder. These changed bread and cake-making recipes a great deal.

Custard powder, blancmange powder and concentrated egg powder.

Bottled, gelatine-based jellies, and later, stiffer table jellies in packets. These let housewives with little time and money make elaborate desserts like those of the wealthy.

Factory-style bulk-made cheese (replacing farm cheese).

Sweetened, condensed milk; dried milk.

Margarine, at first made from beef fat and milk; it was cheap although it tasted insipid and 'oily' to begin with.

Bulk-dried vegetables and dried packeted soups.

Commercially bottled pickles and sauces (also in jars). Some, such as the products of Harry J. Heinz, had a novelty value at first but soon became household names.

Experiments in bottling and canning meat in bulk had been going on since the beginning of the century in both France and England, not to help the housewife but to feed the troops and sailors. In 1865 the Admiralty set up the first large-scale meat-canning factory. Ten years later we were importing canned meats from both Australia and America. (This marked a significant change; by the end of the century Britain relied on imported food.)

Fish supplies to the expanding cities before mid-century had been insufficient and more often than not rotten or tainted. The supply improved rapidly when steam trawlers replaced the old sailing boats, and the invention of trawling made cod an every-day fish instead of a luxury one. As the railways spread and speeded up, fish even reached inland towns safely, in ice

Tinned food became popular in the late nineteenth century.
This is a can of Libby's tripe with a printed paper label c.1880

imported in bulk from Iceland and Norway. The ice man who brought a great dripping block of ice to a well-to-do Victorian home before a dinner party became a familiar sight. Another familiar sight which now disappeared, however, was the oyster stalls in poor quarters of London. Suddenly, about 1850, the oysters which had been a staple food for the very poor became an almost unobtainable luxury, due to over-fishing and pollution.

Chilling or freezing meat in bulk was not practical until a cheap way of making ice was found in 1861. Even then, it took until 1880 to find a way of refrigerating and transporting bulk meat in good condition; so chilled and frozen meat became a major source of supply only at the end of the century.

The 1890s: A cook's store cupboard and larder in a middle-class city home of the 1890s was as full of packets and cans as any housewife's now. With the help of bottled sauces, canned vegetables and fruit, and essences, she could choose between as many flavours (if less subtle ones) as a skilled chef who still made all his kitchen 'basics' by hand.

Most fresh foods came to her door. The baker and muffin-man called daily. The fishmonger with his ice-laden cart brought cod, hake, salmon, skate, eels, herring and shellfish; even lobsters were still a reasonable price. She could buy most vegetables in season from the greengrocer's cart, from asparagus in spring to pumpkin at Hallowe'en, although she would have to prepare all her vegetables (like her fish) herself. Her milkman would still fill her jug with milk or cream from his churn; bottling and pasteurization did not come in until the 1920s. However, railway transport from the country, machine milking and cooling gave her cleaner milk than before 1860 – although she would still be wise not to look too closely at its blueish tint.

She would really only have to leave her basement kitchen to visit the butcher and poulterer. Veal was still the cheapest meat to use for everyday meals and white stock; the family would not despise a well-dressed calf's head, and the feet still made the best-reputed jelly. Mutton had gone down a bit in the social scale; Irish stew was now made from scrag and was a servants' dish, although a roasted joint looked handsome on the dinner table. A fine chicken or capon was as much a party dish as a pheasant. Small birds such as woodcock and snipe were popular savouries.

Amongst the working class, some poorer slum children still had only bread and jam, or porridge for seventeen meals out of twenty-one in the week, and there were many waifs who got less. But there was a strong humanitarian movement now to help the needy. Well-meaning people produced dozens of cook-books for instance to teach the poor how to use their small resources well – although these were not as a rule very practical because few ordinary people knew anything about nutrition yet, or the real problems involved.

In the country, conditions and wages varied, and in some parts, labourers and their families still did not get enough to eat. On the other hand, many farmers gave their workers food 'perks', or let them 'buy' food by doing a bit of overtime, and most still let women and children into the fields to glean after the harvest. Children got off school to go nutting in season, or to pick field mushrooms.

This was at the lowest end of the scale. There were many grades of working people, and some (such as skilled craftsmen or the upper servants in a big house) now lived almost as well as their employers.

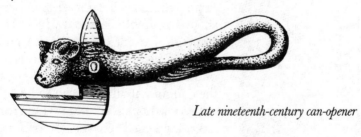

Late nineteenth-century can-opener

Cooking Methods and Tools

A cook's working methods and tools are dictated by the kind of heat she uses, and how it is contained, so we must look at these first.

In a poor home, around 1800, the fire was still set on a raised slab in the ground, against a wall, and was fuelled by wood, peat or furze. A cauldron, pot or kettle (the name varied from place to place) hung by an iron chain or rod with hook attached, from a bar in the chimney, or might be perched on the fire on its three stubby legs. This container was used for boiling stirabout (plain or flavoured porridge) or whatever else the family might have.

The poor housewife did not fry or broil (cook on a griddle) for lack of fat. Roasting, if done at all, was primitive. The meat might hang from the pot hook or be suspended by a piece of worsted from the front of the fireplace mantel, with a dish under it for the drips.

Some oatcakes or small loaves might be baked on the hearth on a flat hot bakestone, perhaps under an upturned crock or in a dry pot placed in the hot ashes. A beehive-shaped portable earthenware oven was sometimes used, covered with embers. But anyone in the country who had time or money for it, sent their dough or pies to the communal village oven to be baked. City cookshops and bakers would roast or bake, for a small charge, for artisans.

A reflector oven or roasting screen which was placed in front of an open fire with meat suspended inside. Hanging at the top is a bottle-jack, or clockwork mechanism which turned the meat. The door at the back allowed the cook to baste the meat

In a more affluent home, the fire was in a grate, and fuelled by coal. Boiling was done in cast-iron pots like the ones in cottages, raised and lowered by a ratchet or a chimney crane. But roasting was a much more elaborate procedure in which the meat or bird was rotated on a spit in front of the fire over a drip-tray. Spits and the mechanisms for turning them were like those in the eighteenth century and remained almost unchanged, except for extra decoration, until the 1880s.

One development at the beginning of the nineteenth century, however, was to place the meat in a concave iron or tinplate 'reflector oven' like a screen, with the concave side open to the fire to reflect the heat on to the food. A door in the screen let one get at the food from the back, to baste it. Later, smaller similar roasters were developed with shelves for baking batch cakes or spikes for holding apples or bread for toasting.

Another nineteenth-century development was a clockwork bottle jack for turning the spit which did not depend on the heat of the fire to turn it.

Spit-roasting survived even after gas ovens came in. Oven-cooked meat, according to a cook-book editor in 1886, did not have the same flavour.

Broiled meat however was popular; chops could be broiled or pancakes fried over the open fire in a cast-iron frying pan or on a gridiron (griddle) with a long handle.

The cast iron open range – like cast iron itself, and tinplate – had been developed in the late eighteenth century. By about 1830 it was commonplace in upper- and middle-class kitchens and in many solidly built smaller homes, because it could easily be built into an existing fireplace. The fire was still open for roasting and toasting, but had a cast-iron oven on one side. Early models had a swinging trivet at the other side to hold a kettle, and the grate could be made smaller by winding in the side or by folding down the top bars. In later models of this Yorkshire range, as it was called, a set of hinged bars might fold down over the fire to support pots and pans, and by the 1860s a hot water boiler was generally installed on the side opposite the oven.

In February 1802, George Bodley, a Devon iron-founder

patented a closed-top range. The design of this Kitchener range was much like that of the Yorkshire type, but it had a cast-iron hotplate over the fire with removable boiling rings. The front of the fire could often be enclosed too by movable panels or a door, to redirect the heat for boiling or baking instead of roasting.

This combination stove became popular in affluent homes in southern England, because the cook could boil, fry and bake at the same time, just as we do today. But it was expensive to buy, very hard work to keep clean, and a glutton for fuel. North country people stuck to the open range. (Poor people everywhere still cooked on a small open grate by balancing a kettle, frying pan or saucepan on the top.)

Experimental gas cookers and grills were tried out from 1824 onwards, but did not become popular until the 1880s in spite of promotion by enthusiasts. However, the experiments led to the development of gas cookers much as we know them today; so when the gas companies decided to promote them in the 1880s, they had an efficient product to offer, available in sizes and shapes to suit all homes. Vitreous enamel, wipe-down surfaces replaced the old black-leading needed for iron stoves. Well-insulated ovens with see-through doors made baking easy, although one still had to guess the exact heat. One new development was the grill which

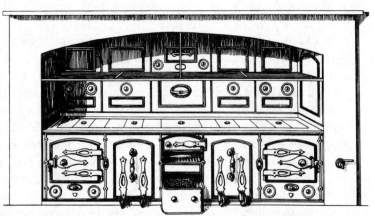

A closed range made by Barnard, Bishop and Barnard, 1881. Suitable for hotels and other large catering establishments

toasted food placed under it. It replaced the old gridirons on which food was broiled over the heat.

Penny-in-the-slot gas meters let even quite poor people use gas. They could hire gas cookers cheaply too. By 1898, one home in four that had a gas supply, had a cooker as well.

The first electric power station for domestic consumers did not open until the 1880s, and although electric cookers were being demonstrated in the 1890s along with other electrical cooking equipment, their history really belongs to the twentieth century.

The development of the closed cast-iron cooking range

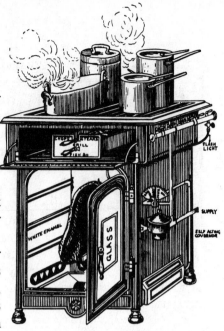

The Charing Cross Kitchener, 1890, an early example of a gas cooker. Although there was a temperature gauge the only effective way of controlling the heat was by turning the gas up or down

changed the shape of cooking pots and pans. They now needed to be flat-bottomed and no longer needed long handles. They also got smaller because the range could hold more of them, and as fancy cooking became popular with the rising middle class, they became more specialized. A mid-Victorian cook might have, for instance, an omelette pan, a sauté pan and frying pan, and separate fish kettles for flat and round fish, and for salmon. Luckily for her, all these were no longer made of copper or brass which needed hard scouring, but of tinplated cast iron, varnished black. Towards the end of the century, vitreous enamel began to be used as a finish, and lightweight aluminium cookware first appeared.

Ladles, spoons, chopping knives, mashers, herb choppers, and other traditional implements did not change, but a number of more specialized tools and gadgets were added to them, many of them metal versions of earlier ones. Mass-produced tinware

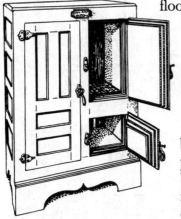

Segers Patent Dry Air Syphon Refrigerator c.1890. Made in USA. Blocks of ice were kept in the top right-hand cupboard which cooled food in the other compartments

flooded middle-class kitchens. For example, pastry and biscuit cutters, patty pans and pikelet rings, jelly moulds, moulds for brawns and raised pies. A boiled tongue could be curled up and pressed in a tinplate screw-down press like a cheese-press. Tinplate biscuit and sweet tins, often gaudily painted, replaced bottles, jars and boxes. The essential tin-opener was introduced during the 1860s to open cans of corned beef.

Free-standing toasters of various shapes were elaborated for making some of the more delicate dishes eaten at long formal dinners. A common type was a tripod with a multi-pronged attachment and a drip-tray beneath which could be used for cooking small birds, fruits, nuts or cheese as well as for toasting bread.

After 1865, tinned cast iron and tinplate were combined in many mechanical labour-saving gadgets. A grater, bread rasper, potato peeler, mincer, bean slicer, marmalade cutter, knife sharpener and an enormous, complicated apple corer, peeler and slicer were just some of them. There was even a chopper and mixer (but no blender).

Ice had been cut in blocks and stored in underground or well-insulated ice-houses since 1660 and this supply, together with imported block ice from Norway and America, cooled late Georgian and Victorian food for parties. About 1840, tin or zinc-lined boxes came into use. They were packed with ice with the food on top. About fifteen years later, similar ice chests were patented which had a top, aerated compartment for crushed ice, a drainage system for melted ice-water, and a lower chilled compartment for food. The prototype refrigerator (which it was called) had been created.

The sorbets, ice-creams and iced puddings which had become immensely popular for formal upper- and rising middle-class dinners could not be frozen in a small quantity of crushed ice alone. Experiments in making artificial ice led to the discovery that ice mixed with saltpetre or salt made a colder, longer-lasting freezing mixture, and about 1864, it was found in America that churning ice-cream while it froze improved its texture greatly. Ice-cream makers or freezers were therefore developed which were like a box or pail with a cylinder inside which contained the flavoured cream and was cranked by a handle; in later models, a paddle inside the cream container was worked by turning a handle. We still use similar churn freezers.

In fact, cooking the Victorian way was not unlike cooking today except that the cook still prepared her own meat, fowls and fish, and kneaded, mixed and whisked by hand. Her gadgets were still clumsier than her fingers.

Late Victorian pots and pans including a double saucepan (left) and long fish kettle

SERVICE, SETTINGS AND MANNERS

To see how the new foodstuffs, materials and appliances changed the way people ate in the nineteenth century, we must focus on the meals of the people who used them – the rising middle class. **1800-1840:** At first, breakfast was taken between 9 and 10am as in the eighteenth century, but it became more substantial. The aristocratic eighteenth century custom of having just chocolate, coffee or tea, toast and hot sweet rolls still held for some people (Jane Austen was one) but a cooked breakfast was popular with men; Jane Austen mentions boiled eggs and pork chops.

Luncheon, still a light snack meal, was taken about 1 o'clock to fill the gap between breakfast and the new, but variable, later dinner hour. This was rapidly getting later because more and more men worked in their own, or other people's, offices. Jane Austen regarded 5 or 6pm as a reasonable dinner hour in 1805, with evening tea – an eighteenth-century introduction – two or three hours later and, for the greedy or when entertaining, a late supper before bedtime.

A plain everyday dinner at home might consist of only three or four savoury dishes, with a couple of sweet dishes afterwards or perhaps cheese. But a formal dinner was still set out in eighteenth-century style in two or three courses or 'services' – in fact, two complete self-service meals were served, one after the other.

One new feature of such a dinner however was that, although servants were at hand to change the plates and pour wine, gentlemen carved for and served their lady neighbours, and only from the dishes close by; it was not thought polite to stretch or to demand a dish at the other end of the table.

Dishes and tableware had already, in the eighteenth century, begun to have the shapes we know now, but there were some novelties; for instance, early in the nineteenth century it became fashionable to use silver servers, knives and forks for eating fish, and also for fruit, because it was thought that using steel spoiled the

An épergne or table centre

flavour, and that the acid foods corroded the metal. More
important, bone china with its translucent body and sparkling
glaze was developed to beautify dinner tables.

Two cloths were laid on the table, one for removal between
courses or before the dessert. (Table mats, leaving the table bare,
now began to be used at lunch but never at dinner.) In the centre of
the tablecloth was placed a grand food dish, a plateau or an
épergne. A plateau was a chased silver or glass oblong tray with
rounded ends, on small feet. An épergne was a tall ornament, with
branches which held small dishes of sweetmeats or flowers. Later
in the century, it would often be replaced by a flower arrangement
or by a tazza; this was a stemmed shallow bowl or plate like a cake-
stand for fruit, sweetmeats or trailing floral decorations.

One marked change in dining habits occurred early on. Instead of the ladies entering the room first in order of precedence, followed by the gentlemen, so that the sexes were seated separately, it became the custom for each lady to be escorted into dinner by a gentleman, who then sat next to her, However, in spite of this 'promiscuous seating' as it was called, etiquette demanded that all the ladies should be served first as in the past; and from this grew the habit of every gentleman serving his lady companion before himself. He must also (since a lady might not ask for wine) make sure that she was served, both during and after dinner, with the wine she preferred. He should call for the same wine for himself, and when the glasses came, bow to his companion and drink with her.

Separate styles of glasses were now beginning to be used for different wines. The number of wines served with a meal also increased. By mid-century, a different wine would be served at each stage of the meal, each in a special glass, and these would be arrayed on the table beside each diner instead of being called for.

Another early nineteenth century feature was the refinement of the use of the 'finger glasses'. These were small glasses of water supplied before the dessert for rinsing out the mouth. However, early in the century, they began to be used instead to wet the corner of the napkin to wipe the mouth and then to rinse the fingertips.

There were not many other refinements yet. Men still stayed drinking in the dining room long after dinner, and their manners were as coarse as in the previous century. Ladies stayed only after the dessert for perhaps two glasses of wine, then retired.

1840-1900: Three important changes took place in Victorian well-to-do eating patterns: mealtimes changed, meals became larger and more elaborate and the serving system changed completely.

As the pattern of 'going to the office' developed, breakfast got slightly earlier and dinner a lot later. A man might go to his club after his office day, before returning home to change his clothes and have one of the newly popular aperitifs; so dinner seldom took place before 8, 9 or 10 pm if entertaining.

The Victorian breakfast was a hearty affair. Mrs Beeton in

1861 suggested any cold joint in the larder might be placed 'nicely garnished' on the sideboard along with collared and potted meats or fish, cold game or poultry, veal and ham pies, game pies, cold ham and tongue – pressed in the new-style tin press. These were to supplement a choice of hot dishes, such as broiled mackerel or other fish, mutton chops and rump steaks, broiled sheeps' kidneys, sausages (now prepared and sold by butchers), bacon and eggs, other kinds of eggs, muffins, toast, marmalade, butter, jam, tea and coffee. She suggested adding fruit in the summer.

Lunch was still lightish; the same cold dishes would do as at breakfast, or a mother might eat the same hot meal as the children. If a woman entertained, the dishes would be dainty rather than filling, but this was not common, and she was more likely to have soup or chicken sandwiches alone. However, if it was her At Home Day, she would serve a new meal of afternoon tea, with hot teacakes, thin sandwiches, an array of small cakes and biscuits, and at least one large cake made with baking powder instead of yeast.

Breakfast table setting from Mrs Beeton's Book of Household Management, *1891*

And then there was dinner. The quantity which well-to-do Victorians served and ate at a dinner party was prodigious. Even a small dinner for six given by people of modest means in 1861 contained at least thirteen dishes and dessert. A wealthier dinner later in the century was a lot more lavish. Note, however, that Mrs Beeton, alongside these meals, suggests menus for Plain Family Dinners such as bubble and squeak made from remains of cold beef, and curried pork followed by baked semolina pudding.

Copying French custom, a new way of serving meals had begun to creep in during the early 1800s, but it was not really adopted in middle-class homes until mid-century, and even then Mrs Beeton is dubious about it. More staff were needed to serve it, and more cutlery to eat it with.

The new style consisted of sending to table one kind of dish at a time, beginning with soup and fish, then made-up meat dishes (entrées), roasts, poultry and game, then vegetable and sweet dishes called entremets and finally dessert.

Fashionable dining also demanded that all the serving (including carving) be done in the kitchen so that diners were issued with a ready-prepared plate.

English hostesses wavered but finally, towards the end of the century, settled for a compromise in which modern-style courses (soup, fish, etc.) were sent to table in turn, any carving was done at a side table, and the dish, or choice of dishes, was handed round to the diners.

What made such a dinner so very different from ours was that there were usually six or seven courses and a choice – sometimes a wide choice – in each. At a really long, large dinner, the cook might also serve an iced sorbet after the main course to revive the palate.

It was as well that dishes were now handed round, because there was no room for them on the table among the clutter of assorted wine glasses, rows of knives and forks, tasse, vases of flowers and napkins twisted into fancy shapes. All these were larger than before and more elaborate. The Victorians engraved, embossed, curled or chased every surface. (Curiously, they standardized the shapes of cutlery, such as knife-blades and the

*A Victorian method of making
a table napkin look decorative*

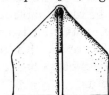

The Collegian

The Mitre

Fold the napkin in three, lengthways

Fold the napkin in four, lengthways

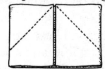

Fold the ends to the middle

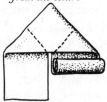

*Turn down the ends diagonally
from the centre*

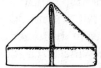

Fold over the top corners

*Turn the folded napkin over and
roll up the ends*

*Turn the folded napkin over, raise the
outer corners and tuck into each other to
form the finished mitre design*

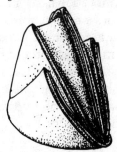

*Turn the rolls under as indicated
by the diagonal dotted lines
Note: Resembling a mortar board, this
form of napkin could have either a
bread roll or a small posy of flowers
slipped under its square top panel*

*The Victorian table napkin was a 30 inch square of starched and crisply ironed linen
damask, which was folded into a variety of ornamental forms and set beside each place
setting on the dining table*

tines of forks. The development of EPNS (electroplated nickel silver) tableware for modest homes in the latter part of the period encouraged this.)

No mid-Victorian table would have been complete without a vase of flowers. Mrs Beeton even stresses that one should be placed on the breakfast table. At dinner parties, the height of flower arrangements tended to make conversation impossible across the table. However, this hardly mattered since good manners demanded that polite conversation should be confined to one's neighbours.

By mid-century, dining-table manners had become genteel. Fish, for instance, should be eaten with just a fork and a scrap of bread; one should only toy with one's silver (or EPNS) fish knife. One should eat only a little of each dish, and that delicately. It was no longer 'done' to wet one's napkin to dab the mouth; ladies especially, should dabble only the fingertips in the finger-bowl. It was not done, either, to gulp down a glass of wine. Even gentlemen drank slowly of the different wines served with each course, until the ladies left the room and they could settle to their port; and even then, they were expected to appear in the drawing room quite soon after the ladies' coffee-tray had been removed.

Between dinner parties, the average, reasonably affluent Victorian family lived relatively plainly. Nevertheless, by our standards, they spent a disproportionate amount of their time thinking about food and drink, and in entertaining for show. A well-to-do married couple with business connections, say in the food trade, might well give four dinner parties a month, for 12-16 guests each, and serve 20-30 dishes each time at considerable cost. One wonders how their cook would have managed without her mincer, bean slicer, bread rasper and new wire egg whisk, her packet jellies and custard powder, her ice-box, freezer pail and above all her combination Kitchener, to produce the showy dishes on the sparkling plate which these occasions required.

RECIPES
Dinner party dishes

POULET SAUTÉ
À LA PLOMBIÈRE

A decorative hot entrée for a formal dinner in 1895 which would make a practical main dish by itself today.

2 small chickens, about 2 lb (900 g) each
4 oz (100 g) streaky bacon
2 oz (50 g) unsalted butter
2 shallots, finely chopped
1 tbls (15 ml) flour
1 tbls (15 ml) mild curry powder
2 tsps (10 ml) desiccated coconut
4 fl oz (125 ml) white wine
1 tbls (15 ml) brandy
1 pt (575 ml) white stock
4 parsley sprigs and ½ bay leaf, tied in muslin
salt
pepper
a pinch of grated nutmeg
1 tsp (5 ml) redcurrant jelly
juice of ½ sour orange
6 oz (175 g) long grain rice
a little extra stock (optional)
rind of ½ orange, pared thinly and cut into 'matchsticks', to garnish
6-8 warm fleurons (half-moons) of cooked puff pastry, to garnish

Joint the chickens, and dice the bacon, discarding any rind. Melt the butter in a saucepan or flameproof casserole. Fry the bacon for about 2 minutes, shaking the pan, then add the chicken pieces and shallots, and sauté until lightly browned on all sides. Mix together the flour, curry powder and coconut, and sprinkle over the chicken. Stir round, and pour in the wine, brandy and stock. Add the herb bundle, then bring to the boil and add the seasoning, nutmeg, redcurrant jelly and orange juice. Reduce the heat and simmer uncovered for 30 minutes or until the chicken pieces are tender. While the meat is simmering, cook the rice in boiling, salted water until tender, then drain and keep warm. Skim any fat off the curry sauce, and thin with a little stock if wished. Simmer the shreds of orange rind in water for 2 minutes and drain. Arrange the rice in a circle, pile the chicken, bacon and sauce in the centre, and garnish the top with shreds of rind and warmed fleurons.

Charles Herman Senn:
Recherché Cookery

RICE À LA SOEUR NIGHTINGALE
(Sister Nightingale's Rice)

Today it would be a doubtful honour to have even a royal chef's version of kedgeree named after one.

6 oz (175 g) long grain rice
salt
1 lb (450 g) smoked haddock fillet
2 square slices bread, crusts removed
3-4 oz (75-100 g) unsalted butter
3 hard-boiled eggs
pepper
a pinch of grated nutmeg
1 tbls (15 ml) grated Parmesan cheese

Cook the rice in plenty of boiling, salted water until tender. While it is cooking, pour boiling water over the haddock, and leave to stand for 5 minutes. Drain the rice when ready.

Cut each bread slice into four triangles. Fry in 1½ oz (40 g) of the butter until golden on both sides. Remove with a fish slice, leaving any fat in the pan, drain on absorbent paper, then keep warm.

Separate the whites and yolks of the hard-boiled eggs into separate bowls. Chop the whites. Remove any bones and skin from the fish and flake the flesh coarsely. Mix with the chopped egg whites. Add the remaining butter to the frying pan, and toss the rice in it over gentle heat, adding seasoning and nutmeg to taste. Mix in the fish and egg white mixture, and pile in a cone or pyramid on a hot dish. Sieve the egg yolks and cheese together, and sprinkle over the mixture. Put in the oven at gas mark 4, 350°F (180°C) for 4-5 minutes until the cheese begins to colour. Garnish with the triangles of fried bread and serve at once.

Charles Elmé Francatelli: The Cook's Guide and Housekeeper's and Butler's Assistant

WHITE SOUP À LA REINE

This was a popular cream soup offered at affluent dinner parties throughout the period. Notice that the stock is made with veal. Calves were slaughtered early, and the meat was as plentiful and cheap as chicken (the modern substitute) is now.

1 chicken, cooked
3 pt (1.7 L) water
1 lb (450 g) veal, cubed
1 carrot
1 stick celery
1 onion
12 oz (350 g) rice
3 pt (1.7 L) veal or chicken stock
1 oz (25 g) butter
salt
pepper
½ pt (275 ml) single cream
croutons, to serve

Remove the meat from the cooked chicken and set aside. Put the carcass in a saucepan, add the water, veal, carrot, celery and onion and simmer for about 2 hours to make a broth. Strain. Meanwhile, simmer the rice very gently in the veal or chicken stock for about 40 minutes until all the stock is absorbed.

Work the chicken meat in a food processor with the butter and ¼ pint (150 ml) of the broth. When it is reduced to a smooth pulp, add the rice and work into the mixture. Mix with 2 pints (1.1 litres) of the broth then strain the soup through a nylon sieve lined with cheesecloth. Heat the strained soup in a saucepan, season to taste, then stir in the cream. Serve with croutons.

Charles Elmé Francatelli: The Cook's Guide and Housekeeper's and Butler's Assistant

---

CALF'S FOOT JELLY

Chefs and good cooks still considered it essential to make calf's foot jelly in the late nineteenth century, not only as nourishment for invalids, but as by far and away the best basis for their many (often elaborate) jellied desserts. Isinglass was accepted as an alternative but was less esteemed. Gelatine, made by boiling hooves and hides, came into its own when the first cheap jellies became an 'instant' sales success at the Great Exhibition of 1851, but made any high-class cook wince.
Today, calves' feet are not, officially, sold for human consumption, but here, for interest, is the great Alexis Soyer's recipe for 'jelly stock'.

'Take two calf's-feet, cut them up and boil in three quarts of water; as soon as it boils remove it to the corner of the fire, and simmer for five hours, keeping it skimmed, pass through a hair sieve into a basin, and let it remain until quite hard, then remove the oil and fat, and wipe the top dry. Place in a stewpan one gill of water, one of sherry, half a pound of lump sugar, the juice of four lemons, the rinds of two, and the whites and shells of five eggs, whisk until the sugar is melted, then add the jelly, place it on the fire, and whisk until boiling, pass it through a jelly-bag, pouring that back again which comes through first until quite clear; it is then ready for use, by putting it in moulds or glasses.'

Alexis Soyer: The Modern Housewife or Ménagère

MACARONI À LA REINE

Miss Acton's 'excellent and delicate mode of dressing macaroni' makes delightful reading but long-winded instruction. Its essentials in modern terms are these.

8 oz (225 g) macaroni
salt
10 oz (275 g) white Stilton or other rich white quick-melting cheese without rind (see note)
2 oz (50 g) unsalted butter
12 fl oz (350 ml) double cream or thick rich white sauce
pepper
a good pinch of ground mace
a pinch of cayenne pepper
fried breadcrumbs, finely crushed

Cook the macaroni in boiling salted water until tender, then drain. While it is cooking, flake the cheese and the butter. Heat the cream or sauce almost to boiling point. Add the cheese and butter in small portions, with salt and pepper, the mace and cayenne, and stir until dissolved. Pour over the hot, drained pasta, and toss to mix. Turn into a warmed serving dish, and sprinkle thickly with golden crumbs before serving.

Eliza Acton: Modern Cookery for Private Families, 1874 edition

● Miss Acton suggests using Stilton without the blue mould.

Perhaps young Stiltons were less blued in those days.
White Stilton–a good cheese in its own right–is available from speciality suppliers.

PHEASANT GITANA

Week-end shooting and house-parties were a feature of upper-class Victorian life. This was a useful way to handle a badly shot bird for formal dining.

1 pheasant, trussed
8 oz (225 g) streaky bacon, rinded and cut into 1 in (2.5cm) squares
1 oz (25 g) butter
1 garlic clove
2 large Spanish onions, sliced
4 ripe tomatoes, sliced
¼ pt (150 ml) sherry
1 tsp (5 ml) paprika

Put the pheasant in a large flameproof casserole with the bacon, butter and garlic. Fry, turning the pheasant, until it is browned all over. Pour off excess fat, then add the onions, tomatoes and sherry. Cover and simmer for 45-60 minutes until the pheasant is tender, shaking the pan occasionally. Just before serving, stir in the paprika.

Charles Elmé Francatelli: The Cook's Guide and Housekeeper's and Butler's Assistant

SAVOY CAKE

A grand dinner or banquet always featured large and small cakes, especially Savoy cake, among its sweet entremets or desserts. Since stale Savoy cake was also the basis of creamy desserts such as Coburg pudding and trifle, a shrewd chef included these in his menu too.

This is Alexis Soyer's basic Savoy cake, probably made, as was common, in a fancy mould, like a jelly mould. (Hot steamed and similar puddings were also made in fancy moulds, so that they looked elaborately carved when turned out.)

clarified butter for brushing
8 oz (225 g) caster sugar,
    plus a little extra
1-2 drops lemon essence
7 eggs, separated
3 oz (75 g) plain flour
3 oz (75 g) potato flour

Brush the inside of a 4½ pint (2.5 litre) decorative mould or an 8 inch (20 cm) diameter, 3 inch (7.5 cm) deep cake tin with clarified butter. Invert it to drain. When the butter has set, sprinkle the inside of the mould or tin liberally with caster sugar, and shake out the excess.

Add the lemon essence to the caster sugar, then beat with the egg yolks in a large bowl until thick and almost white.

Separately, whisk the egg whites until stiff but not dry. Sift into the egg yolk mixture a little of the flour and potato flour, mixed. Fold it in with a metal spoon. Fold in about half the egg whites, then sift and fold in about half the remaining flour mixture. Repeat, using all the ingredients.

Using a spatula, turn the mixture into the prepared mould or tin as lightly as possible. Bake at gas mark 4, 350°F (180°C) for 1-1¼ hours. Test for readiness by running a hot thin poultry skewer into the cake. Turn out to cool on a wire rack. (Leave for 1-2 days before cutting up to make into a dessert.)

Alexis Soyer: The Modern Housewife or Ménagère

● Herman Senn, a well-known late-century chef, baked the quantity of Savoy cake mixture above in a large ring mould. When it was cold, he filled the centre with a good half-pint of vanilla-flavoured, sweetened whipped cream, and titled it 'Gateau de Savoie à la Chantilly'. International menu French had become 'the thing' for even middle-class formal dinners by his day. Perhaps that was why he called his big cookbook of 1893 *Practical Gastronomy and Culinary Dictionary: A Complete Menu Compiler and Register of Most Known Dishes in English and French.*

ICED PUDDINGS

One or more elaborately moulded ice-creams or iced puddings were served at any formal Victorian dinner or banquet. This description of how to freeze an ice-cream pudding was written by Samuel Hobbs, a freelance chef who prepared many dinners for royalty among others. His puddings were made with about 2¼ pints (1.2 litres) cream custard and were meant for 14 people, a fairly small number for a Victorian dinner party.

'…freeze the pudding as follows: place the same in a three-quart pewter freezer; break up or pound as fine as possible twenty pounds of rough ice and put the cover on your freezer, mix three or four double handfuls of fine salt with the pounded ice well and rapidly together; place the same round the freezer in a tub or pail and by holding the handle, turn the freezer round and round for about ten minutes; then take off the lid of the freezer and with the ice spatule, remove the pudding which you will find has frozen to the side of the freezer and mix the same with the unfrozen part of the pudding; now put on the lid and proceed again as in the first instance… again remove the lid and mix the frozen with the unfrozen part… till it becomes smooth and uniform in appearance. You should now turn the freezer by the aid of your spatule, beating the pudding with the same, so as to make the freezer spin round; this should be continued till the pudding is sufficiently frozen and by this process becomes very smooth

A variety of pewter ice-cream moulds, an ice pick and an American ice-cream freezer

and firm… Then fill your pudding mould as follows: remove the freezer from the ice and scoop the remainder of the ice into a pail, mix fresh salt with the same as before, and then with your spatule, or a spoon, fill the ice pudding mould with the frozen pudding, tapping the same so that the pudding will, when turned out of the mould, show smooth and compact. The pudding should be well embedded in ice, under and over it; and if more ice is needed, proceed to prepare as in the first instance; let the pudding remain in this till required for dinner, when remove the mould from the ice and dip it into a pail of water, slightly warm; then dry it in a cloth, remove the lid, also the bottom of the mould, and the pudding with a little shake will leave the mould and fix itself on to the silver dish upon which it should be sent to table.'

Samuel Hobbs: One Hundred and Sixty Culinary Dainties for the Epicure, the Invalid and the Dyspeptic

● A modern ice-cream maker should produce the same effect as a Victorian churn freezer, although the ice-cream quantities will have to be adapted to fit its smaller capacity.

PETITES BOUCHÉES

These little pastries were offered among Victorian sweet entremets or desserts at formal dinners, and were also among the offerings at evening parties.

6 oz (175 g) whole almonds
4 oz (100 g) caster sugar
rind of ½ lemon, pared thinly
1 egg white
10 oz (275 g) puff pastry

Blanch the almonds, by plunging in boiling water for about 3 minutes, then rub off the skins and chop very finely. Pound together the sugar and lemon rind in a mortar, then sift to remove any solid rind. Mix in the almonds. Beat the egg white until liquid, and mix into the almonds and sugar to make a paste – you may not need it all. Roll out the puff pastry to a thickness of ¼ inch (5 mm), and cut into diamonds, rounds, ovals, etc. Reroll and recut trimmings. Spread the pastry shapes thickly with the almond paste. Bake at gas mark 6, 400°F (200°C) until gilded. Cool on a rack.

Mrs Isabella Beeton: The Book of Household Management, 1886 or 1888 edition

BAVARIAN CREAMS

Soyer, in The Modern Housewife, *explains how these 'creams' can be flavoured like jellies with ripe fruit in syrup or with preserves. He then gives a basic, standard recipe for a plain one, using generous Victorian quantities. It has been adapted slightly for use now.*

1 vanilla pod, split
1 pt (575 ml) milk
5 egg yolks
6 oz (175 g) caster sugar
3 tbls (45 ml) any sweet liqueur
1 oz (25 g) gelatine
¾ pt (425 ml) whipping cream

Simmer the vanilla pod in the milk for 10 minutes. Meanwhile, beat the egg yolks and sugar together in a saucepan until thick and quite white. Still beating, add the hot milk gradually, and place over low heat until the custard thickens. Strain into a bowl and cool.

While cooling, heat the liqueur in a small pan until very hot; sprinkle in the gelatine little by little and stir until it dissolves. Do not boil. Stir it into the cooling custard, and chill until the mixture begins to thicken at the edges. While chilling, whip the cream fairly stiffly. Fold it into the thickening custard. Pour into a wetted 3 pint (1.7 litre) ornamental mould and leave for at least 2 hours. Turn out on to a chilled serving dish.

Alexis Soyer: The Modern Housewife and Ménagère

CHARLOTTE RUSSE

This is one of Soyer's recipes using the recipe above.

'Line the inside of a plain round mould with Savoy biscuits, cutting and placing them at the bottom to form a rosette, standing them upright and close together [round the sides]… fill with any [liqueur-flavoured] cream, place the mould in ice, let it remain until ready to serve, turn over on a dish and remove the mould.'

Alexis Soyer: The Modern Housewife and Ménagère

● Use sponge fingers for the Savoy biscuits.

Everyday dishes

MOCK CRAB

This version of a Victorian luncheon dish was put by a dour Scots cook in her book Superior Cookery. *Not all Victorian cookery was rich and showy. Simple as this is, the recipes in Mrs Black's other books were drab by comparison.*

1 hard-boiled egg
1 tbls (15 ml) salad oil
½ tsp (2.5 ml) salt
½ tsp (2.5 ml) caster sugar
½ tsp (2.5 ml) made English mustard
1 tbls (15 ml) white wine vinegar
a few drops of onion juice
4 oz (100 g) red Cheshire or Leicester cheese, coarsely grated
1 tbls (15 ml) cooked chicken, finely chopped
1 crab shell or lettuce leaves, to serve
thin slices of brown bread and butter, rolled, to serve

Separate the egg yolk and white. Sieve the yolk into a small bowl. Separately, finely chop the white and keep aside for garnishing. Work the sieved yolk to a smooth paste with the oil, using the back of a spoon. Mix in the salt, sugar and mustard, then blend in the vinegar and onion juice to make a thin cream. Mix together the cheese and chicken lightly with a fork, keeping the cheese shreds separate, then blend in the vinegar mixture lightly. Chill. To serve, pile in the crab shell or on lettuce leaves and garnish with the chopped egg white. Serve with rolls of thin bread and butter.

Mrs Black: Superior Cookery

BOILED SALAD

'Take Beetroot. Boil it well and slice it neatly. Take Celery. Boil it well and cut it in large pieces. Some slices of Potato, also boiled and neatly cut. Some Brussels Sprouts are sometimes added. Add a rich Salad Sauce, composed of cream, Eggs, and mustard. To be eaten cold. Like a Lobster salad – to which dish it bears a very great outward resemblance.'

Janey Ellice's Recipes 1846-1859

STEWED TROUT

A nineteenth century cook had no frozen, farmed supermarket trout, only river fish which might be much larger if old and wily. The cooking time below has been adapted to suit both; otherwise the author's tasty recipe is almost unchanged.

2 medium-sized trout
3 oz (75 g) butter
1 tbls (15 ml) flour
a good pinch of ground mace
a good pinch of grated nutmeg
a pinch of cayenne pepper
¾ pt (425 ml) veal or chicken stock
3 parsley sprigs
1 bay leaf
1 broad strip lemon peel, rolled
salt
2 tbls (30 ml) dry white wine (optional)

Clean the fish, and trim the tails and fins; remove heads if you wish. Rinse inside and pat quite dry. Melt the butter in a large deep frying pan or skillet. Stir in the flour, mace, nutmeg and cayenne together. Add the trout, and brown them on both sides, shaking the pan to prevent them sticking. Now add the stock, parsley, bay leaf, lemon peel, salt and the wine if using. Half-cover the pan, and reduce the heat to a gentle simmer. Cook for 15-35 minutes, depending on the size of the fish. When ready, the fish should be tender when pierced with a thin poultry skewer, but should not be soft enough to break up.

Remove the fish to a warmed serving dish. Skim all the fat off the cooking liquid, and strain some or all of it over the fish. Serve at once.

Eliza Acton: Modern Cookery for Private Families

HODGE PODGE

This is Isabella Beeton's leftovers version of stewed, well-aged spring lamb with summer vegetables. Other writers, such as Eliza Acton, had made it with raw meat and called it China chilo. However, from mid-century even great chefs granted that most people sometimes ate leftovers. In 1853, Alexis Soyer called his similar dish simply 'Remains'. Even thriftier than Mrs Beeton, he suggested using leftover peas and other vegetables served with the original roast.

1 lb (450 g) lightly cooked lamb or
*   mutton*
8 oz (225 g) firm-hearted lettuce
*   without outside leaves*
6 spring onions, including green stems
2 oz (50 g) butter or margarine
salt
pepper
4 fl oz (100 ml) water
10 oz (275 g) shelled garden peas

Mince the meat coarsely, discarding skin and excess fat. Slice the lettuce and spring onions and put them in a saucepan with the meat. Add the fat, and season generously. Pour the water over the dish. Cover, and simmer over very low heat for 45 minutes. Meanwhile, boil the peas for about 10 minutes or until just tender. Drain and add them to the meat just before serving. (Cooked peas as recommended by Soyer can just be added to the meat a few minutes before the end of the cooking time, to heat through.) By then, at the end of the cooking time, the liquid in the pan should almost all have been absorbed.

Mrs Isabella Beeton: The Book of Household Management

● This dish is much better-flavoured if like Eliza Acton's China chilo, it contains a large finely chopped onion, and 1½-2 tsps (7.5-10 ml) curry powder.

DORMERS

Between dinner parties, much Victorian cookery was in the boiled-cod-and-cabbage class to make up for the cost of the parties. These 'sausages' were probably eaten as a supper dish, but would be good for breakfast or as part of a mixed grill with bacon instead of gravy.

8 oz (225 g) cold cooked lamb or mutton, without skin or bone
3 oz (75 g) cold cooked rice
2 oz (50 g) shredded suet
salt
ground black pepper
1 large egg
1 oz (25 g) fine dried breadcrumbs
dripping or bacon fat for frying
leftover gravy

Chop or mince the meat, rice and suet together fairly finely. Season highly. Turn on to a board and divide into six equal-sized portions. Squeeze and shape each portion into a small roll or sausage shape.

Beat the egg with a fork on a plate. Scatter the breadcrumbs on a sheet of greaseproof paper. Roll the 'sausages' in beaten egg, coating completely, then cover with crumbs. Leave to stand for 15-30 minutes. Heat the frying fat in a frying pan, and turn the 'sausages' over in the hot fat until crisp and browned on all sides. Drain on absorbent paper, then place on a warm serving dish. While the 'sausages' are resting, skim the surface of any leftover gravy, and dilute it if needed. Bring to simmering point in a small saucepan while frying the 'sausages', then pour the gravy around them just before serving.

Mrs Isabella Beeton: The Book of Household Management

IRISH STEW

Irish stew seems to have been christened as such only in the early nineteenth century. At first it was a middle-class dish using loin or best end chops.

2 lb (900 g) neck chops of well-aged lamb or mutton
2 lb (900 g) potatoes, sliced
1 slice of ham, diced (optional)
6 small onions, weighing about 14 oz (400 g), sliced
1½ tsps (7.5 ml) salt
½ tsp (2.5 ml) white pepper
2 tsps (10 ml) mushroom ketchup
¾ pt (425 ml) stock or leftover gravy

Ask the butcher to cut through any long rib bones. Take them off, and use for stock or soup. Place a layer of potatoes in the bottom of a deep flameproof casserole or pot holding about 5 pints (2.8 litres). Cover with chops and a few squares of ham, if using, then with a layer of onions. Sprinkle with seasoning. Repeat the layers until the dish is full, ending with potatoes. Mix the ketchup into the stock or gravy and pour over the dish. Cover tightly, and place over a very low heat. Simmer gently until tender, about 1½ hours for best end or loin chops, 2-2½ hours for middle neck or scrag.

William Kitchiner: The Cook's Oracle, 1836 edition

● Eliza Acton, writing a little later than Dr Kitchiner, omits ham, makes onions optional and doubles the quantity of potatoes, which she says should be boiled to a mash for a real Irish stew. Most other nineteenth-century cooks, however, follow Dr Kitchiner's recipe fairly closely.

CAROTTES NOUVELLES À LA FLAMANDE

In formal Victorian menus, vegetables whether used for garnishing or served as a separate course were almost always sculptured, stuffed or richly sauced – and overcooked. This is a fairly simple recipe.

1¼ lb (600 g) young spring carrots
salt
1 oz (25 g) butter
pepper
a pinch of grated nutmeg
2 pinches of caster sugar
½ tbls (7.5 ml) flour
½ pt (275 ml) white stock
2 egg yolks
2½ fl oz (65 ml) single cream
2 tsps (10 ml) chopped parsley
croutons, to garnish

Wash and scrape the carrots (they should all be one size, if possible), quarter them neatly and parboil them for 10 minutes in salted water. Drain. Melt the butter in a pan, add the carrots, season with salt, pepper, nutmeg and caster sugar. Sprinkle in the flour and toss over the heat for a few minutes. Add the stock, cover the pan tightly and simmer gently for about 20 minutes, stirring occasionally. When the carrots are cooked, beat the egg yolks and cream together then add to the pan, stirring gently until thickened. Pour on to a warm serving dish, sprinkle with parsley and garnish with a few croutons.

Charles Herman Senn: Practical Gastronomy and Culinary Dictionary

---

STEWED OX-KIDNEY

Hardly what we would call a stew today! But it is still good for its original purpose, as a 'plain entrée or side dish for every-day fare'. Notice that even this top-class chef did not scorn bottled sauces.

1-1¼ lb (450-600 g) ox kidney
3 tbls (45 ml) butter
2 oz (50 g) mushrooms, chopped
2 tsps (10 ml) chopped parsley
1 shallot, chopped
salt
pepper
1 tbls (15 ml) flour
2 tsps (10 ml) Harvey's sauce
1 tsp (5 ml) lemon juice
¼ pt (150 ml) beef stock or water
very small squares or triangles of dry toast

Skin and core the kidney, and cut it across into thin rounds. Heat 2 tbls (30 ml) of the butter in a frying pan and sear the kidney slices on both sides briefly; they should still be pink in the centre. Add the mushrooms, parsley and shallot, and toss in the butter until well coated. Add the remaining butter if needed. Season well, then sprinkle in the flour and stir in the Harvey's sauce and the lemon juice. Add the stock or water slowly, and stir over fairly low heat for 4-5 minutes until the shallot is tender and the sauce is almost reduced to a glaze. Add a little more stock if needed. Arrange the toast triangles or squares around a warmed serving dish with the sauced kidney in the centre.

Charles Elmé Francatelli: The Cook's Guide and Housekeeper's and Butler's Assistant

● Harvey's sauce was a popular Victorian condiment. It had been one of the first commercially successful bottled sauces, along with Lazenby's Anchovy Essence; both had been created at the end of the previous century by innkeeper Peter Harvey and his sister Elizabeth Lazenby.

D'ARTOIS OF APRICOT

Both chefs and domestic cooks gave similar recipes for these popular little pastries; Francatelli's is one of the clearest. The only changes in the recipe below are one or two ideas from Victorian cook-books, suggesting, for instance, a size for the d'artois.

1 lb (450 g) puff pastry
apricot jam
1 well-beaten egg mixed with a few
    drops of water
caster sugar

Take one-third of the pastry, and roll it out on a lightly floured surface into an oblong which will just fit on to a baking sheet about 14 x 12 inches (35 x 30 cm) in size. (You could use a standard 14 x 10 inch (35 x 25 cm) Swiss roll tin, turned upside down.) Lay the pastry on the tin. Spread a thick even layer of apricot jam over the pastry to within 1 inch (2.5 cm) of the edge. Brush the edge with beaten egg, using a brush dipped in cold water. Roll out the remaining pastry to fit the first sheet. Lay it over it, and press down the edges to seal.
With the back of a knife, mark the pastry into small oblongs about 3 inches (7.5 cm) long and 1 inch (2.5 cm) wide. Brush evenly all over with egg. Using a small knife, flick up tiny nicks of pastry in rows, making a kind of feather

pattern on each cake. Bake at gas mark 6, 400°F (200°C) for 15-20 minutes.
When risen and gilded, sprinkle evenly with sugar. Return to the oven for 2-3 minutes to melt it, then place under a moderate grill for a moment or two to glaze. Cool and cut into oblongs. To serve, arrange a row in a circle on a doily, place another on top, then another until all are arranged.

Charles Elmé Francatelli: The Cook's Guide and Housekeeper's and Butler's Assistant

● Pastry cream, apple marmalade or any other kind of preserve can be used in the d'artois.

● The d'artois are less fragile if made 1½ inches (3 cm) wide.

Charity food

POOR MEN'S PIES

Nineteenth-century reformers and writers were always conscious that the poor needed help, but generally believed that the best way to give it was to teach them to make the best use of their small resources. Well-meaning ladies and great chefs alike poured out instructive recipes for the wives of city artisans and rural labourers, assuming that they had the means and facilities to use them, and the time and energy to read and act on them. Soyer, who pioneered soup-kitchens for the destitute, created a 'Labourer's Pie' with 4 lb of meat, and long instructions on how to make a well-fitting pastry crust.

Here is a more practical pie where ingredients are concerned, although the author's knowledge of nutrition was nil, and she assumed that all her readers had ovens and fuel to heat them. It is meant to feed 4-6 people.

3 oz (75 g) tapioca
4 oz (100 g) dripping
8 oz (225 g) onions, sliced
3½ lb (1.6 kg) potatoes, sliced
salt
pepper
8 oz (225 g) flour
1 tsp (5 ml) baking powder

Wash the tapioca and soak for 1 hour in cold water. Take 1 oz (25 g) of the dripping and put a little of it at the bottom of a pie dish. Add some onion, tapioca, potatoes and seasoning. Repeat the layers until the onions, tapioca and potatoes have all been used.

Mix the flour, baking powder, some salt and the remaining 3 oz (75 g) dripping, adding enough cold water to make a smooth paste. Roll out and use to make a lid for the pie. Bake at gas mark 6, 400°F (200°C) for about 1¼ hours. Serve hot.

Martha H. Gordon: Cooking for Working Men's Wives

POOR MAN'S SOUP

Soyer's soup-kitchen meal for the starving was widely publicized and copied. Although only slightly more nourishing than other soup handouts which he condemned, it did a lot to jolt the consciences of the affluent who accepted his flamboyant (and sometimes specious) arguments and appeal to them.

2 oz (50 g) dripping
*4 oz (100 g) meat, cut into 1 in
  (2.5 cm) dice*
4 oz (100 g) onions, thinly sliced
*4 oz (100 g) turnips, cut into small dice
  ('the peel will do')*
*2 oz (50 g) leeks, thinly sliced ('the
  green tops will do')*
3 oz (75 g) celery
12 oz (350 g) wholemeal flour
8 oz (225 g) pearl barley
3 oz (75 g) salt
¼ oz (7 g) brown sugar
2 gals (9 L) water

M Soyer's New Food for the Poor: 'I first put two ounces of dripping into a saucepan (capable of holding two gallons of water), with a quarter of a pound of leg of beef without bones cut into squares of about an inch; and two middling-sized onions, peeled and sliced; I then set the saucepan over a coal fire, and stirred the contents round for a few minutes with a wooden (or iron) spoon until fried lightly brown. I had then ready washed the peeling of two turnips, fifteen green leaves or tops of celery, and the green part of two leeks; (the whole of which, I must observe, are always thrown away). Having cut the above vegetables into small pieces, I threw them into the saucepan with the other ingredients, stirring them occasionally over the fire for another ten minutes; then added

A soup kitchen set up for poor Coventry weavers, 1862

one quart of cold water and three quarters of a pound of common flour and half a pound of pearl barley, mixing all well together; I then added seven quarts of hot water, seasoned with three ounces of salt, and a quarter of an ounce of brown sugar, stirred occasionally until boiling, and allowed to simmer very gently for three hours; at the end of which time I found the barley perfectly tender... The above soup has been tasted by numerous noblemen, members of parliament, and several ladies who have lately visited my kitchen department and who have considered it very good and nourishing...

As regards the peelings and ends of vegetables which I use in my receipts, it is a well-known fact, that the exterior of every vegetable, roots in particular, contains more flavour than the interior of it...

It will be perceived that I have omitted all kinds of spice except in those dishes which are intended expressly for them, as I consider they only flatter the appetite and irritate the stomach and make it crave for more food; my object being not to create an appetite but to satisfy it.'

Alexis Soyer: Soyer's Charitable Cookery or the Poor Man's Regenerator

TEA-CUP BREAD PUDDING

Even before Soyer, Francatelli wrote a cookery book 'for the working classes', which like most similar ones mixed good ideas and unpractical nonsense. This comes from the pathetic section of sick room receipts.

'Bruise a piece of stale crumb of bread the size of an egg, in a basin, add four lumps of sugar and a very little grated nutmeg, pour half a gill of boiling milk upon these, stir all well together until the sugar is melted, then add an egg, beat up the whole thoroughly until well mixed; pour the mixture into a buttered tea-cup, tie up in a small cloth... [Francatelli's instructions here become rather muddled.]...boil the pudding for twenty minutes, at least, and as soon as done, turn it out on a plate. This, or any similar light kind of pudding, constitutes safe food for the most delicate.'

Charles Elmé Francatelli: A Plain Cookery Book for the Working Classes

Advertisement for Liebig Company's 'Extract of Meat'. In 1900 the product was renamed 'Oxo'

Twentieth-Century Britain

Gill Corbishley

ttitudes to food and cooking among British people as the twentieth century began varied enormously. 'The rich man in his castle, the poor man at his gate' were words from the hymn *All Things Bright and Beautiful*, written only fifty years earlier.

For the well-to-do food was still exclusively the responsibility of servants. Among the large portion of the population unable to afford servants, the poorer people who lived in the countryside ate better, despite the agricultural depression, than people who lived in towns.

Throughout history people have thought of the times in which they are living as changing – almost invariably into something worse. The nineteenth century had seen enormous developments in industry and empire. People had become so wealthy in such large numbers that they even had time to worry about the squalid and unhealthy lives of the workers in industrial towns. Public Health and Employment Acts had made conditions better by 1900. Publications like *The British Workman* were full of articles about philanthropists such as Dr. Barnardo and the work of the National Society for the Prevention of Cruelty to Children. Yet the differences of quantity and variety of diet between those who produced *The British Workman* and those who attempted to feed themselves on a workman's wage in an industrial town were still more pronounced than the difference in diet between rich and poor had ever been.

Socialist idealists such as William Morris blamed industrialisation for the country's condition. The Arts and Crafts movement sought a return to medieval values, glorifying the image of the healthy, rosy-cheeked country labourer and rejecting machines and factories. But in reality the twentieth century has seen industrial and technological change undreamt of by Morris.

304

THE CHANGING DIET

omparison of food and cooking for rich and poor in 1900 and comparison in the 1990s demonstrates immediately what have been the major changes during the twentieth century. Today the very poorest families have access to a variety and quantity of food which was inconceivable in 1900. Developments in transport, food production and preservation and communication have all contributed to this.

But perhaps the most striking contrast between 1900 and the 1990s is the way in which the differences between food and cooking in rich households and in poor households have been narrowed. There are still obvious differences caused by lack of money, but instant communication, beginning with radio and films and compounded by advertising and television, has led to far greater uniformity of aspiration and appearance in the kitchen than there was in 1900. Just as blue jeans are worn by both rich and poor, burgers and coke are available to everyone.

From the end of the nineteenth century advertisements were making their impact. The 'Liebig Company's Extract of Meat' (renamed 'Oxo' in 1900) showed elegant china and a smartly-dressed cook, while the pictures on posters displayed for Fry's and Terry's chocolates and Peek Frean cakes and biscuits conveyed the message that upper-class and up-to-date people such as the lady cyclist in the Peek Frean advert ate these products. It is interesting that these advertisements have been re-issued in the 1990s as part of the 'nostalgia industry'. Modern advertisements for food items such as bread, butter and cereals exploit that nostalgic feeling. In the cinema people were able for the first time to see the dining-tables and kitchens which were normal for people other than their close neighbours.

In 1927 the British Broadcasting Corporation was established and at the end of that year a book called *Home, Health and Garden* was published which printed the texts of talks ranging from 'Planning an Ideal Kitchen' to national dishes from the West Indies. As more homes became equipped with a wireless, the broadcasters' messages reached thousands more people than the increasing number of cookery books being published could ever hope to do.

But it was the trauma of the Second World War, from 1939 to 1945, which made 'listening in' a national occupation. Eighteen million people listened every day to Charles Hill, 'The Radio Doctor', and learned which foods were good for them and how to cook them. The German sea blockade and the commandeering of food for the troops and those engaged in war work had created all sorts of shortages. The British government also recognised the need to keep the nation healthy. As a result the public was bombarded with help and guidance, including a daily five-minute radio programme 'Kitchen Front', which was on every morning after the eight o'clock news.

The process begun at the turn of the century with the publication of dozens of magazines such as *Home Notes*, all with regular pages of recipes and advice about the home, was expanding and gathering momentum. Although cookery books had been in circulation in Britain since the middle ages, most people's knowledge of food and cooking had been limited to what they ate and saw in the homes of family and friends. Food was treated in different ways in different parts of the country. During the war, families from Canterbury to Chester, rich and poor, in town and country were at the mercy of the Ministry of Food and were plied with recipes which used only carrots, potatoes and dried eggs!

If the spread of the wireless between 1927 and the 1950s had led to a narrowing of the difference in attitudes to food and cooking between different sections of the British population, this effect was quite eclipsed by the impact of television.

By 1953, the year in which Elizabeth II was crowned and in which thousands of people bought their first television in order to watch the coronation ceremony, a book called *Cooking with Harben* by Philip Harben, 'The Television Chef', had already been published. From almonds, anchovies and artichokes (globe) to whitebait, Yorkshire pudding and Zabaglione, Mr Harben passed on to his audience an accumulation of cookery ideas and experience. His fame was equalled by that of Fanny and Johnnie Cradock, who were ready with recipe suggestions for the recently-invented 'teenager' in 1970. News magazine programmes such as 'Nationwide' and 'Town and Around' invariably featured a cookery item during the 1960s and 1970s.

By the 1980s this sprinkle of television advice on food and cooking had become an avalanche. In the 1990s children begin by learning to cook with the 'Blue Peter' programme. Adults can learn how and what to cook from programmes such as 'Food and Drink' and 'The Roux Brothers', but there is also constant information, from both the Department of Health and from programmes such as 'Food File', about food production and healthy eating.

There are still elaborate, expensive meals eaten every day in Britain at the end of the twentieth century, just as there were at the beginning of the century. The rich man may still be in his castle. One major difference is that the poor man at his gate is quite likely to be as knowledgeable as he is about the variety and the processes involved in food and cooking.

In 1970, following a television series, Fanny and Johnie Craddock published a recipe book which included a section called 'A Teenager's Party'

FARMING AND FOOD PRODUCTION

T he final quarter of the nineteenth century had been a difficult time for small farmers, faced with the enclosure of the last vestiges of common land and competition from imports of grain and other food from the Empire. But by 1900 a balance had been achieved and farm owners and tenant farmers alike were enjoying Victorian prosperity. Machinery, for drilling corn, hay-making, reaping, binding and threshing, was in use. Steam engines travelled from farm to farm, pulling their ploughs, or their mole-drain layers, from side to side of the fields on cables.

By the outbreak of the First World War in 1914, the country was dependent on imports for one half of all its food. Seventy-five percent of its bread corn was coming from overseas. By 1915 losses of shipping were causing food shortages. It was not until 1917 that a Food Production Department was built up throughout the country with County Executive Committees vested with powers to order the ploughing and cultivation of fields. Some men were provided from the army to work on this extra cultivation. But they had to be augmented with prisoners of war, schoolboys and women from the Land Army.

Ironically, it was the threat of disaster presented by the Second World War which really revolutionised British farming in the twentieth century. With the experience of shortage during the First World War still a vivid memory, the Government was quick to act. 'Dig for Victory' was the slogan, and the farming population responded magnificently. Nearly six million acres of grassland were ploughed, including Windsor Great Park, which became the largest wheat field in Britain. Crops were grown on the Sussex Downs for the first time since Saxon days. By 1944 food production, in terms of

From a photograph in The British Workman and Home
Monthly Annual *for 1907*

calories, had almost doubled, wheat production had increased
by 90% over its pre-war level and vegetable production by
almost 50%.

Over half of all manual workers kept either allotments or
vegetable gardens. Allotments sprang up in the London
parks – even in the moat at the Tower of London! Pig Clubs
were started up throughout the country because farmers had
turned from animal farming, which must be supported by
imported feed-stuffs which were no longer available, to growing wheat and potatoes.

In 1939 the Government began a system of food rationing
which was not completely dispensed with until 1954. Because
of the changes in food production at home and the scarcity of
imported food, many things which were eaten every day were
almost unobtainable. Ingenious substitutes were made for the
variety of ordinary foods like onions, eggs, cheese, bananas,

tomatoes, sausages, meat, fish, cakes, biscuits, chocolate, apples, oranges and lemons. The war brought its own crop of recipes. Today we admire the invention of the wartime cook – though we are usually only tempted to taste the products of those recipes as a novelty!

For farmers this successful concentration on home agriculture was an unqualified success. The Agricultural Act of 1947, passed by the new Labour Government, was designed to save the farmer from the insecurities of pre-war farming. Since then British farming has been increasingly helped by capital grants, tax concessions and price supports.

While imports of cheap animal-feed from the developing countries were used to produce intensively reared stock, pigs and poultry, a large proportion of grain for bread manufacture was also still imported. In 1973 Britain's entry into the European Economic Community guaranteed more subsidies for farmers, as prices for products were fixed at the Community's headquarters in Brussels. Food imported from countries outside the Community, such as America, Canada and New Zealand was, at the same time, subject to high import duties.

For the first few years after this radical change, the relationship between farmers and the consumer was strained. Post-war expansion, the destruction of hedges and ditches to create 'prairie' fields of corn and the over-enthusiastic use of fertiliser and pesticide now came in for sharp criticism as food prices shot up and stories of milk lakes and butter mountains circulated.

As the century ends, there has been some tempering of these extremes. Production quotas seem to have decreased the size of the surplus food stocks; farmers are being forced to diversify their crops, even to 'set aside' some land from agriculture. At the same time the Green movement has prompted some farms to return to organic farming, without artificial fertilisers and pesticides, and the worst excesses of intensive pig- and chicken-rearing are the subject of constant criticism.

FOOD ADULTERATION

ood adulteration with an eye to profit can be documented from the Middle Ages, when flour was 'extended' by the addition of chalk. The first British Food and Drugs Act was passed in 1860 in order to control additions such as brick dust to cocoa and copper to green pickles. There were still insufficient laws to control the ingredients which were put into the first manufactured foods. Various chemical dyes were used to colour jam, egg powders were made which contained no egg and raspberry juice without a hint of fruit. It was during the Second World War that scientists first began putting back into foods vitamins which the manufacturing process had removed. Bread, for example, was required to contain specified proportions of iron, vitamin B and nicotinic acid, and these regulations still apply today.

During the 1940s great advances were also made in the development of fertilisers and pesticides to help farmers gain a better yield from their crops. Twenty years later people had realised that DDT (dichloro-diphenyl-trichloroethane) could spread through the food chain after killing the insects at which it was aimed, threatening even human beings.

It was also in the 1960s that people became wary of 'additives' to food which might be harmful. Monosodium glutamate, much used in Chinese restaurants, was the first cause of alarm. It was said to cause Kwok's Disease, an allergic reaction. Tests made in 1986 have now cast doubt on this diagnosis. Over the following thirty years scares included cyclamate sweeteners; nitrates and nitrites used as preservatives in bacon and sausages; saccharin sweeteners; tartrazine colouring and fruit preservatives and waxes.

Perhaps it is not surprising that, by 1992, increasing num-

bers of people yearn to eat 'natural', unadulterated fruit, eggs
and vegetables and meat from animals which have not been
fed on and injected with chemicals. Salmonella, to be caught
from chickens and eggs, and Bovine Spongiform Ence-
phalopathy (BSE), the disease which destroys cows' brains and
makes them 'mad', are just two of the threats offered to
people's health by food today.

There are still many gaps in biochemical knowledge, although it is known that chemicals in many of the 'natural'
foods we eat and drink, like oxalic acid in spinach, caffeine in
tea and coffee and carotene in egg yolks and carrots can also
damage the human body. The enormous increase in choice of
food which the century has brought has supplied a whole
range of problems which are irrelevant to the starving and
undernourished.

From a photograph in the Market Strand, Falmouth, Cornwall, 1905

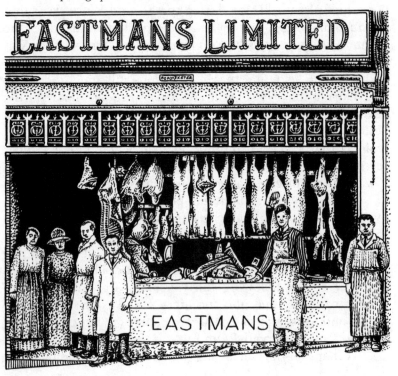

TWENTIETH-CENTURY SHOPPING

The High Street in even the smallest town in the 1990s looks very different from the way it looked a hundred years earlier.

The motor car is responsible for a great many of the changes, both directly and indirectly. Roads have been widened and decorated with yellow lines in many former High Streets to make room for the ubiquitous car, but most shops have also been enlarged and altered out of all recognition to provide selling space for the enormous range of goods which modern transport now supplies everywhere.

Advances in transport and manufacture of food were well under way by 1900. Canning and freezing were possible and margarine had been invented in the late 1860s. It was possible to bring goods close to their destination by rail. But a typical street scene would still have shown many age-old features. Shops were small and specialised, the butcher's adorned with hanging carcasses, the grocer's full of anonymous sacks and packages from which tea, sugar, flour and bacon must be taken and weighed out in the correct measure. But things were ready to change. By 1900 numerous foodshops over the whole country were part of multiple-ownership chains. John Sainsbury opened his first shop in Drury Lane in 1869, the Maypole Dairy was founded in 1819 and taken over by the Home and Colonial in 1924. Liptons was established in Glasgow in 1871. By 1900 each of these retailers owned many branches in different parts of the country. The variety of goods which could be offered for sale was increasing all the time, as items such as tinned sardines and salmon, condensed milk and bananas became available. From the early part of the century onwards the development of motor-driven transport meant that shopkeepers were increasingly able to get goods on sale quickly.

With a shop full of goods, the next obvious step was to find methods of selling as much as possible. There was no restriction on shop hours, apart from that on Sunday opening, and for the Sainsbury branch in Kingsland High Street in east London this meant opening at 7.30 am every day and closing at 9.15 pm from Monday to Thursday, 10.45 pm on Fridays and at midnight on Saturdays. After closing, many shop salesmen in working-class areas would take the empty beer tankards left on their counters back to the pubs. The beginning of the week was always slack, but then time could be spent making up the blue bags for sugar and weighing and parcelling out goods ready for sale.

It was towards the end of the 1920s that more and more proprietary brands began to come into the shops and Sainsbury branches created separate grocery departments and increased the range of own-label groceries. At this time there were still 80,000 independent grocers, 20% of which were part of a chain. Now the advertising industry was able to make its mark in food retailing, promoting Kellogg's cornflakes, Quaker oats, Horlicks, Ovaltine, John West salmon and Heinz (57 Varieties) baked beans, among others, throughout the 1930s. Even the lack of supplies during the Second World War was turned to good account, as each manufacturer promised to 'be back' as soon as supplies and rationing allowed.

The founder of another of today's giant supermarket chains, Jack Cohen, was the first shop owner in Britain to introduce a revolutionary change in shopping. He launched Tesco self-service stores in 1947. Wages had begun rising sharply after the war, all groceries could now be obtained pre-packaged (although it was still possible to buy them loose as well) and he believed it would be profitable to follow the self-service model introduced in America in the 1930s. For a few years Tesco Stores had little success but in 1950 twenty new stores were bought and converted to supermarkets and business continued to grow until, in the last decade of the century, shops have become so big that they are invariably located in

A London milkman in the 1940s, from a photograph

purpose-built retail parks, which are completely outside the town.

Important scientific breakthroughs were, of course, as necessary to the shopping revolution as the motor-car and the power of advertising. Clarence Birdseye set up his first fish freezing plant in New York in 1923. Although it had been possible to transport frozen goods for many years, it was his method of quick-freezing which made the production of frozen fish, peas and, later, thousands of other delicacies possible. Canned goods have continued to sell well but the development of foil and film-based packaging materials has meant that an ever-widening range of goods is available for sale in food shops. In 1992 air freight brings chilled exotic fruit and vegetables into every town's supermarket several times a week. The season for eating peas disappeared from the calendar in the 1960s and by the 1990s even strawberries and new potatoes could be produced which were almost indistinguishable from their 'natural' seasonal equivalents.

IN THE KITCHEN

he nostalgia industry has made the picture of a nineteenth-century kitchen, dominated by its range in more well-to-do houses and built around table and fireplace in poorer ones, familiar to most people at the end of the twentieth century. By 1900 one in four houses with gas had a cooker, but these were of course all in towns. Other signs of the approaching revolution were refrigerators, introduced in about 1890. Blocks of ice were kept in an insulated cupboard at the top and cooled food in the other compartments. Labour-saving gadgets included mincers, potato-peelers, apple-corers and knife-sharpeners. The first electric cookers were manufactured with hot-plates made with coiled wires inside, which did not last long. In 1900 an electric kettle was made, with its element outside.

It was not until the early 1930s that problems of the means of electrical supply and production were sufficiently overcome to allow the possibility of the mass production of electric kitchen appliances.

As new appliances began to be installed in the majority of kitchens, two themes predominated. The first was the escape from drudgery: labour saving devices! An Electrical Development Association pamphlet issued in 1925 gave this promise:

> Indeed, Electricity comes as a timely solution of the servant and other problems, which threatened to disturb that most potent factor in civilisation – THE HOME; Electricity provides the modern housewife with a perfect servant – clean, silent, economical. What used to be the labour (hard labour) of hours is now accomplished almost without effort in a matter of minutes.

A 'modern' kitchen of 1927 from The Electrical Age for Women: the Official Journal of the Electrical Association for Women, *quoted in* A Woman's Work is Never Done *by Caroline Davidson*

It is hard to deny that this glowing picture does contain a degree of truth. A survey by the Electrical Association of Women in 1934 found that the jobs of tending to lamps, cooking stoves, fires, washing, ironing and cleaning which took 26 hours per week without electricity were reduced to 7 hours per week with the help of electricity. The fresh-smelling, shiny-surfaced kitchen and instant hot meals which are the norm in late twentieth-century Britain are not achieved by hours of brushing, scrubbing and polishing, peeling, chopping, frying and boiling but with electric cleaners, chemical air fresheners and surface sprays and ready-made meals.

All those inventions freed time for and made possible the second important change in the kitchen during this century: the attempt to produce absolute cleanliness and hygiene.

Early kitchen machinery, used by a tiny minority of rich people's servants, was heavy and cumbersome. The first gas and electric stoves looked like smaller versions of cast-iron ranges and the furniture in kitchens was still wooden or upholstered. Mass production coincided with rapid developments in car and aeroplane manufacture and with the Rural Water Supplies Act in 1934, after which two thousand parishes were supplied with piped water within ten years. Scientists were also finding more proof of the importance of hygiene for health. The result of all these influences was the ideal of the modern, streamlined, shining white, fully fitted kitchen.

The frozen food industry, and therefore the domestic freezer, did not exist until the second half of the twentieth century. Its arrival, the development of the microwave oven from 1968 onwards, and the invention of polythene, tinfoil and clingfilm has made the ideal of a kitchen free from the brutish realities of muddy vegetables and dead animal carcasses quite feasible.

An electric cooker from the early 1920s

EATING IN

t the beginning of the twentieth century it is immediately obvious is that nobody was eating deep-fried foods which had been manufactured and processed before they were bought. By 1900 self-raising flour, yeast and baking powder were available to be bought. Cheese, jelly, custard and blancmange, sauces and pickles, margarine and dried vegetables such as peas and lentils were also being processed in the new 'garden factories'. Porridge had become popular as part of the middle-class breakfast towards the end of the nineteenth century and, by the 1920s, Mr Kellogg's cornflakes and the Shredded Wheat Company's product from their new factory at Welwyn Garden City were also appearing on breakfast tables. A combination of convenience and advertising has kept cereals continuously popular ever since. Chocolate, which first appeared in its solid form in 1866, has increased in quantity and diversity as people were increasingly able to afford to buy it.

As in most other aspects of British life, the Second World War provides a convenient watershed in the history of twentieth-century food. 'Before the War' there were no wrapped, sliced loaves, no sugar-coated cereals, no instant desserts or instant coffee. Rationing ended in 1954 and ten years later those items were all commonplace. The refinement of freezing techniques, followed by 'freeze-drying' and vacuum-sealing coupled with the earnest efforts of importers to obtain exotic raw materials and exotic dishes from all over the world has led to the bewildering choice of menu offered to supermarket shoppers and television viewers today.

The rationing of almost all foodstuffs during the Second World War provides an interesting fixed point for comparison with a modern diet. Amounts allowed varied between 1940 and 1954 but for one week were approximately those listed here:

Milk – 3 pints, sugar – 225 gm (8 oz), butter – 50 gm (2 oz), margarine – 100 gm (4 oz), cooking fat 85 gm (3 oz), cheese – 85 gm (3 oz), bacon – 100 gm (4 oz), meat – to the value of 1s 2d (2d had to be spent on corned beef), eggs – 1 (if available) and 1 packet of dried eggs per month, sweets – 60 gm (2.1 oz), jam – 50 gm (2 oz), tea – 50 gm (2 oz).

In their sixty-fifth anniversary magazine published in May 1989, the Good Housekeeping Institute concluded that general food trends during those years showed people eating not so much beef, lamb and fish but more poultry, pork and eggs than they had fifty years previously. They found that less bread was eaten, but more pasta, rice and breakfast cereals; less butter, margarine, lard and whole milk, but more cheese, low-fat and dairy spreads and skimmed milk; fewer potatoes but more vegetables and less sugar and preserves but more alcohol!

No other food can equal Quaker Oats in richness and delicacy of flavour. It is the food for the man who swings a hammer — or for the man who wields a pen.

Quaker Oats is truly economical, because there is more delicious eating and more nourishment in a pound of Quaker Oats than in an equal weight of any other food.

Quaker Oats Cookers are Free. SEND FOR DETAILS.

Our Consumers' Benefit Plan will help you save money on hundreds of things you need. Send for Catalogue.

Quaker Oats

11-12 FINSBURY SQUARE, LONDON, E.C.

An advertisement from 1904

Nutrition – Eating To Live Or Living To Eat

lthough previous generations had known that food is essential to life, it was not until the very beginning of the twentieth century that scientists discovered that certain foods, and certain parts of food, such as the outer covering of rice and wheatgerm in bread, contained elements necessary to keep people healthy.

After doctors had realised, during the Boer War and the First World War, that almost half the male population called up to enlist in the army were not in good enough health to serve, efforts were made during the 1930s to redress the balance. The School Medical Officer for Glossop designed a free school meal to supply children suffering from malnutrition with elements missing from their home food. The Glossop Health Sandwich consisted of:

85 gm (3 oz) wholemeal bread

21 gm (¾ oz) butter or vitaminised margarine

21 gm (¾ oz) salad; mustard and cress, or watercress, or lettuce or tomato or carrot

42.5 gm (1½ oz) cheese, or salmon, or herring, or sardine or liver

6 gm (3/16 oz) dried brewers' yeast

To accompany the sandwich was 1 pint of milk and 1 orange, when obtainable; if no fruit 7 gm (¼ oz) chopped parsley was included in the sandwich filling.

By the time the Second World War began, the nation's health, both on the battlefield and at home, had become a Government priority. Rationing provided a good opportunity to redistribute vital foodstuffs, like milk, eggs and orange-juice, to the fighting men, mothers and babies who needed them most.

As shortages became a memory and the country moved into the 'Swinging Sixties', the concept of eating for health ceased to be quite so mainstream. Coffee-Bars were booming (the first espresso coffee machine was imported in 1952) and self-service restaurants selling fried food were springing up all over the country. Two minorities remained obsessed with the content of the food they ate – the slimmers and those who chose to live an 'alternative' life in communes, often guided by a 'guru' from an Eastern country and eating food such as brown rice, lentils and vegetables.

Thirty years later both these attitudes have become pre-occupations for many thousands of people. There are no longer many people living in communes but a survey of 2,000 consumers by the *Independent* newspaper in 1986 reflected a strong interest in 'healthy eating'. Of the people interviewed 63% said they had increased their fruit and vegetable intake, many had changed from white bread to brown, 33% said they were eating more fish and most said they were eating more fibre and less meat. Strangely, market statistics recorded at the same time showed that fruit and vegetable consumption had actually fallen in the previous five years and that the nation was eating more meat per head than it had done ten years earlier!

'An apple a day keeps the doctor away' is still an acknowledged truth at the end of the twentieth century, but children are far more likely to eat a daily packet of crisps than to eat a daily apple.

In the 1990s, however unwholesome the food we eat may be, the British nation has information constantly presented to it about the advisability, and the virtue, of eating with discretion in order to remain slim and healthy. Particular elements in foods have been blamed for causing the diseases of civilisation, cancers, thrombosis and heart disease.

But it might be argued that both healthy food and slimming are more useful today to manufacturers and advertisers as a means of selling more food than they are to the British public as a whole.

Meanwhile a Gallup Poll to discover the Briton's perfect meal found, in 1947, that it was tomato soup, sole, roast chicken with roast potatoes, peas and sprouts, trifle and cream, cheese and biscuits, coffee and wine. And in 1986? The answer to the same question was vegetable soup, prawn cocktail, steak with chips, peas, carrots and salad, gateau, cheese and biscuits, coffee and wine.

A gas cooker from 1974 (left) and an electric cooker from the 1958 Belling catalogue

EATING OUT

world in which a large proportion of the population never ate a meal outside their own home seems remote from life in the 1990s. But a hundred years ago restaurants were only available to limited numbers and categories of people. Chop-houses, where a middle-income man could eat his lunch, existed, and there had, of course, been facilities for the rich to eat in hotels and inns for centuries. The poor made do with take-away food from street vendors, eel and pie shops and the occasional sprat supper. The first fish and chip shops were opened around 1870, when it became possible to keep fish frozen and transport it away from the coast.

The coming of the railways meant that Tea Rooms began to be provided, where gentlemen and ladies could eat out. By the turn of the century, both Lyons and the ABC ran chains of tea rooms, while many smaller concerns also sprang up.

What the railways had done for tea rooms, the motor-car did for coaching inns. Between the two world wars the Bright Young Things flocked to road-houses to eat and drink. During and immediately after the Second World War restaurants, struggling with their ration 'points', were generally used more from necessity than as a luxury.

But from the late 1950s onwards several things began to happen which brought a dramatic change in the number and variety of restaurants.

First came a flood of refugees from Communist China. By the mid 1960s every medium-sized town in Britain had its Chinese restaurant. They provided excitingly original food cheaply and unpretentiously. The growing student population and the teenage workforce with spare money for luxuries could

Thorogood's 'Japanese Tea Rooms' in Clacton, c.1903, from a photograph. Courtesy of Norman Jacobs

enjoy this new kind of food without having to worry about wearing the right clothes for the restaurant or which knife and fork to use.

Young people also provided the custom for milk bars, coffee bars and cafeterias such as Steak Express and The Golden Egg. Less adventurous family parties were also looking for alternatives to home cooking and these were soon provided by places like the Quality Inn, the Chicken Inn and, after 1965, by Pizza Express, followed by Pizzaland and Pizza Hut. Burger bars, like Wimpy, MacDonalds and Burger King, were direct competition for restaurants serving fried chicken or pizzas. By 1992 public distaste for red meat and fatty foods has prompted MacDonalds to diversify: now they too are selling pizzas.

It is once again people's increasing mobility which is cited as the reason for their interest in foreign food and the enormous popularity of foreign restaurants in Britain since the 1970s. Cheap air travel and foreign holidays have created a demand for a great variety of food and drink in British restaurants.

Soho, in London, has been a home for refugees and expatriates from France, Russia, Hungary, Greece and Italy who have been running restaurants there since the early years of this century. Now they have been joined by Turkish, Mexican, Malaysian, Chinese, African, Lebanese and Indian restauranteurs. In smaller towns the Indian restaurant first followed the pattern set by Chinese immigrants a few years earlier. By employing family members and staying open late the restaurants were able to offer cheap, tasty food when nothing else was available. In the last ten years a far more varied and interesting range of food has been offered in many Chinese and Indian restaurants, as they have become a more up-market option.

An interesting development in restaurants during the 1980s was begun by Paul Bocuse, a French chef. His 'nouvelle cuisine' and 'cuisine minceur' was both very popular and very expensive. His

Akbar Tandoori
Takeaway

TAKE AWAY MENU

A take-away menu from 1992

326

own doctrine was: 'Never cut corners, but look for the very finest meat, vegetables and so on ... one of the tenets of la nouvelle cuisine is that the food must keep its own taste, making the most of its original flavour. Previously in French cooking there was a concern with ostentatious effect which had little to do with cooking.'

This led to the exquisite presentation of small portions of food, which failed to find popularity with a general public who wished, at least, to feel full for their money. Although it no longer seems possible to find a restaurant which still calls what it serves 'nouvelle cuisine', it did serve to encourage a trend towards fresher ingredients and better cooking in some sorts of restaurant.

The only style of restaurant it is rather difficult to find among the thousands which exist at the end of the twentieth century is one which is typically English. It is still possible to find a chop-house, though only the grandest sort, in London and there is still the odd eel and pie shop in existence, but these are a tiny minority. In 1992 it is the Happy Eater which, together with the Little Chef and Trusthouse Forte, supplies a range of sandwiches, salads, burgers, jacket-potatoes, fried foods and sweets to the traveller, which shows the fastest growth in sales since 1986 (79%). Fast Food is the name given to this sort of catering – its nationality is not specific and its popularity seems limitless.

SOMETHING
TO DRINK

'I say, I hope there'll be something to drink tonight. The wine outlook becomes increasingly desperate since France went. One didn't expect to have to fight a war on an occasional half-pint of bitter, and lucky if you find that.'

The Soldier's Art, Anthony Powell 1966

All sorts of drinks, tea and Horlicks as well as the wine mentioned by Anthony Powell, became luxury items during the Second World War because of the blockade of shipping and the rationing system.

The story of what people were drinking from 1900 onwards, like the story of food, is one of steady expansion of both volume and diversity of manufactured products which was only briefly interrupted by the world wars. At the beginning of the century poorer people drank tea or home-brewed beer almost exclusively. Barley water and fruit syrups were made at home for invalids and children. For the more well-to-do it was becoming possible to buy commercially produced beer and beverages in ever-greater variety.

The commercial beer trade was encouraged when duties on beer and glass were repealed in the 1830s and by 1880 Whitbread's beer was so popular that the labels carried the request: 'When empty please destroy the label'. The temptation to re-sell the bottle full of home-brew was obviously widespread!

Fizzy drinks, kept bubbly by delightful devices such as the Hamilton cap, where the bottle was stored on its side to keep the cork moist, and the Codd, with its marble held tight against the rubber ring by gas pressure, were a rare treat for English children in 1900. Soda-water was originally so named because sodium bicarbonate was used to make it fizzy, but it then became a general title for many highly-flavoured American drinks. Flavours like sarsaparilla (an extract from the dried roots of a Jamaican shrub) and orgeat (a mixture of barley or almond extract with orange-flower water) are now almost forgotten. The simpler flavours of orange and lemon dominated the fruit squashes, which were ubiquitous in the 1950s, 60s and 70s.

Changes in drinking habits, for soft drinks at least, followed the 'healthy eating' doctrines of the 1980s. Squashes, with their high sugar content and synthetic colourings, became less popular and packaging made pure fruit juice, treated to retain a long-life and with all-natural sugar content, an attractive alternative. Mineral waters remain as popular as ever and are consumed in ever-greater quantities, although many people prefer to buy 'traditional', cloudy lemonade,

Bank holiday crowd on Hampstead Heath, London, from a 1902 photograph

ginger-beer with nineteenth-century pictures on the cans and flavours such as dandelion-and-burdock which give a spurious impression of nutritive value. In the 1990s it is also possible to buy an infinite variety of 'natural', 'healthy' spa waters to which only bubbles, preservatives and a twist of flavouring have been added!

But the most popular fizzy drink in Britain at the end of the twentieth century must be Coca-Cola. It is no longer made from the products of the addictive cola plant. What it is made from is a closely-guarded secret. Factories all over the world, constructed in exactly the same way, are sent Coca-Cola ingredients from America in steel drums and make up the drink to be sold in their own country. In the 1880s Coca-Cola was first marketed as a cure for headaches and the distinctively-shaped bottle was introduced in 1915. Cans, which appeared in the 1950s, have almost completely replaced the bottle in this country, although they can still be bought in many other countries. 'Coke' has become more than just a drink: it is also a design icon and cultural statement.

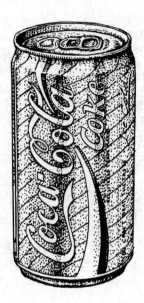

Coca-cola cans appeared in the 1950s

Benefit to health has always been an advertising claim for the other new sorts of drinks which were appearing at the beginning of this century. Fry, Cadbury and Rowntree all produced cocoa drinks in the second half of the nineteenth century. These were quickly rivalled by Horlicks, which was patented in Chicago in 1883 and produced in Slough in 1906, and Ovaltine from the British Ovaltine Company, which was formed in 1909. A milky drink before retiring to bed was promoted as the *only* method of ensuring adequate, healthy rest. The continuing presence of all these products on sale demonstrates their appeal to large numbers of people.

Perhaps the story of coffee through the twentieth century is an accurate reflection of the sorts of change which have occurred. At the beginning of the century only a small number of better-off people drank coffee. Beans were bought, roasted and ground at home on the whole, although Thomas Lipton had already begun to sell packages of ready-ground coffee in his shops. Coffee essence had also been sold since the 1850s, and the arrival of Camp coffee in 1885 eventually made sales higher than those of real coffee. The invention of instant coffee, which was first sold in England in 1939, completely changed the market; Camp was relegated to cake-making and the nation began to drink coffee by the gallon.

The next change, prompted by the move from 'synthetic' to 'real' in people's minds and by the development of vacuum-sealed ground coffee and a variety of efficient kitchen machinery for making coffee at reasonable prices, was a return to coffee without additives which began in the 1980s. Today, as with most other things we eat and drink, there is a bewildering range of choice: instant, filter, espresso, percolator, de-caffeinated, with chicory, with chocolate! Today, it seems, we can consume almost anything, as long as we can afford to buy it.

A Hamilton bottle for mineral waters

RECIPES

These recipes have been chosen from the thousands printed and circulated since 1900 in order to demonstrate the most important changes in food and cooking through the century.

Traditional Tastes: Recipes from before the Second World War

SHEEP'S HEAD SOUP

This is a nourishing soup, and the head itself can be served afterwards for the meat course. Clean the head and chop it in half, take out the brains; the end of the nostril should be chopped away altogether, on account of the mucus. Place the head in three quarts of cold water, with a little salt, 12 leeks cut in small pieces, and a little carrot and turnip; when it has gently simmered three hours remove the meat and keep it hot. Thicken the soup with 3 oz of fine Florador*, previously wetted with a little milk or water; this should be boiled in the soup, from fifteen to twenty minutes; it is then ready for serving. The scum which rises during the preparation must be carefully removed with a wooden spoon; no straining is required. If desired clear, omit the Florador.

To serve the head, make a nice thick parsley or sharp sauce, and pour over it in the dish. The brains should be boiled separately tied up in muslin, and placed in boiling water; they will take about twenty minutes to cook, and should then be chopped with a leaf or two of sage, and some pepper and salt. Serve on a separate dish, with the sheep's tongue in the middle.
* use plain flour
Vera: Middle-Class Cookery, c.1900

TASTY AND CHEAP

1 Fresh Haddock (about 2 lb, 900 g)
3 fresh herrings
2 eggs
1 small teacup of breadcrumbs, or broken pieces of any dry biscuits, cream crackers or thin lunch pounded into crumbs
4 or 5 spring onions

small sprig of parsley
saltspoonful of salt
shake of pepper

Have the large bone taken out of the fish, and as many of the small ones as possible. Have the fish thoroughly clean and cut into convenient pieces, and put all through the mincer. Chop the onion and parsley finely, and add the minced fish; add salt and pepper, now add 1 egg and white of the other, and mix all together very thoroughly with a wooden spoon, and make the mixture into balls about the size of an egg.

Have some boiling water ready and put the fish balls in, with just enough water to cover the fish. Sprinkle a little salt and pepper over, and allow to boil 30 minutes. Take off the gas and allow to cool. Now beat the remaining yolk of egg, and add to contents of saucepan, put over gas for a few minutes to thicken the gravy. This dish can be eaten hot with boiled potatoes for dinner, or is delicious when cold.

Daily Express Prize Recipes For Fish Cookery, c.1925

RISSOLES OF GAME

8 oz (250 g) any cold game
4 oz (100 g) cooked ham or bacon
one truffle cut in dice
6 mushrooms
5 or 6 tbls (80 ml) of sauce or thick
  gravy
8 oz (250 g) shortcrust pastry
1 egg beaten
breadcrumbs or vermicelli
salt
pepper

Remove all skin and bone, chop meat and ham finely and add mushrooms and truffle. Add enough sauce to moisten, shape into balls the size of large chestnuts. Roll out pastry thinly. Cut out circles.

Lay a ball of mixture on each round of pastry. Brush round edges with a little cold water, fold one half over the other and press edges together. Brush each one with beaten egg. Cover with breadcrumbs or vermicelli, broken small. Fry each one in hot fat until golden brown.

Mrs J. M. Pile, Great Oakley, 1911

'Over the Kitchen Fire' was a regular cookery column in
the magazine Home Notes

FIG PUDDING

8 oz (250 g) dried figs (sliced)
4 oz (125 g) moist sugar
6 oz (175 g) chopped suet
4 oz (125 g) fine white breadcrumbs
4 oz (125 g) flour
a pinch of salt
a saltspoonful of grated nutmeg
two beaten eggs
half a gill of milk

Mix the dry ingredients thoroughly, then moisten with the eggs and milk; pour into a buttered basin, tie down with a pudding cloth, and boil for two hours and a half.
The Smallholder magazine, 1913

*BATTENBURG CAKE

Foundations:
6 oz (175 g) margarine
6 oz (175 g) sugar
6 oz (175 g) flour
3 eggs
little lemon rind
½ tsp baking powder
carmine
Almond Paste:
5 oz (150 g) ground almonds
5 oz (150 g) icing sugar
5 oz (150 g) castor sugar
flavouring
1 egg (about)
jam, butter icing or royal icing

Cream the butter and sugar, add beaten egg slowly; sift in flour and baking powder, add lemon rind; mix well. Put half the mixture into flat dripping-tin, colour the other half pink, and bake in a similar tin. Bake in moderate oven about 30 minutes; when cold; cut into strips about 1½ inches square. Spread the outside of each strip with jam, place a white and pink one, then on top a pink and white strip. Roll out almond paste, wrap neatly round the four strips, make even sides, trim the ends, decorate top with coloured icing or royal icing. Method for Almond Paste: Mix almonds, sieved icing sugar, and castor sugar, add flavouring top the egg, mix all to a very stiff paste.
*Battenburg was the original name of the Mountbatten family.
Lindsay and Mottram: Manual of Modern Cooking, 1927

BOSTON CREAM

The whites of two eggs
1 lb (450 g) sugar
1 quart cold water
1 oz (25 g) tartaric acid
six drops of essence of lemon

Put the sugar and water into a pan, boil fast for half an hour. Strain through fine muslin. Allow it to stand until cold, and then add the acid crushed to powder and essence of lemon. Beat the whites to a stiff froth on a plate, and stir well together until all is dissolved. Pour into bottles. Will keep two or three months.

To make a drink: Put two large tablespoonfuls into a glass, fill to within an inch of the top with cold water, stir in as much carbonate of soda as will lie on a sixpence; it is ready for drinking when it froths up to the top.
The Smallholder magazine, 1913

Reason for Change:
The Second World War

LIQUID MILK

To prepare liquid milk – from dried milk

3 tbls (50 g) dried milk
2 breakfastcups water

Mix the dried milk with 2 tablespoons of the water and beat very hard with a wooden spoon or a whisk until smooth. Add the rest of the water gradually and stir or whisk well.
HMSO: Food from Overseas, 1941

COD PANCAKES

½ lb (225 g) salt cod cooked and flaked in small pieces
1 level tbls (15 ml) chopped parsley
salt and pepper

2 level tbls (30 ml) mixed herbs
6 oz (175 g) mashed carrots

Batter:
4 oz (125 g) flour
1 level tbls (15 ml) dried egg (dry)
2 level tsps (5 ml) baking powder
salt
½ pt (300 ml) water
(Makes four helpings)

Make the batter by mixing together all the dry ingredients, adding sufficient water to make a stiff batter. Beat well and add the remainder of the water. Add to the batter the flaked cod, parsley, seasoning, herbs and carrots. Melt some fat in a pan and when smoking hot drop in large spoonfuls of mixture. Brown the pancakes on one side then turn over and brown the other.
Ministry of Food Pamphlet

TWO MINUTE SOUP

4 tbls (60 ml) dried milk
2 breakfastcups cold water
1 tsp (5 ml) vegetable or meat extract
or
2 tbls (30 ml) chopped parsley or
pinch of salt

Mix milk as above. Bring to boil and stir in the extract or parsley and salt.
HMSO: Food from Overseas, 1941

'LORD WOOLTON PIE'

5 to 6 persons

Take 1 lb each of diced potatoes, cauliflower, swedes and carrots, three or four spring onions, if possible one teaspoonful of vegetable extract and one tablespoonful of oatmeal. Cook all together for 10 mins, with just enough water to cover. Stir occasionally to prevent the mixture from sticking. Allow to cool; put into a pie dish, sprinkle with chopped parsley, and cover with a crust of potatoes or wholemeal pastry. Bake in a moderate oven until the pastry is nicely brown and serve hot with a brown gravy.
Ministry of Food, 1940

ORANGE FLAVOUR WHIP

1 lb (450 g) stewed or bottled plums
2 ½ level tbls (35 ml) dried milk
3 level tbls (45 ml) of new sweet
marmalade

Strain the plums and keep the juice for a sauce or jelly. Mash the plums and mix with the milk and marmalade. Beat well. Serve in individual dishes topped with marmalade or custard.

Other delicious combinations are apples and plum jam; rhubarb and raspberry jam – and you can think of many others. When you use a somewhat colourless fruit it is best to combine it with a red one.

These fruit whips are very easy to make and are favourites at children's parties.
Ministry of Food Pamphlet, 1945

Wartime Food Facts *from the Ministry of Food*

336

PLAIN WHEATMEAL CAKE

4 tbls (60 ml) N.W. flour
4 tbls (60 ml) white flour
1 ½ tbls (20 ml) sugar
1 ½ tbls (20 ml) chopped dates or any
* other dried fruit*
1 tsp (5 ml) spice
1 tbls (15 ml) dried milk
1 medium carrot (grated)
1 tbls (15 ml) dripping, cooking fat or
* margarine*
1 tbls (15 ml) treacle or syrup
1 ½ tsp (7.5 ml) baking powder
salt

Rub the fat into the flour. Add the rest of the ingredients and mix to a dropping consistency with water. Put into a greased or lined baking tin and bake in a moderate oven for 1 ½ to 2 hours.
HMSO: Food from Overseas, 1941

COCOA WITH DRIED MILK

3 tbls (45 ml) dried milk
2 breakfastcups water
cocoa powder

Mix the milk powder with the cocoa powder; stir in the boiling water gradually; boil one minute.
HMSO: Food from Overseas, 1941

Wind of Change:
1950s–1970s

SHELLFISH AND GRAPEFRUIT SALAD

This sounds an unusual combination, but when prepared it is a real palate tickler.

1 pt (575 ml) picked prawns or other
* shellfish*
1 grapefruit
¼ cucumber
lettuce and tomato for salad
French dressing as required

Prepare the lettuce and arrange in a salad bowl with the tomatoes. Peel grapefruit removing pith, pips, and skin from the segments and put into a bowl with the juice. Peel the cucumber and cut into dice. Add cucumber and shellfish to the grapefruit, and stir in gently sufficient dressing.

Pile the mixture into the centre of the salad bowl, and garnish with a few prawns. Serve at once.
Zena Skinner: Town and Around Recipes, 1965

DUCK IN ORANGE SAUCE

4–6 people

A duck, unless specially fattened for the table, is usually a disappointing bird to carve; the yield is markedly less than from a chicken of the same weight. This recipe is designed to make the bird go further by enrobing it in a sauce that is rich and luscious. The result is a somewhat sumptuous dish, not to be attempted by those who prefer austerity.

*1 duck; a wild duck would do
  particularly well in this recipe*
*2 oranges, or other citrus fruits in this
  order of preference: Seville oranges,
  grapefruit (1 enough), sweet
  oranges, lemons, tangerines (4
  would be needed)*
1 large onion
1 large carrot
2 bay leaves
1 tbls (15 ml) flour
*4 oz (125 g) mushrooms (omit if
  unprocurable),*
*1 glass (4 fl oz, 125 ml) port or
  sherry – Empire wine will do
  admirably, or, failing that, use 1 pt
  of rough cider in a manner to be
  described later*

Two hours before dinner put the trussed duck in a slow oven (gas oven mark 2; electric 300°F). Do not put it in a baking tin of fat, but let it stand on the grid shelf with a baking tin on the shelf below to catch the fat that will drip from the bird in liberal measure. Put the giblets on to boil with half the onion, half the carrot, the bay leaves, the juice and rinds of the oranges, water to cover. If you are unable to use port or sherry, let the covering liquid be 1 pint cider made up to quantity with water. Cook this stock gently for 1 hour. Strain, and make up (or reduce by rapid boiling in an open pan) the liquid to 1 pint. If you have a pressure cooker you can make the stock in a quicker and simpler way; put the giblets, etc, in the pressure cooker with exactly 1 pint water (or cider, if that is what you are using) for 15 minutes. About 1 hour before dinner start making the sauce. Chop the remaining onion and carrot as finely as possible. Into a heavy saucepan, or a frying pan if you are more used to working that way, measure not more than 2 oz of the fat that has dripped from the duck – there should be plenty by now. Make this fat hot in the pan and in it fry the finely chopped onion and carrot until they are browned. Stir in the 1 oz of flour and cook till that too begins to brown. Now add the stock gradually, stirring well, and bring it up to boiling point so that it thickens. Add the wine and the stalks of the mushrooms; simmer for 10 minutes. Adjust the seasoning and colour the sauce with gravy browning if it looks pale.

About ½ hour before dinner remove the baking tin from the oven and from it drain every particle of fat – a most valuable bonus. Put the duck – nearly cooked by now – into the empty tin and pour the sauce right over it, see that it is all covered. Lay the mushroom tops, whole and washed, but not peeled, along the breast of the bird in a neat and decorative manner. Put it into the oven for another half hour's cooking. Soon the coating sauce will dry on the bird: spoon some more sauce over it to give it a fresh coat. Repeat this several times. Ten minutes before time, put the duck into a dish fit for the table, and put it into the lowest part of the oven to keep it hot. Pour the sauce from the baking tin through a strainer into a cold basin. Let it stand for 5 minutes, then skim off the top layer to remove all fat. (Set this aside for clarifying later – another little bonus.) Return the sauce to the saucepan and re-heat, beating well to work in any fat there may still be, and send it to the table separately in a sauce boat.

Although it has taken some time to give this recipe in detail (many of the instructions will be superfluous to advanced cooks), it is really not at all difficult. The achieving of it will give you great satisfaction, and the eating of it will give you a passing glimpse of that better time which still seems so far away.

Philip Harben: Cooking with Harben, 1953

FRENCH ONION SOUP

Quantities for six people:

2 tbls (30 ml) butter
2 tbls (30 ml) oil
1 ½ lb (700 g) onions, thinly sliced
2 cloves of garlic, crushed
½ tsp granulated sugar
2 pt (1.1 l) good beef stock
½ pt (275 ml) dry white wine
6 slices French bread
8 oz (250 g) Gruyère cheese
salt and freshly milled black pepper

Heat the butter and oil together in a large saucepan. Stir in the sliced onions, garlic and sugar and cook over a fairly low heat for about 30 minutes, or until the base of the pan is covered with a nutty brown, caramelized film (this browning process is important as it helps the colour of the resulting soup, and also helps considerably with the flavour). Now pour on the stock and wine, bring the soup to the boil, cover and simmer gently for about an hour.

Then taste and season the soup with salt and freshly milled black pepper (and if you really need a stomach-warmer add a

339

tablespoon or two of brandy). Now toast the slices of French bread and spread them with butter. Place each slice in a fireproof soup bowl, ladle the soup on top, and when the toast surfaces sprinkle grated Gruyère cheese over the surface of each bowl. Grill until golden brown and bubbling.
Delia Smith: The Evening Standard Cook Book, 1978

TIFFIN

Base: 1 lb (450 g) crushed biscuits (malted milk)
2 tbls (30 ml) drinking chocolate / cocoa
4 oz (125 g) margarine
1 tbls (15 ml) sugar
2 tbls (30 ml) syrup
Top: 4 oz (125 g) cooking chocolate
4 tbls (60 ml) icing sugar

Melt margarine, syrup, cocoa and sugar in pan. Add biscuits. Set in swiss roll tin in fridge. Melt cooking chocolate, add icing sugar and a little milk if needed to mix to a spreadable butter cream. Spread on base. Leave to set, before cutting into fingers.
Grange Park Women's Institute Recipes, 1975

CHABLIS CUP

1 bottle Chablis
1 sherry glass of sherry
1 pt (575 ml) boiling water
6 lumps of sugar
1 thin strand of lemon peel
1 tumbler soda water
any chosen small summer fruits
8 ice cubes

Dissolve sugar in the boiling water, add lemon peel and leave for 30 minutes. Strain, add Chablis and sherry, chill thoroughly for 30 minutes. Just before service add chosen fruits, soda water and ice cubes, and serve.
NOTE: Skinless segments of sweet orange; thinly sliced unskinned cucumber (which is not a fruit!); peeled, stoned, halved grapes; peeled segments of pear cut like skinned, sliced peaches – with a silver knife, stoned, black or white cherries, and always when available – a sprig or two of the mixed drinks herb – borage.
Fanny Cradock Invites, 1970

LEMON SWEET

Base

8 oz (250 g) digestive biscuit
  (crumbled)
4 oz (125 g) melted butter
1–2 oz (25–50 g) soft brown sugar

Grease and line a fire-proof dish.

Filling

small tin condensed milk
small carton double cream
juice of 1 lemon

Mix the ingredients together, put into the biscuit base and chill for at least one hour in the fridge.

Grange Park Women's Institute Recipes, 1975

Fin de Siècle

CARROT SOUP WITH ORANGE AND TARRAGON

4 Servings

Carrot and orange soup is often spoilt, I feel, by the use of far too much oil to sauté the vegetables initially and adding cream at the end. Neither is necessary. Nor does the soup need much, if any, salt – it will spoil the delicate, rather sweet flavour and light texture. Fresh tarragon is wonderful for this soup, but dried is perfectly all right – it reconstitutes itself quickly in the liquid.

1 lb (500 g) carrots
1 onion
1 medium potato
1 orange
6 cardamom pods
1½ pints (1 l) chicken stock
1 tbls (15 ml) fresh chopped tarragon,
  or 1 tsp (5 ml) dried

Roughly chop the carrots, onion and potato. Brush out a heavy saucepan with oil and sauté the vegetables for about 3 minutes.

Meanwhile, grate the peel of the orange, then squeeze its juice and rind, the cardamom, and stock. Bring to a simmer, cover and cook for 25 minutes. Add the tarragon in the last 5 minutes of cooking. Blend very well: the texture should be as smooth as possible. Serve with triangles of wholemeal toast or warmed brown rolls.

Jenny Rogers: Healthy Food in Half an Hour, 1987

BUCKS FIZZ

Fill a tall tumbler with crushed ice. Fill a quarter of the glass with orange juice and top up with champagne. Decorate with an orange slice.

Joe Turner: The Sainsbury Book of Cocktails and Party Drinks, 1982

341

TROUT MARINATED WITH YOGHURT AND SPICES

6 Servings

The wise man dismisses nothing.
He stands at the banks of a
fast-flowing river.
Not dismayed by the raging
torrent that blocks his path.
He wonders where it is going.
And while pondering upon these
thoughts, he will sip a glass of
lassi.

This iced and salted yoghurt,
flavoured with aromatics will
free his mind of concern and
liberate the gastric juices and
turn his thoughts to the fragrant
spices of the orient. Which, my
friends, can be yours if you
follow these instructions.

6 trout
½ tsp paprika
4 tbls (60 ml) coriander seeds
½ tsp salt
6 cardamom seeds
2 onions, finely chopped
2 cloves garlic
¼ tsp ground black pepper
1 tbls (15 ml) dill
½ green pepper, deseeded
2 tbls (30 ml) freshly chopped mint
Juice of 1 lemon
6 oz (175 ml) natural yoghurt
Butter for basting

Instead of trout, you can use
whiting or perch, or thick fillets
of white fish such as hake or cod.

Place all the other ingredients,
except the yoghurt, in your
liquidizer (or pestle and mortar).
Whizz or grind until you have a
paste which you then mix with
the natural yoghurt. Clean the
fish and spread the paste over
and inside them. Leave to
marinate for 1 hour.

Grill over a wood fire or
under a preheated grill until
crisp and cooked. During the
cooking process, you should turn
the fish from time to time, and
baste with butter and the
remainder of the marinade.

As you sip your iced lager and
flake the flesh of the fish into
freshly baked nan bread,
uplifted with a fine lime pickle,
you may wonder what the first
sentences of this recipe signify.
But, as they say in the East, if you
have to ask you will never know.
Keith Floyd: Floyd on Fish, 1985

STIR-FRIED GINGERED BEEF

Serves 4

2 tsps (10 ml) soy sauce
1 tbls (15 ml) sherry
1 tsp sesame oil
1 tsp cornflour
2.5 cm (1 inch) piece fresh root ginger,
  grated
grated rind of 1 orange and 1
  tablespoon juice

14 oz (400 g) beef olives, shredded into strips 1 cm (½ inch) wide
1 tbls sunflower oil
4 oz (125 g) mangetouts
½ × 8 oz (230 g) can waterchestnuts, drained and sliced
orange segments to garnish

Place the soy sauce, sherry, sesame oil, cornflour, ginger, orange rind and juice in a bowl. Stir in the beef and leave to marinate for at least 15 minutes. Remove the beef with a slotted spoon; reserve the marinade.

Heat the sunflower oil in a large frying pan or wok, add the beef and stir-fry for 3–5 minutes, until browned.

Stir in the marinade, mangetouts and waterchestnuts and cook for 5 minutes.

Serve immediately, garnished with orange and accompanied by rice noodles.

Preparation time: 5 minutes, plus marinating

Cooking time: 8–10 minutes

Freezing: Not recommended

Clare Gordon-Smith: Good Fast Food, 1986

IMAM BAYILDI

You too will faint at the taste of these aubergines! In Turkey imam bayildi are all too often seen floating in a puddle of luke warm grease. Not so our version.

6 Servings

3 plump aubergines
1 large onion, chopped
2 courgettes, chopped
1 red and 1 green pepper, chopped
2 fat garlic cloves, crushed
4 tbls (60 ml) olive oil
2 bay leaves
1 tbls (15 ml) marjoram
1 tbls (15 ml) basil
½ tbls (7.5 ml) cumin
½ tbls (7.5 ml) cardamom
6 oz (175 g) toasted almonds, roughly chopped
juice of 1 lemon
8 oz (250 g) lexia raisins
7 fl oz (200 ml) red wine
1½ lb (700 g) cooked rice
1 lb (450 g) strong cheddar, grated
6 tomatoes, sliced

Halve aubergines lengthwise, and scoop out middles with a soupspoon. Roughly chop the removed flesh.

Sauté vegetables and chopped aubergine in oil with bay leaves. When onion softens, add the rest of the herbs and spices, cover, and continue cooking until aubergine is soft. Remove from heat.

Add nuts, lemon juice, fruit, wine, rice and cheese (reserving a little for topping), and mix well. Check seasoning.

Pile mix into aubergine shells. Decorate with tomato slices and remaining cheese. Bake at 180°C for 1 hour, covered with foil.

Hilary Howard and Julia Stapleton: Cooking with Stones, 1989

REDCURRANT FLANS

6 Servings

These delightful little flans are ideal for al fresco summer parties. If fresh redcurrants cannot be found, use canned or frozen ones.

2 oz (50 g) castor sugar
¼ pt (15 ml) rosé wine
1 lb (450 g) redcurrants
2 tbls (30 ml) redcurrant jelly
6 individual sponge flan cases

Place the sugar and wine in a saucepan and heat gently until dissolved. Add the redcurrants, cover and cook gently for 3 minutes. Remove with a slotted spoon and set aside.
Boil the liquid for a few minutes, until reduced and syrupy. Stir in the redcurrant jelly and heat gently until melted.
Divide the redcurrants between the flan cases and brush them with the glaze.
Serve with Greek strained yoghurt or whipped cream.

Variation
Replace the redcurrants with blackcurrants.
Preparation time: 10 minutes
Freezing: Not recommended.
Clare Gordon-Smith: Good Fast Food, 1986

PEACH CAKE

3 lb (1.5 kg) peaches (about 13)
8 oz (250 g) sugar
1 lemon
7½ oz (200 g) butter
4 eggs
10 oz (300 g) self-raising flour
3½ oz (100 g) ground almonds
1 tsp (5 ml) ground aniseeds
grease for baking tray
5 oz (150 g) cranberries

Pour boiling water over peaches, skin them, half them and stone them. Bring 50 g sugar and ¼ of litre of water with lemon juice to the boil. Steam peach-halves in that liquid for about 8 minutes on low heat. Sieve juice off and let peaches cool (sieve off into saucepan). Mix butter, rest of sugar, eggs and grated rind of lemon peel. Mix into smooth dough with flour, almonds and aniseeds. Pour out onto greased baking tray. Put peaches on dough and cranberries on top of peaches and dough. Bake at gas mark 4/180°C for about 40 minutes. Mix cornflour with little water, bring the juice sieved off earlier to boil and stir in cornflour. Use as glazing on finished cake.
Gill Corbishley, 1985

BIBLIOGRAPHY

GENERAL FOOD HISTORY

Ayrton, Elizabeth, *The Cookery of England*, André Deutsch (London, 1974); Penguin Books (Harmondsworth, 1977).

Berriedale-Johnson, Michelle, *The British Museum Cookbook*, British Museum Press (London, 1987).

Brett, Gerard, *Dinner is Served*, Rupert Hart Davis (London, 1968).

Brooke, Sheena, *Hearth and Home: a short history of domestic equipment in England*, Mills and Boon (London, 1973).

Davidson, Caroline, *A Woman's Work is Never Done*, Chatto and Windus (London, 1982).

Drummond, J. C., and Wilbraham, A., *The Englishman's Food*, Jonathan Cape (London, 1969 edition).

Feild, Rachael, *Irons in the Fire*, Crowood Press (Marlborough, 1984).

Grigson, J., *English Food*, Macmillan (London, 1974); Penguin Books (Harmondsworth, 1977).

Hartley, Dorothy, *Food in England*, Macdonald (London, 1954).

Harrison, Molly, *The Kitchen in History*, Osprey (London, 1972).

Tannahill, Reay, *Food in History*, Penguin Books (Harmondsworth, 1988).

Wilson, C. A., *Food and Drink in Britain*, Constable (London, 1973); Penguin Books (Harmondsworth, 1976).

PREHISTORIC BRITAIN

Cobbett, W., *Cottage Economy*, 1822, reprinted by Oxford University Press (Oxford, 1979).

Darvill, Timothy, *Prehistoric Britain*, Batsford (London, 1987).

David, E., *English Bread and Yeast Cookery*, Allen Lane and Penguin Books (Harmondsworth, 1977).

Evans, E. E., *Irish Folk Ways*, Routledge and Kegan Paul (London and Boston, 1957).

Firth, J., *Reminiscences of an Orkney Parish*, Rendall (Stromness, 1975).

Fowler, Peter, *The Farming of Prehistoric Britain*, Cambridge University Press (Cambridge, 1983).

Grigson, G., *The Englishman's Flora*, Phoenix House (London, 1958); Paladin (St Albans, 1975).

Grigson, J., *Jane Grigson's Fruit Book*, Michael Joseph (London, 1982); Penguin Books (Harmondsworth, 1983).

Hill, J., *The Wild Foods of Britain*, A. and C. Black (Publishers) Ltd (London, 1939).

Longworth, I. H., *Prehistoric Britain*, British Museum Publications (London, 1985).

Mabey, R., *Food for Free*, Collins (London, 1972); Fontana (London, 1976).

Manley, J., *Atlas of Prehistoric Britain*, Phaidon (London, 1989).

Phillips, R., *Wild Food*, Pan Books (London, 1983).

Richardson, R., *Hedgerow Cookery*, Penguin Books (Harmondsworth, 1980).

Simmons, J., *A Shetland Cook Book*, Thuleprint Ltd (Sandwick, Shetland, 1978).

Stout, M. B., *The Shetland Cookery Book*, T. and J. Manson (Lerwick, 1968).

ROMAN BRITAIN

André, J., *L'Alimentation et la cuisine à Rome*, Librairie C. Klincksieck (Paris, 1961).

Birley, E., *Research on Hadrian's Wall*, Titus Wilson (Kendal, 1961).

Boon, G. C., *Silchester, the Roman Town of Calleva*, David and Charles (Newton Abbot, 1974).

Breeze, D. J., *The Northern Frontiers of Roman Britain*, Batsford (London, 1982).

Breeze, D. J., and Dobson, B., *Hadrian's Wall*, Penguin Books (Harmondsworth, 1978).

Davies, R. W., *Roman Military Diet*, Britannia (1971), pp. 122–142.

Edwards, J., *The Roman Cookery of Apicius*, Rider (London, 1984).

Flower, B., and Rosenbaum, E. (eds.), *The Roman Cookery Book, a critical translation of The Art of Cooking by Apicius*, Harrap (London, 1958; reprinted 1974).

Frere, S., *Britannia*, Routledge and Kegan Paul (London, 1967).

Gillam, J. P., 'Types of Roman coarse pottery vessels in Northern Britain', *Archaeologia Aeliana*, 4th ser. XXXV, 1–72.

Greeve, K., *The Archaeology of The Roman Economy*, Batsford (London, 1986).

Hartley, B. R., *Roman Samian Ware (Terra Sigillata)*, Hertfordshire Archaeological Society Print No. 1 (1970).

Johnson, S., *Later Roman Britain*, Routledge and Kegan Paul (London, 1980).

Johnston, D. E., *Roman Villas*, Shire Publications (Aylesbury, 1979).

London in Roman Times, London Museum Catalogue No. 3 (London, 1946).

Potter, T. W. and Johns, C., *Roman Britain*, British Museum Press (London, 1992).

Richmond, I. A., *Roman Britain*, Penguin Books (Harmondsworth, 2nd ed. 1963).

Salway, P., *Roman Britain*, Clarendon Press (Oxford, 1981).

Wacher, J. S., *The Towns of Roman Britain*, Batsford (London, 1974).

Wacher, J. S., *Roman Britain*, Dent (London, 1978).

Wacher, J. S., *The Coming of Rome*, Routledge and Kegan Paul (London, 1979).

West, L. C., *Roman Britain: the Objects of Trade*, Blackwell (Oxford, 1931).

Woodman, M., *Food and Cooking in Roman Britain*, Corinium Museum Publications (Cirencester, 1985).

MEDIEVAL BRITAIN

Anon, *Ancient Cookery*, 1381. In *Antiquitates Culinariae*, Richard Warner, 1791, facsimile edition by Prospect Books (London, 1983).

Anon, *Ashmole MS 1439*, c.1430. In Austin (ed.), *Two Fifteenth Century Cookery Books*, Early English Text Society, Oxford University Press (Oxford, 1964).

Anon, *The Forme of Cury*, c.1390. In *Antiquitates Culinariae*, Richard Warner, 1791, facsimile edition by Prospect Books (London, 1983).

Anon, *Harleian MSS 279*, c.1430, and 4016, c.1450. In Austin (ed.), *Two Fifteenth Century Cookery Books*, Early English Text Society, Oxford University Press (Oxford, 1964).

Black, Maggie, *The Medieval Cookbook*, British Museum Press (London, 1992).

Braudel, Fernand, *The Structures of Everyday Life*, translated by Sian Reynolds, Collins (London, 1983).

Buxton, Moira, *Mediaeval Cooking Today*, Kylin Press (Waddesdon, 1983).

Clair, Colin, *Kitchen and Table*, Abelard Schuman (New York, 1964).

John Russell's Boke of Nurture, c. 1460. In F. J. Furnivall (ed.), *Early English Meals and Manners*, Early English Text Society (1868).

Layton, T. A., *Five to a Feast*, Duckworth (London, 1946).

Mead, W. E., *The English Mediaeval Feast*, George Allen and Unwin (London, 1967).

R. Howe (ed.), *Mrs Groundes-Peace's Old Cookery Notebook*, Rainbird Reference Books with David and Charles (Newton Abbot, 1971).

Sass, Lorna J., *To the King's Taste*, Metropolitan Museum of Art (New York, 1975).

Wildeblood, Joan, and Brinson, Peter, *The Polite World*, Oxford University Press (Oxford, 1965).

TUDOR BRITAIN

Aikin, Lucy, *Memoirs of the Court of Queen Elizabeth* (London, 1819).

Anon, *The Boke of Cokery*, printed by Richard Pynson without Temple Bar (London, 1500). [The only known copy of this work is in the collection of the Marquis of Bath, Longleat House].

Anon, *The Book of Kervinge*, printed by Wynkyn de Worde (London, 1508) [Cambridge University Library Sel. 5.19.19].

Anon, *A Proper Newe Book of Cokerye*, printed by John Kynge & Thomas Marche (London, probably before 1572) [Corpus Christi College, Cambridge, Archbishop Parker Collection].

Anon, *The Good Hous-wives Treasurie*, printed by Edward Allde (London, 1588) [British Library 1038.d.43].

A. W., *A Book of Cookrye Very necessary for all such as delight therein*, printed by Edward Allde (London, 1591) [Bodleian Library, Oxford, Douce W.23].

Boorde, Andrewe, *A Compendyous Regyment or Dyetary of Helth*, printed by Robert Wyler (London, 1542).

Dawson, Thomas, *The good huswifes Jewell*, part 1, printed for Edward White (London, 1596); part 2, printed for Edward White by Edward Allde (London, 1597) [Bodleian Library, Oxford, Douce D.49 (1 & 2)].

Hope, W. H. St. John, *Cowdray and Easebourne Priory* (London, 1919).

Partridge, J., *The Treasurie of Commodious Conceites and Hidden Secrets* (London, 1573, 1600).

Partridge, J., *The Widowes treasure . . .*, printed for Edward White by Robert Walde-grave (London, 1585) [Leeds University, Preston Collection P/K1 1585].

de Rosselli, Giovanni, *Epulario or the Italian Banquet wherein is shewn the maner how to dress . . . all kinds of Flesh, Foules or Fishes*, translated from the original Italian and printed for William Barley by Abel Jeffes (London, 1598) [British Library 7955.b.8].

Society of Antiquaries, *A Collection of Ordinances and Regulations for the Government of the Royal Household* (London, 1790).

Turberville, George, *The Noble Arte of Venerie of Hunting* (London, 1575).

SEVENTEENTH-CENTURY BRITAIN

Anon, *The Second Book of Cookery* (London, 1641).

Anon, *A Book of Fruits & Flowers*, 1653, reprinted with an introduction by C. Anne Wilson, by Prospect Books (London, 1984).

Avery, Madam Susanne, *A Plain Plantain*, 1688 (Ditchling, Sussex, 1922).

Brears, P. C. D., *The Gentlewoman's Kitchen*, Wakefield Historical Publications (Wakefield, 1984).

Cromwell, Elizabeth (Joan), *The Court and Kitchen of Mrs Elizabeth Commonly called Joan Cromwell*, 1664, reprinted by Cambridgeshire Libraries (Cambridge, 1983).

Digby, Sir Kenelm, *The Closet of Sir Kenelm Digby Opened*, 1669 (London, 1910).

Driver, C., and Berridale-Johnson, M., *Pepys at Table*, Bell and Hyman (London, 1984).

Evelyn, John, *Acetaria, a Discourse of Sallets*, 1699, reprinted by Prospect Books (London, 1982).

Fairfax, Henry, and others, *Arcana Fairfaxiana*, mid 17th century (Newcastle, 1890).

May, Robert, *The Accomplisht Cook* (London, 1660).

Mosley, Jane, *Jane Mosley's Derbyshire Recipes 1669-1712*, Derbyshire Museums Service (Derby, 1979).

Murrel, J., *A New Booke of Cookerie*, 1615, reprinted by Da Capo Press (New York, 1972).

Platt, Sir Hugh, *Delightes for Ladies To adorne their Persons, Tables, Closets, and Distillatories with Beauties, Banquets, Perfumes and Waters*, printed by Humferey Lownes (London, 1608).

Price, Rebecca, *The Compleat Cook*, 1681, Routledge and Kegan Paul (London, 1974).

W. M., *The Compleat Cook and Queen's Delight*, 1671 edn. reprinted by Prospect Books (London, 1984).

GEORGIAN BRITAIN

Anon, *Adam's luxury, and Eve's cookery*, 1744, reprinted by Prospect Books (London, 1983).

Bradley, Richard, *The Country housewife and lady's director*, 6th edn. London, 1736, reprinted with an introduction by Caroline Davidson, and glossary, by Prospect Books (London, 1980).

Carter, Charles, *The complete practical cook*, 1730, reprinted by Prospect Books (London, 1984).

Cook, Ann, *Professed cookery*, 2nd edn. Newcastle, 1775; 3rd edn. reprinted as *Ann Cook and Friend*, with introduction and notes by Regula Burnet, by Oxford University Press (London, 1936).

Glasse, Hannah, *The art of cookery made plain and easy*, 1747, reprinted with glossary and index by Prospect Books (London, 1983).

Maclean, Virginia, *A short-title catalogue of household and cookery books published in the English tongue 1701-1800*, Prospect Books (London, 1980).

Mennell, Stephen, 'Food at the late Stuart and Hanoverian courts', *Petits Propos Culinaires*, Vol. 17 pp. 22–9.

Nott, John, *The cook's and confectioner's dictionary*, 3rd edn. London, 1726, reprinted by Lawrence Rivington (London, 1980).

Raffald, Elizabeth, *The experienced English housekeeper*, 10th edn. Manchester, 1786; 8th edn. 1782, reprinted by E. and W. Books (Publishers) Ltd (1970) and Redwood Press for Paul Minet reprints (1972).

Smith, Eliza, *The compleat housewife*, London, 1727; 15th edn. 1753, reprinted with a foreword by Lord Montagu of Beaulieu, and the addition of a glossary compiled by C. H. Hudson, by Literary Services and Production Ltd (London, 1968).

Stead, Jennifer, 'Quizzing Glasse: or Hannah scrutiniz'd', *Petits Propos Culinaires*, Vol. 13 pp. 9–24, Vol. 14 pp. 17–30.

Swift, Jonathan, *Directions to servants in general* (London, 1745).

Trusler, John, *The honours of the table, or, rules for behaviour during meals* (London, 1788).

Verral, William, *The cook's paradise*, London, 1759, reprinted with Thomas Gray's cookery notes in holograph, with an introduction and appendices by R. L. Megroz, by Sylvan Press (London, 1948).

VICTORIAN BRITAIN

Acton, Eliza, *Modern Cookery for Private Families*, Longmans Green, Reader and Dyer, 1855, facsimile edition by Elek Press (London, 1966).

Beeton, Isabella (ed.), *The Book of Household Management*, Ward Lock and Tyler, 1861, facsimile edition by Jonathan Cape (London, 1968).

Black, Mrs, *Superior Cookery*, William Collins, Sons & Co. (Glasgow, c. 1898).

Burnett, John (ed.), *Useful Toil*, Allen Lane (Harmondsworth, 1974).

Burton, Elizabeth, *The Early Victorians at Home*, Arrow Books (London, 1972).

Currah, Anne (ed.), *Chef to Queen Victoria: the recipes of Charles Elmé Francatelli*, William Kimber (London, 1973).

Davis, Michael Justin (ed.), *In a Wiltshire Village: scenes from rural Victorian life*, Alan Sutton (Gloucester, 1981).

Francatelli, Charles Elmé, *A Plain Cookery Book for the Working Classes*, 1852, reprinted by Scolar Press (London, 1977).

Francatelli, Charles Elmé, *The Cook's Guide and Housekeeper's and Butler's Assistant*, Richard Bentley & Son (1877).

Gordon, Martha H., *Cookery for Working Men's Wives*, Alexander Gardner (1888).

Hickman, Peggy, *A Jane Austen Household Book with Martha Lloyd's Recipes*, David and Charles (Newton Abbot, 1977).

Hobbs, Samuel, *One Hundred and Sixty Culinary Dainties for the Epicure, the Invalid and the Dyspeptic*, Dean & Son (c.1890).

Janey Ellice's Recipes 1846–1859, J. Wentworth (ed.), Macdonald and Jane's (London, 1975).

Kitchiner, William, M. D., *The Cook's Oracle* (1817).

Margetson, Stella, *Leisure and Pleasure in the Nineteenth Century*, Cassell (London, 1969).

Norwak, Mary, *Kitchen Antiques*, Ward Lock (London, 1975).

Senn, Charles Herman, *Recherché Cookery* and *Practical Gastronomy and Culinary Dictionary*, Spottiswoode and Co. (London, 1895).

Soyer, Alexis, *The Modern Housewife or Ménagère* and *Soyer's Charitable Cookery or the Poor Man's Regenerator*, Simkin, Marshall and Co. (1853).

TWENTIETH-CENTURY BRITAIN

Braithwaite, Brian, Walsh, Noelle and Davies, Glyn (compilers), *The Home Front: The Best of 'Good Housekeeping' 1939–1945*, Ebury Press (London, 1987).

Carlton, Paul, *Simple Vegetarian Cooking*, Harrap (London, 1931).

Coates, Doris, *Tuppeny Rice and Treacle: Cottage Housekeeping 1900–1920*, David and Charles (Newton Abbot, 1975).

Corbishley, Gill, *Ration Book Recipes: Some Food Facts 1939–1954*, English Heritage (London, 1990).

Forty, Adrian, *Objects of Desire: Design and Society 1750–1980*, Thames and Hudson (London, 1986).

Hudson, Kenneth, *Food, Clothes and Shelter: Twentieth-Century Industrial Archaeology*, John Baker (London, 1978).

Kitchen, Penny (compiler), *For Home and Country: Women's Institute Magazines 1919–1959*, Ebury Press (London, 1990).

Patten, Marguerite, *We'll Eat Again*, Hamlyn (London, 1985).

Marrack, J. R., *Food and Planning*, Victor Gollancz (London, 1942).

Plimmer, Violet G., *Food Values in Wartime*, Longmans and Green (London, 1941).

Vera, *Middle-Class Cookery*, R. S. Cartwright (London, c.1900).

349

INDEX

Compiled by Jane Parker

351